Elizabeth Fry

Newshot House 1879. NRS

Elizabeth Fry

JUNE ROSE

TEMPUS

For Verily and Paul

First published by Macmillan, 1980
This edition first published 2007

Tempus Publishing Limited
The Mill, Brimscombe Port,
Stroud, Gloucestershire, GL5 2QG
www.tempus-publishing.com

British Library Cataloguing in Publication Data.
A catalogue record for this book is available from the British Library.

ISBN 978 0 7524 4245 7

Typesetting and origination by Tempus Publishing Limited
Printed and bound in Great Britain

Contents

	About the Author	6
	List of Illustrations	7
	Acknowledgements	9
	Genealogy	11
	Prologue	13
I	'A Fly-away State'	15
II	The Transformation	41
III	'A Careworn Wife and Mother'	65
IV	'Laudable Persuits'	91
V	'Quite a Show'	111
VI	The National Crusade	139
VII	The Crash	169
VIII	More Cruelty than Before	193
IX	Royal Commands	217
X	Heroine of Europe	239
	Sources	267
	Bibliography	271
	Index	275

About the Author

June Rose is the author of several biographies, including *Marie Stopes*, the fascinating precursor of modern attitudes towards women and sex (also by Tempus), *Modigliani*, the twentieth-century Italian painter and *Susan Valadon: Mistress of Montmartre*. She lives in Highgate, London.

List of Illustrations

Frontispiece.   Plashet House, drawn by Katharine Fry

1.   Joseph Fry in 1823
2.   Elizabeth Fry in 1818
3.   Earlham Hall, the home of the Gurneys
4.   A satirical aquatint of Mrs Fry at Newgate
5.   Mrs Fry reading to the prisoners at Newgate
6.   Elizabeth Gurney at the age of nineteen
7.   Rachel Gurney
8.   Joseph John Gurney
9.   Portrait of Elizabeth Fry
10.   J. J. Gurney and his family in 1842
11.   The Fry children living at home in 1830

The endpapers contain part of Elizabeth Gurney's journal entry for 7 February 1798. This was three days after she had first met William Savery, an American Quaker and one of the most important early influences in her life.

Grateful acknowledgements are due to the Library of the Society of Friends, London, for permission to reproduce these illustrations.

Acknowledgements

There are many people I should like to thank for helping me with this book. First of all, Edward Milligan, Librarian to the Society of Friends, who gave me so much valuable help and advice whilst I was working at Friends House Library. I am deeply indebted to him and to his assistant, Malcolm Thomas, for guiding my researches so knowledgeably. I am very grateful to Doris Eddington, who took me on a 'pilgrimage' of the city of Norwich and showed me her own mementos of Elizabeth Fry, including family papers, tract books and a shawl lined with ermine. Verily Anderson and Paul Paget offered me generous help and hospitality and took me to visit their Gurney relatives and I would like to thank them all. In particular I am indebted to Mr Richard Gurney for showing me family portraits and journals which were most useful and for permission to reproduce material from the Norwich Record Office. Mrs Frank Thistlethwaite very kindly showed me round Earlham, which is now the Administration Building of the University of East Anglia. Lotte Lowenthal spent many hours in libraries and Record Offices searching on my behalf and her help was invaluable.

I should also like to thank: the staff of the Manuscript Department of the British Library; the staff of the Guildhall Library; Mrs S. Hamlyn, the Local Studies Librarian of Newham Reference Library; David Doughan, the Assistant Librarian of the Fawcett Society and Amanda Golbey who worked there;

E.M. Kelly, the Curator of the Bank of England Museum and Research Department; Roger Whitworth, the Curator of the Museum of Iron Research Project; and the staff of the Department of Paleography and Diplomatic, Durham University.

Gabrielle Morrison typed the manuscript with efficiency and discernment and offered valuable suggestions. Finally I would like to thank my editor, Hilary Gibbs, for her advice, encouragement and patience.

Genealogy

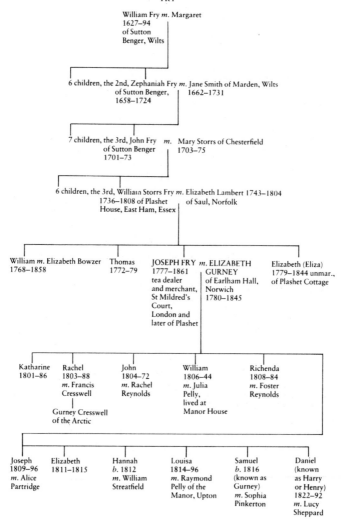

FRY

William Fry *m.* Margaret
1627–94
of Sutton
Benger, Wilts

6 children, the 2nd, Zephaniah Fry *m.* Jane Smith of Marden, Wilts
of Sutton Benger,   1662–1731
1658–1724

7 children, the 3rd, John Fry   *m.*   Mary Storrs of Chesterfield
of Sutton Benger   1703–75
1701–73

6 children, the 3rd, William Storrs Fry *m.* Elizabeth Lambert 1743–1804
1736–1808 of Plashet   of Saul, Norfolk
House, East Ham, Essex

William *m.* Elizabeth Bowzer	Thomas	JOSEPH FRY *m.* ELIZABETH	Elizabeth (Eliza)
1768–1858	1772–79	1777–1861 GURNEY	1779–1844 unmar.,
		tea dealer of Earlham Hall,	of Plashet Cottage
		and merchant, Norwich	
		St Mildred's 1780–1845	
		Court,	
		London and	
		later of Plashet	

Katharine	Rachel	John	William	Richenda
1801–86	1803–88	1804–72	1806–44	1808–84
	m. Francis	*m.* Rachel	*m.* Julia	*m.* Foster
	Cresswell	Reynolds	Pelly,	Reynolds
			lived at	
	Gurney Cresswell		Manor House	
	of the Arctic			

Joseph	Elizabeth	Hannah	Louisa	Samuel	Daniel
1809–96	1811–1815	*b.* 1812	1814–96	*b.* 1816	(known
m. Alice		*m.* William	*m.* Raymond	(known	as Harry
Partridge		Streatfield	Pelly of the	as Gurney)	or Henry)
			Manor, Upton	*m.* Sophia	1822–92
				Pinkerton	*m.* Lucy
					Sheppard

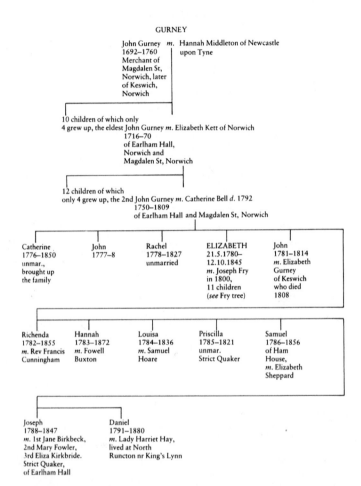

GURNEY

John Gurney *m.* Hannah Middleton of Newcastle
1692–1760   upon Tyne
Merchant of
Magdalen St,
Norwich, later
of Keswich,
Norwich

10 children of which only
4 grew up, the eldest John Gurney *m.* Elizabeth Kett of Norwich
1716–70
of Earlham Hall,
Norwich and
Magdalen St, Norwich

12 children of which
only 4 grew up, the 2nd John Gurney *m.* Catherine Bell *d.* 1792
1750–1809
of Earlham Hall and Magdalen St, Norwich

Catherine	John	Rachel	ELIZABETH	John
1776–1850	1777–8	1778–1827	21.5.1780–	1781–1814
unmar.,		unmarried	12.10.1845	*m.* Elizabeth
brought up			*m.* Joseph Fry	Gurney
the family			in 1800,	of Keswich
			11 children	who died
			(*see* Fry tree)	1808

Richenda	Hannah	Louisa	Priscilla	Samuel
1782–1855	1783–1872	1784–1836	1785–1821	1786–1856
m. Rev Francis	*m.* Fowell	*m.* Samuel	unmar.	of Ham
Cunningham	Buxton	Hoare	Strict Quaker	House,
				m. Elizabeth
				Sheppard

Joseph	Daniel
1788–1847	1791–1880
m. 1st Jane Birkbeck,	*m.* Lady Harriet Hay,
2nd Mary Fowler,	lived at North
3rd Eliza Kirkbride.	Runcton nr King's Lynn
Strict Quaker,	
of Earlham Hall	

Prologue

'We long to burn her alive', wrote the Reverend Sydney Smith in 1821 of Elizabeth Fry. 'Examples of living virtue disturb our repose and give birth to distressing comparisons.'

Even in her lifetime there was a daunting purity about Elizabeth Fry, which chilled her own sisters and occasionally led bolder spirits to mock her. In her everyday life she pursued an ideal of perfection so remote from the concerns of most men and women that it seemed possible only to exalt or deride her.

Through the veil of history she appears pious, elevating, benevolent, braving the horrors of Newgate prison to tame the half-crazed women inside through her message of Christian love. She martyred herself for her cause and came gradually to believe in her own saintliness.

Her actual achievement was extraordinary. A portly matron with ten children, she had gatecrashed into public life, into an exclusively male preserve, when the very idea was unthinkable. Through her passionate crusade she succeeded in rousing the world's conscience to the pitiable state of women in prison and in creating a glimmer of sympathy for the lunatics and the poor. She also instituted an order of nursing sisters. By the time Queen Victoria came to the throne, Elizabeth Fry had become the figurehead of much of the philanthropic endeavour in the country.

She was almost forty years older than Queen Victoria and Florence Nightingale, admired by them both for her compassionate exercise of feminine influence outside the home. She would have been truly horrified at the fact that she is regarded today as one of the earliest feminists.

Throughout her life Elizabeth Fry suffered from the handicap of her sex and tried to reconcile her role of wife and mother with her work as a reformer. Although her standing as a Quaker minister gave her the authority to follow her calling, strict Quakers at that time disapproved of the involvement with worldly affairs that Elizabeth Fry's public life demanded. Her life was a martyrdom, but not in the sense that has been popularly supposed.

After her death she was canonised by her biographers. Her own daughters contributed largely to the myth, editing forty-four volumes of her journals, correcting her curious spelling, improving her grammar and carefully removing all trace of individuality and of human weakness. The fair copy of her journals made by her daughter Katharine, now in the Manuscript Department of the British Library, forms the basis of nearly all the biographical material about her.

After reading through the original 561,000 words of her journals now in Friends House, London, scrawled almost illegibly in scrappy notebooks, a portrait began to emerge of a far more complex and tormented human being than has ever been allowed to appear. This book is largely a result of that study.

I

'A Fly-away State'

Elizabeth Gurney was born on 21 May 1780 in Magdalen Street, the shopping centre of the busy old town of Norwich. Her home, Court House, stood back from the street, a dignified building with pedimented doorways and sash windows surrounding two gardens, separated by a railing. The house still stands, although the gardens have disappeared and the street has become the main route north out of the town.

In later years Elizabeth Fry was immensely proud of her Gurney birth. For generations Gurneys had helped to establish Norwich as a leading centre of the cloth trade and her father, John, had inherited both the house and the woolstapling and spinning factory nearby. They had also been Quakers, members of the Society of Friends, from the early days, and still suffered from certain civil disqualifications. As a Friend, John Gurney had been barred from attending university and was unable to hold civil office. By the time Betsy was born, he had banking interests in Gurneys Bank, founded by his cousin Bartlett, and fifteen years later became a partner in it. His wealth and popularity in the town had long dispelled any prejudice against him and the family had begun to weaken in their strict observance of the 'peculiarities' of Friends.

Perhaps in some ways it had been easier to remain faithful when they had been persecuted. A hundred years earlier one of her ancestors had been sent to prison for keeping his faith:

in 1682, John Gurney defied the authorities by attending a meeting for worship held in the street, after Friends had been banned from assembling at their own Meeting House.

During the eighteenth century the fierce intolerance of Dissenters had abated and the enterprising Gurneys had become middlemen in the woollen industry, buying wool and yarn from small farmers, putting it out to spinners and weavers, and then marketing the cloth. As they prospered, they began to lend money to the growers and weavers. The family reputation for good credit and honest dealing served to foster what developed naturally into a banking business. During Sir Robert Walpole's term of office, another Gurney ancestor, a successful woollen manufacturer, had pleaded at a Committee of the House of Lords so eloquently against the importation of calico and cotton from abroad that he convinced his audience and became known in Norwich as 'the weavers' friend'. Walpole himself was impressed by Gurney's oratory and offered him a safe seat in Parliament, but John Gurney declined since he would not swear the oath of allegiance on grounds of religious conscience.

Betsy's own grandfather, John Gurney, had in his turn benefited the city by importing yarn from southern Ireland when the local supply threatened to run out. His initiative saved hundreds of weavers from wretched poverty and earned him, besides, a fortune. By then the Gurney family felt a personal sense of responsibility for the prosperity of the town. John Gurney remained a devout and active member of his religious Society, despite his commercial success, but he had the foresight to realise that it might be difficult for his children to resist the temptations of a more worldly way of life. When he died he left a fortune of £100,000.

To this day Quakers place an emphasis on simplicity in worship and inner discipline, in order to experience the presence of God directly, in shared silent worship. During the eighteenth century, they appeared an inward-looking body, anxious to retain the increased tolerance towards them and reluctant to proselytise. They felt strongly that they possessed special spiritual blessings and had a special witness to bear within their ranks. Membership was regarded as a birthright and Quakers who married 'out' or offended against their moral code were expelled. To keep themselves separate, barriers were raised. 'Plain' male Friends wore 'Plain' dress, stripped of all ornament. Powdered hair or ruffles on the shirt, pockets, buttonholes or waists on coats, were considered vain and impious. Quaker women looked simple but attractive in gowns of a sober colour, without frills and feathers. Since Friends ignored rank and regarded all men as equal before God, they addressed everyone as 'thou'. Worldly pleasures, such as the theatre, dancing, music, singing and cards, were forbidden. In practice, it was difficult for Plain Quakers to mix with their neighbours, since no self-respecting Plain Friend would take off his hat when he entered a house.

For a young couple, popular and accepted in Norwich society, the puritan self-denial required was too much to ask, although both John and his wife, Catherine, remained firmly wedded to the broad principles of their faith. Two years before Betsy was born, John had refused to allow Gurney's Bank to become involved in a scheme for raising money for privateers. It appears that Catherine, the mother that Elizabeth Fry was to claim as the most profound influence in her life, was a sweet-natured, pious woman, better educated and more reflective than her husband. Catherine's great-grandfather, Robert Barclay, had been a leading Quaker theologian and she herself had read widely on the subject. She was firm in her faith, but broadminded and cultured. The young couple compromised, attending Meeting once instead of three times a week as pious Quakers did, mixing freely in Norwich society and bringing up their children more liberally than Plain Quakers demanded.

By 1780 they had been married for five years. Both parents were good-looking; John Gurney, 'handsome Johnny' with his bright red hair, was regarded as the best looking young man in the county, an astute businessman, a keen sportsman and a great catch. His attachment to the graceful and cultivated Catherine

Bell had disappointed the Gurneys since she came from a family of very limited means. They married despite the opposition and their home was warm and loving. Besides Betsy, there were two older girls, Kitty aged four and Rachel aged two. A son had died in infancy. John's mother, Elizabeth Kett, lived in a wing of the Court house with her housekeeper, Molly Neale. The two elderly ladies were always finding an excuse to bring the little girls presents of sugar-plums and finger cakes. Despite her large income, Grandmother Kett was often out of pocket because she spent so much on her charities.

Catherine Gurney too put aside time each day for 'the claims of the poor'. She was a careful housewife, dividing her day between the needs of her husband, the children, the servants and poor neighbours. Each day she would visit the children in their nurseries before breakfast and read the Scriptures herself if she had the time. She supervised the kitchen and the servants and visited the children again before her husband came home for dinner. They dined alone, at about three, but afterwards the girls were brought in by their nurses. During the short afternoon, she would write letters, read or tell the children simple Bible stories. Before they went to bed she would read another passage from the Bible to them, usually a psalm. Although Betsy was to say later that in early life religion filled her with gloom, the Bible soaked into her being.

Their life seemed calm, ordered and content, in a settled world. Every summer the family moved to the country, as did most of the wealthy Norwich families. They rented a simple little house on the Common at Bramerton, four miles outside Norwich. Those early summers at Bramerton were to make up Betsy's happiest memories. Here her mother would take her by the hand and walk round the old-fashioned garden with her, pointing out the shrubs and trees and her own wild-flower beds. The garden, with its summer fruits and the cherry orchard beyond, was always confused in Betsy's mind with the Garden of Eden.

Often her mother would have a basket on her arm covered with a clean linen cloth, containing a chicken or some small delicacy for the cottagers. Betsy loved those visits and remembered them all her life. There was a neighbour with strawberry beds called Greengrass, and one-armed Betty, and their gardener – who often brought a present of fresh fish that he had caught in the village pond to the kitchen door. Sometimes they would make an expedition to the sea and Betsy could sit happily on the pebbles collecting shells.

Her mother's journals reveal that, as a tiny girl, Betsy was, if anything, a favourite. Writing to a relative of her children's progress in March 1783, Catherine Gurney remarked: 'Kitty's good propensities by no means fail her [Kitty was seven]. My lively Rachel [who was five] has an ardent desire to do well, yet cannot always resist a powerful inclination to the contrary. But my dove-like Betsy scarcely offends.'

The delightful little girl with her fair hair and downcast blue eyes was always to be found close to her mother. From her birth in 1780 until she was six, a new brother or sister arrived every year, demanding her mother's attention and love. Betsy obviously felt a deep sense of unease, although Catherine Gurney tried conscientiously to 'enjoy each child individually'. 'I watched her when asleep in the day with exquisite anxiety and used to go gently to her bedside to listen, from the awful fear that she did not breathe,' she wrote later. Elizabeth soon became painfully shy. Perhaps modern psychologists would have been disturbed by the apparent lack of spirit in the child and advised some form of therapy or counselling but, in the late eighteenth century, her low spirits and the physical symptoms they produced were put down to 'delicate health'. With so many brothers and sisters who enjoyed almost aggressive good health, Betsy began to feel her weakness as a source of shame and to indulge it more. She grew from an amiable small child into an obstinate little girl, stubborn and withdrawn. Although she lived in an agony of desire to please, she could not bring herself to deny her own instincts.

Anxiety gnawed at her and spoilt most of the outings and pleasures of childhood.

By the late eighteenth century the quality had begun to take trips to the seaside to inhale the sea air or even to dip in the sea. When the Gurneys visited Cromer, Betsy would start to cry at the first glimpse of the water. Her brothers and sisters squealed with delight, but Betsy wept bitterly when she was ducked by her nurse in the cold water, considered so health-giving. Loud noises and bangs terrified her. Most of all she feared the dark and, when she was left without a nightlight, sobbed herself to sleep, longing for her mother. As Mrs Fry recalled years later, she 'cried when she was looked at', and tried to pretend that her eyes were weak, to avoid comment.

Even the Bible stories that her mother told her with so much love and piety frightened Betsy. In her fearful imagination, the story of the sacrifice of Isaac was so real that, after hearing it, she refused to go to Meeting with her parents, for fear that they might sacrifice her. One afternoon when her parents were taking the children out on a pleasure trip, she stubbornly refused to get into the carriage when she noticed her father's sporting gun lying on the seat.

Betsy was so nervous that she could not concentrate on her lessons. She fidgeted and dozed off into daydreams and the other children, who alternately teased and felt sorry for her, easily outstripped her. To the end of her life she apologised to her eldest sister Catherine for her poor writing and spelling. She was vulnerable and sensitive about what the others thought of her. 'Having the name of being stupid,' she said, 'really tended to make me so and discouraged my efforts to learn.' Fortunately Catherine Gurney did not scold her, although she must have been disappointed. She took immense trouble over her daughters' education since Quakers had always accepted the idea that men and women were equal in the sight of God. She drew up a curriculum for them that was exceptionally demanding for the time. They studied Latin, French, 'the simple beauties of mathematics', modern history, geography, chronology, 'approved branches of natural history' and drawing. Since she was a practical woman and realised that the mistress of a household needed practical skills, she also insisted on the girls learning to sew neatly, cut out linen, understand how to manage household economy and plan a menu for a family. She desired them to acquire that gentleness of manner 'indispensably necessary in women, to say nothing of that polished behaviour which adds charm to every qualification', and to be virtuous and good on the 'broad basis of Christianity'. Intellectually it was a far more stimulating education than most contemporary young ladies received. The Gurney girls were expected to study academic subjects seriously, not merely to learn to speak French, sing, dance and paint prettily.

By the time Betsy had begun to learn her lessons, a ninth child, Priscilla, was on the way. The family, with their retinue of servants, had outgrown the house in Magdalen Street, business was prosperous and John Gurney could afford to live in the style of a country gentleman. He rented Earlham Hall, a large seventeenth-century mansion, surrounded by a wooded park and situated about two miles from Norwich. The spacious house, built of flint and redbrick, was gabled, with two bay windows and star-shaped chimneys. With its well-kept lawns, stables, shrubberies and dove-cote, Earlham became part of the Gurney legend. Generations of the family grew up to love the place, with its winding staircases and attics and its eighty cupboards and powder closets. It was a marvellous house for hide-and-seek. John Gurney could fish and shoot in the grounds and the children could ride in the park on their ponies or go boating on the river Wensum which flowed by. Yet, to a timid six-year-old like Betsy, with her terror of the water and the dark, the rambling old house must have seemed frightening.

She was a delicate child, subject to 'languor of body and mind that rendered study irksome' and nervous attacks of mysterious origin. She drew a veil over these childish attacks, 'her most tender, nervous system', whilst her sisters, caught up in the romanticism of the age, rather revelled in them. 'Betsy is so ill … I look forward with the most gloomy ideas concerning her,' wrote Louisa Gurney, four years her junior, in 1796.

Her ill-health, the 'nerves' and the inexplicable apathy have a curious echo in other great women reformers of the period, notably Florence Nightingale. Whether little Betsy sensed that she was a unique personality and unconsciously 'used' her illness to allow her self space and solitude in which to develop is at least worth considering. At night, when she was weeping in the dark, she was prey to the most morbid fancies. She wished sometimes that 'two large walls might crush us all together that we might die at once and thus avoid the misery of each other's death'. In her fantasy, at least, she coped with the pain of rivalry with her siblings and of separation from them. She also had a recurrent nightmare of being stranded on the seashore and washed away by wild waves.

If she had a friend among the children, it was Rachel, two years older than Betsy, with high spirits and a sweet nature. Their mother encouraged the friendship between the girls, hoping perhaps that the lively spirits of the elder girl would counteract Betsy's tendency to mope and fret. The girls shared a 'pretty light closet' where they kept their own books, pictures, teaset, sea shells and other treasures they collected. 'As far as I can recollect,' Betsy Fry wrote when she was a matron in her forties, 'we unitedly partook of these pleasures without any of the little jealousies or the quarrels of childhood.' In the same passage, she contradicts herself by adding that she felt very inferior to her two elder sisters.

There were days, however, when Betsy could join in wholeheartedly with what appeared to outsiders as the charmed life of Earlham. In the summer, the dashing young Gurneys roasted potatoes over an open fire in the fields or rode into Norwich on their ponies. Betsy rode well and enjoyed it. In the city they would drink syllabub through a straw and listen to the band. On evenings when they had company, a blind fiddler would walk up through the avenue of limes to play to them, and the old house echoed to the children's dance. Sometimes Rachel and Betsy would sing duets at the piano, but Rachel outshone her sister in everything. With her dark blue eyes and sparkling nature, she was universally admired.

They were great tomboys, these good-looking sisters. They liked to jump in the barn and sit on top of the high straw stack and they played practical jokes on their visitors. When their cousin, Hudson Gurney, came to call one evening, they locked him in the pantry. One fine day in spring, the seven tall Gurney sisters linked arms across the main road and forced the mail-coach to a halt. As well as a governess, the children had a riding master, a drawing master (Old Crome, the founder of the Norwich school) and, later, a French master. They worked hard at their lessons, but there was always time for strolling in the park, where herons could be found nesting, for writing their journals and for endless gossip.

Unfortunately Betsy burnt her early journals, so we only see oblique glimpses of her at this time. Her sisters found her 'preachy' and 'tetchy'. As a young girl, she disliked the long Quaker Sunday quite as much as the others. She dreaded going to 'Goats', the old Dutch Meeting House in Goats Lane, and again and again the girls would note in their diaries that Goats was 'Dis' [family word for disgusting]. They were wealthier, better educated and more worldly than most of the congregation. When they entered in their rustling, brightly-coloured silks, the children were conscious of causing a stir and fidgeted through the Meeting.

Quaker worship demands an inner discipline that requires stilling the conscious mind and heart so that the spirit of God may work while the unifying silence gathers. Only when a message comes to the worshipper with compelling force can he, in conscience, speak. Those who were drawn into the vocal ministry were 'recorded' as ministers by their area meeting, if acceptable, although not ordained. For the children, the long silences, broken occasionally by tedious sermons, were painfully boring. Catherine Gurney tried to induce the right mood in her children by written advice:

Since we know that He who gave us life, health and strength of body has given us an understanding mind, we ought to consider whether it is. not right to love and obey that excellent Being, who has certainly placed us here on earth and surrounded us with blessings and enjoyment … it is necessary to retire with our friends and neighbours from hurry and business, that we may think of Him who delights to bless us.

She warned her children against allowing their thoughts to wander, and Betsy tried to take the advice to heart. Today Quaker children are required to spend only fifteen minutes in silent worship but at that time they were expected to sit still and quiet for two long hours. All the children found Meeting 'flat, stupid, improving and Sundayish'. Richenda, who was to become a Church of England clergy man's wife, felt quite stifled: 'Oh how I long to get a broom and bang all the old Quakers who do look so triumphant and disagreeable.' Betsy suffered perhaps less than the rest. For her, delicate health became almost a regular excuse to miss Meeting.

Meanwhile the cycle of birth went on. On the morning of 9 March 1791, the younger girls were playing in the kitchen garden with their old nurse, while Betsy, Rachel and Catherine studied indoors. Becky, the maid, came out into the garden to tell them that they had a new baby brother, Daniel. The party of children, headed by Catherine, who was almost fifteen, tiptoed into their mother's room in procession, holding each other's frocks, with little Joseph John, barely two-and-a-half, bringing up the rear.

Daniel was the twelfth and last of the Gurney children. Nineteen months after his birth, their mother became ill. For three weeks the great house was filled with gloom and hushed voices. The children were rarely allowed into the sick-room and then only for a minute or two. Most of the time they were kept out of the way by a detested governess. Betsy suffered appallingly. She was in her thirteenth year, a difficult age, plagued by what she described later as 'the most tender nervous system'. To her chagrin, her beloved mother, who would insist on struggling out of bed to pray for her children, prayed especially for Kitty, the eldest, and two of her sons, John, the eldest boy, and little Joseph, 'her bright morning star'.

On her deathbed, Catherine Gurney called on Kitty, not yet sixteen, to be a mother to all the children. The day she died, 17 November 1792, she repeated over and over again 'Peace, sweet is peace'. The event that Betsy had dreaded all her childhood overwhelmed her when it came. Her mother, the only person who understood her, who never lost patience with her moods, was gone. The silent and frightened children filed past her body.

Betsy was plunged into a frightening depression. She wrote later that she had intended to confide to her mother the symptoms of a mysterious illness but delayed it until it was too late. Since this illness coincided with puberty, it seems likely that the onset of menstruation disturbed the precarious stability of her mind and body. The nature of her physical illness, the bouts of depression that dragged her down before her mother's death, her sense of shame at her own insignificance which agitated almost every waking moment, would today almost certainly be regarded as due, in some degree, to nervous over-anxiety. Now that she had no mother, she felt utterly isolated.

For all the family rallied round Kitty, the popular, bustling eldest sister. Bluff John Gurney, her father, turned to her in his grief. She it was whom he consulted about the children. She became the head of the family, while all the servants, particularly Hannah Judd, the housekeeper, and Sarah Williman, the much-loved old nurse, did their best for Kitty. Only Betsy was difficult. She grew more moody, more prone to mysterious aches and pains. She fell into the habit of rising later than the others, of missing lessons; Latin and French she particularly disliked. To catch up, she had to speak French on walks to Norwich with the younger girls which was a humiliation. If she broke into English, she had to pay a farthing fine.

The others soon adjusted to the situation and the routine of life at Earlham flowed pleasantly on. The children all got up and dressed well before six – all, that is, except Betsy. Before they sat down to breakfast at eight, they had worked for nearly two hours at their lessons. After breakfast, Kitty read aloud from Livy's *History of Rome* or some other lesson book while the girls embroidered. By that date, the two eldest boys, John and Samuel, were away at school, Joseph studied with the governess whilst little Daniel was looked after by a nurse. At twelve they sat down to nooning (lunch) and worked again till three, when they dined. At six the family drank tea. Afterwards, the four younger girls, who were inseparable, put on their little red cloaks – they were free to roam without bonnets in the park and garden – and went out with Kitty. She encouraged glee singing and occasionally invited the neighbours to join in a dance. In their own pleasant world set in the peaceful Norfolk countryside, it seemed impossible that life could ever change.

Yet only two miles away was the city of Norwich, which was then a centre of political, cultural and intellectual activity. A climate of social concern pervaded the family. Even the children took an ardent interest in the politics and welfare of the wider world. As a small boy, Joseph refused to take sugar in his tea because of the 'poor slaves'. Nearer home, the French Revolution had thrilled and disturbed them. A close friend of the family, Dr Alderson, a well-known physician, was a republican and a member of the newly-formed Corresponding Society, which advocated universal suffrage and an annual Parliament. The widower and his daughter, Amelia, (later Amelia Opie), who was ten years older than Betsy, were frequent visitors. In the drawing-room of the Aldersons' house in Colegate or at Earlham, the family would discuss the writings of Thomas Paine, Jean Jacques Rousseau and William Godwin. Everything they had held sacred, from parental authority to the sanctity of marriage, was challenged by these fascinating new thinkers. The Gurney girls admired Amelia greatly. She was

lively and amusing, improvised amateur theatricals and wrote
poetry and plays. She seemed to know everyone, from William
Godwin, who was a suitor, to Mrs Siddons, the actress. Through
Amelia the girls heard, enraptured, of the London fashions and
of Mary Wollstonecraft and her startling new book *Vindication of
the Rights of Woman*.

Dr Enfield, a Unitarian Minister and scholar in Norwich, and his
family also helped to undermine the faith of the young Gurneys.
Before her mother's death, Kitty had begun to attend lectures
given by the doctor and had become friendly with his children,
who were atheists. The friendship had caused her mother some
unease, but since she herself had a favourite cousin who was a
Unitarian and the family mixed freely outside the Quaker sect,
she felt unable to object and was, in any case, convinced of the
necessity to allow her children freedom to choose their own path
in the Christian faith.

Had she realised the consequences, she would doubtless have
been pained. Young Henry Enfield and Rachel Gurney fell passionately in love. The sisters found the situation piquant and
helped to conceal the truth from their father. When he did find
out about the love affair, all the young Enfields were forbidden
to visit Earlham. Although John Gurney was liberal in his attitude
about dress or amusements for the children, he drew the line at
marriage into other sects. His brother, Joseph, a more serious
and active Quaker, was constantly upbraiding him for the way in
which he brought up his girls. So the lovers were parted for two
years, with the promise that the matter would be reconsidered if
they were still of the same mind after their separation.

In a sense, his objections came too late. The restless spirit of
the age had unsettled all the family. Their faith in God, which
had been unquestioned, was shaken. In the upper-class circles in
which they moved, men and women of fashion despised religious 'enthusiasm' above all else. Church-going on Sunday had
become a matter of form for the gentry. Some Dissenters were
advocating radical reform, which also unsettled their children.

A sensitive, thoughtful young person like Betsy was, inevitably, deeply disturbed. She became a republican and rode through Norwich with a tricolor in her hat. She mixed more and more with Unitarians and freethinkers. For a time she became enthusiastic about deists, who believed in the existence of God but not in a revealed religion. Like all the sisters, she became infected with the romanticism of the age, and wrote, in ecstasies, about the beauties of nature.

She was a mysterious girl and lived a vivid inner life, as her journals later reveal. In her sixteenth year, in particular, her bouts of depression were so overwhelming – 'in a valley' she called it – that the other girls kept away from her. It seems likely that that particular depression sprang from a brief but painful love affair. James Lloyd, a young man from a rich and scholarly Quaker family, whose father was the founder of Lloyd's Bank, had come to stay at Earlham for several weeks. James had apparently found the tall, sensitive girl the most attractive of the charming sisters. He made her an offer of marriage and she was briefly engaged. What happened to break off the engagement is unknown. She felt the pain of it deeply. 'I dare say he might be said to have done me hurt in his time,' she wrote later.

Apparently she went to London and visited the doctor in February 1796 – her father's account bill records a five-guinea fee to Dr Sims. Betsy's illness at that time almost certainly sprang from her emotional distress. All her life disappointment and unhappiness induced physical symptoms.

Louisa Gurney, the boldest of the girls, who was then eleven, wrote in her journal in April of that year that she did not know what they would do when Betsy came home, 'for we are all afraid of her now, which is very shocking … Dearest Betsy! she seems to have no one for her friend, for none of us are intimate with her.' Betsy's dark moods hung like thunder-clouds over the house and created an oppressive atmosphere.

Her journals, stored for years in an old tea-chest, are in existence from April 1797, just before her seventeenth birthday.

That spring, His Royal Highness, Prince William Frederick, nephew of King George III, was quartered at Norwich with his regiment. John Gurney was highly flattered to receive an invitation to dine with the young Prince. He himself was an unpretentious merchant who had received a very skimpy education for a man of his standing, but his good nature and easy manners made him popular in any company – as, no doubt, did his seven good-looking daughters. John Gurney, in his turn, invited the Prince to dine at Earlham and there was 'an amazing fuss' of preparations. 'Why', wrote Betsy innocently in her journal, 'do I wish so much for the Prince to come?' His visit was a great success. The Prince and his aides were delighted with the lively, graceful girls, unaffected in their manner yet polished in behaviour. But Uncle Joseph, who was worried by the frivolous life the young girls were allowed to lead, disapproved of the visit. He was a conscientious Friend, austere and deeply sincere, and as a good Quaker considered all men as equal and despised the pomp of Court life. He scolded his brother John for his friendship with the Prince, but nevertheless was persuaded to come to Earlham to meet him.

Louisa liked the Prince 'vastly'. So did the other girls. Betsy, however, had mixed feelings about the visit. 'I feel by experience how much entering the world hurts me,' she confided to the 'friend of her heart', her diary. 'Worldly company materially injures me, it excites a false stimulus, such a love of pomp, pride, vanity, jealousy and ambition. It leads us to think about dress and such trifles and when out of it we fly to novels, scandals … for entertainment.' At that stage of her life, Betsy would not have described herself as 'religious', but her desire for self-improvement was already at war with the natural feelings of a girl of seventeen.. 'I met the prince,' she remarked sadly in her journal on 29 April, 'it shows me the folly of the world. My mind feels flat after such a storm of pleasure.' On her birthday, 21 May, she wrote:

> I am 17 today. Am I a happier creature than I was this time twelve-months? I know I am happier: I think I am better. I hope I shall be

much better this day year … I hope to be quite an altered person, to have more knowledge, to have my mind in greater order; and my heart too … it is in such a fly-away state.

All through her life she retained the habit of keeping a stern spiritual balance sheet of her behaviour in her journals. The writing of them seems to have been a release in itself. She was always hard on herself, clear-eyed about her faults and seems to have revelled in self-abasement. In this entry, she upbraids herself for losing her temper with her younger sisters, contradicting the others, exaggerating and telling lies. 'I must not mump [sulk] when they are liked and I am not,' she said of her sisters. Some poor people visited Earlham and Betsy remonstrated with herself for not giving to them with a more open heart. Her tender conscience, her longing for spiritual purification led her into excesses of self-criticism.

Throughout that year she was beginning to flirt with the notion of religion, and her thoughts on it cropped up increasingly. 'My idea of religion is not for it to unfit us for the duties of life, like a nun who leaves it for prayer and thanksgiving, but I think it should stimulate us to perform these duties properly.'

As her diary entries suggest, she found it difficult to behave well with the younger children although she longed so much to do her duty. Louisa complained that she was bossy. When Kitty was away and Betsy had to teach the children their lessons she became so fussed and self-important that there were always scenes. Also she could not help feeling resentful that, although she struggled more than the others to be a dutiful daughter, Richenda, her happy-go-lucky younger sister, was their father's favourite just because she looked so much like her late mother.

That summer when she had turned seventeen, Betsy seemed to blossom and enjoy life openly and with gusto as she never had before. A glimpse of that golden time exists in the journal of John Pitchford, a Roman Catholic friend of the sisters, in the entry for 27 July 1797:

This is a day which I shall ever remember with delight. I have spent seventeen hours with my seven most enchanting friends. I rose at 4 A.M. and walked slowly to Earlham, as I did not wish to disturb them too soon. I had partly made up my mind not to throw pebbles at their windows [the preconcerted signal of my arrival] till six but I found them already risen. The morning was clear and brilliant. Rachel saw me first and knocked at the window. Then Richenda and Louisa came down and soon all the rest except Betsy, who does not rise so soon on account of her health. After a short walk, the four were sent to the schoolroom to do their lessons [the four younger girls, Richenda, Hannah, Louisa and Priscilla]. Kitty, Rachel and I seated ourselves in the shade.

I had brought *Peregrinus Porteus* in my pocket, and read the beautiful description of the farm at Pitane and the glowing language in which the Christian preacher enlarges on the character and manner of our blessed Saviour: they completely enjoyed it …

We enjoyed a charming breakfast together, Betsy having joined us, and then we went into the kitchen-garden to eat fruit. After this, we selected a shady spot on the lawn, where the whole party reclined upon a haycock while I read to them part of my journal, omitting certain passages which avowed my attachment to Rachel … I am not clear whether the sharp-sighted Rachel did not suspect the truth, but her behaviour during the rest of the day was full as kind as ever. They were all interested with my journal. 'Now we really know you,' they exclaimed, 'let us join hands and vow an eternal friendship.' This we did with rapturous feelings and glowing hearts. Rachel now read some of Henry Enfield's journal which he regularly sends her. Betsy read part of her journal, in which she acknowledges all her faults with the most charming candour … After dinner we went to the pianoforte and Rachel and I practised some songs. I taught her the *Stabat Mater*, which she much liked. We then went in the boat and had some most interesting conversation, and after tea chose a delightful spot in the garden facing the setting sun, where Kitty read the poetry of 'The Monk', and I 'The Deserted Village'. Then we went to the village church where I read Gray's 'Elegy' by twilight with great effect. Kitty said, 'We will be your seven sisters'. When we got to the river-side, we again had enchanting singing, finishing by 'Poor John is dead', and, as we returned, promised each other that any of us in danger of death should be visited by the rest. Then we extended our views beyond the grave, and enthusiastically sang till we reached the house 'In Heaven forever dwell'. It was with difficulty that I tore myself away after supper. It was a day ever to be remembered with transport.

In the first week in August, Handel's Oratorio was to be performed in Norwich and Betsy longed to hear it. She was torn between duty and pleasure. 'The Prince is to be there and by all accounts it will be quite a grand sight and there will be the finest musick; but if my father does not like me to go, much as I wish it – I will give it up … without a murmur.' One can sense the intensity of her struggle. John Gurney, however, was far too indulgent a parent to curb her pleasure. 'Betsy went to the assembly and danced a great deal,' wrote young Louisa. 'How most droll! Quite a new excursion.' On the rare occasions when she felt inclined, Betsy could be quite as carefree and charming as the others. And despite the family's pity for her, she seemed to attract the opposite sex. That winter she had an 'offer' from one of the officers. 'How very droll', remarked Louisa. But the round of pleasure could not satisfy Betsy. She revelled in it and then despised herself. 'I am', she observed, 'a dissipated, idle, contemptible fine lady.'

Mutterings of a need for religion filled her journal again. 'I do not know if I shall not soon be rather religious,' she wrote in August, 'because I have thought lately what a support it is through life; it seems so delightful to depend upon a superior power, for all that is good … I think anybody who had real faith could never be unhappy; it appears the only certain source of support and comfort in this life, and what is best of all it draws to virtue ...', and in December, 'A thought passed my mind that if I had some religion, I should be superior to what I am.'

Christmas came, with Norfolk turkey and plum pudding, for, unlike Plain Quakers of the day, the Gurney family thoroughly enjoyed all the trappings of Christmas. The Prince, by now a frequent visitor to Earlham, called three days later. After dinner, the ten young Gurneys and their father gathered round the Prince and 'sang and were very merry'. 'His Royal Highness departed,' Lousia noted, 'after having kept his coach two hours waiting at the door.'

A fortnight later the Prince called again. 'We have had a gay, pleasant bustling time,' Louisa babbles in her diary.

> He had not been here long before he insisted that Rachel should preach him a sermon. He and a great many of us ran up to Betsy's room and Rachel gave a most capital sermon. I never saw anything so droll as it was to see the Prince and all of us locked up in Betsy's room and Rachel ... giving him a good lesson in the Quakers' strain and imitating William Crouch [a dull Quaker preacher] to perfection ... I never saw the Prince so sociable and agreeable as this time ... He does so admire Rachel ... I do like the Prince for liking Kitty so much: I am sure it shows his taste and I don't wonder at it ... Rachel did look beautiful and talked so cleverly all day.

Nothing was said of Betsy. After the Prince left, the company had a dance. Three nights in succession, they danced the night away and on Saturday night they visited Dr Alderson and danced from seven to twelve.

Louisa was intoxicated by the high life. 'What a surprising difference rank and high life make in a person's whole way and manner. I don't know when I enjoyed dancing so much there, such beaux, so superior to the bank boys' (the clerks at

Gurneys Bank). Betsy, however, felt unnerved by the round of pleasure, assailed by a feeling of time passing, with romantic ideas about dying:

> I must die. I shall die! Wonderful death is beyond comprehension. To leave life and all its interests and be almost forgotten by those we love. What a comfort must a real faith in religion be in the hour of death … but I am sorry to say I have no real faith in any sort of religion … If religion be a support, why not get it.

Frustrated by a sense of waste, she wrote, 'I am now seventeen and if some kind and great circumstance does not happen to me, I shall have my talents devoured by moth and rust.'

Like Betsy, Uncle Joseph Gurney of The Grove was unhappy about the worldly state at Earlham. He reproved Rachel for going to dances and she burst into tears. He also spoke severely to their father about the girls and their beaux. To marry out of the Society of Friends was not to be countenanced, even by John Gurney who took his religion easily, so he reprimanded his children and tried to be more 'Quakerly', much to their disgust.

Uncle Joseph also spoke sharply about the lax attitude of the family towards attending Meeting. Betsy stood in great awe of this uncle, and he obviously realised that of all the children, she was the one most likely to respond to religion. On 3 February 1798, an American Quaker, William Savery, arrived in Norwich on a religious visit, 'travelling in the ministry'. Before he came, he had had to lay his 'concern' before the area meeting for business, the Monthly Meeting, which had 'liberated' and provided him with a certificate as evidence of corporate support.

Newspaper reports had reached the Gurneys about Savery which made him sound more interesting than most of the dull old Quakers. He had preached to the Red Indians in America, he had travelled in France and Germany, spoke both French and German, and had visited Holland and Ireland.

The day after his arrival, he was expected at 'Goats'. For once Betsy agreed to go, 'although I had a very bad pain in my stomach'. She sat in the front row facing the Minister's gallery, fidgeting and admiring her new boots, purple, laced with scarlet. William Savery, a wealthy tanner from Philadelphia, was shocked at the bright colours and rustling silks. 'I thought it the gayest Meeting of Friends I had ever sat in … the marks of wealth and grandeur are too obvious in several families.' The Meeting opened with a long, oppressive silence. At last he stood up and began to speak in his attractive American accent.

He spoke of peace, at a time when war fever was rampant and fears of French invasion almost at panic point. He appealed to Christians to 'no more delight in War' when the churches had held services of thanksgiving for a naval victory only four months before. He related with impassioned eloquence the goodness and piety to be found in so-called 'Heathens' to a congregation which was narrow and inward-looking.

For Betsy the man and his message were a revelation.

Legend has overlaid what really happened that day. Long after the event Richenda wrote that when Savery began to speak, Betsy's attention 'became fixed. At last I saw her begin to weep and she became a good deal agitated.' This sounds convincing but Richenda also added that Betsy made her way to the men's side of the Meeting and pleaded with her father to allow her to dine with William Savery at Uncle Joseph's house. Since, according to this account, she had already been invited to her uncle's, the rest of Richenda's version may be discounted.

Betsy herself, curiously, wrote two accounts of the Meeting. In the first she simply says '… after a meeting of three hours I whent with aunt Jane [Uncle Joseph's wife] – all the friends dined there – I felt rather odd as I was the only gay [worldly] person. There was a soft, pleasing manner in friend Savery but I thought he had something of the hoteur of Quakers about him. The [second] meeting was not till six in the evening & uncle

Joseph came to me to say he wished me to go with friend S. alone in the carriage to meeting – we had much talk but not much concerning conversation [about deep spiritual matters] – we whent to meeting which lasted very long & he preached a very excellent sermon.'

Perhaps that account was written on the spot while she was waiting for the carriage. Over two thousand people attended that evening and hundreds must have wanted to say a word to William Savery. Her second account tells us more about her spiritual state:

Today much has passed in my mind of a very serious nature. I have had a faint light spread over [my] mind ... owing to having been much with & heard much *excellence* from one who appears to me a true christian – it has caused me to feel a *little* religion ... at first I was frightened & hurried to think that a plain *quaker* should have made so deep an impression on my feelings but how truly prejudiced in me to think that because good came from a *quaker* I should & must be led away by inthusiesem & folly ...

Today I *felt* there is a God – *I have been devotional* & my mind has been led away from the follies it mostly is wrapt up in – I loved the man as if he was almost sent from heaven – we had much serious talk & what he said to me was like a *refreshing shower* on parched up earth ... it has not made [me] unhappy – I felt ever since *humble* & I have longed for virtue – I hope to be truly virtuous, to let sophistry fly from my mind, not be inthusiastic & foolish but only be so far religious as will lead to virtue – there is nothing seems so little understood as *religion*.

In the first account Betsy tells us that she felt very low during the evening Meeting and thought about her mother in the burying ground and then dwelt on death.

After meeting I rode home to the Grove with friend S & we had a sort of a meeting all the way. As soon as we got to the Grove he had a sort of a regular meeting with me. When I got home, I mixed too much the idea of growing religious and growing the Quaker. I had a painful night. I dreamt nor thought of anything but this man and what had passed. W.S. came next morning. He no longer preached but was kind and affectionate.

William Savery seemed totally unaware of the deep impression he had made. 'J.G. [John Gurney] is a widower,' he records in his journal. 'His children seem very, kind and attentive to him, and he is very indulgent to them.' Savery remarked on the fine library in the house. He felt doubtful whether the young Gurneys, wrapped in luxury, would choose the path of truth.

'Betsy not only admires but quite loves him,' wrote Richenda and added that she herself found him charming and liberal-minded and a most upright Christian. The other sisters laughed at Betsy and teased her about the unexpected impression that the middle-aged preacher had made upon her. But religion, even in the form of Friend Savery, was not powerful enough to claim her undivided attention although she longed for him to come again. Two days later she rode into Norwich in a serious frame of mind but 'being stared at with admiration by a few red coats brought on vanity and I rode home as full of the world as I had ridden to town full of heaven. I should like to have a much deeper and more lasting impression made upon me. I do believe if he had asked me, I should have gone to America,' she wrote innocently. Savery's preaching had come at a time when Betsy was in need of love and groping towards a religious belief. On a freezing night in February 1798 she went to visit her relatives in a state of extraordinary elation:

When I got into the carriage it was full, but with Rachel's singing and a most beautiful starlight night we went over the Castle Hill and for a moment my feelings were open to anything. I looked at the sky and thought of God – I looked at the hill and thought of red coats and my feelings went jumping about most drolly ...

a fine military band went past the carriage, I could have flown after it.

When they arrived at her Uncle Joseph's house, she almost broke her leg getting out of the carriage too eagerly, believing Savery was still there. She was puzzled by her own feelings towards Savery. With him she did not feel uncomfortable and awkward as she had in the past with the narrow-minded Norwich Plain Quakers. On the contrary, she felt that he understood her and that he overflowed with true religion. 'If I were to grow like him a preacher, I should be able to preach to the gay and unbelieving better than to any others for I should ... know their hearts better.'

The following Sunday she went unasked to Meeting although Savery had departed. But the magic was gone. 'Today I felt all my old irreligious feelings ... my mind is so much inclined to scepticism and enthusiasm that if I argue and doubt I shall be a total sceptic; if on the contrary, I give way to it and, as it were, wait for religion I may be led away.' On the whole she hoped she would become religious, and was now openly at odds with the larky Gurney girls, discontented and unsettled. By 16 February she was in a state of great excitement:

> My mind is in a whirl ... In all probability I shall go to London I shall see friend Savery most likely and all those plain Quakers. I may be led away, beware! my feelings are far more risen at the thought of seeing him than all the playhouses and gaieties in the world. One will, do not doubt, balance against the other ... I dare say it will not be half so pleasant as the Earlham heartfelt gaieties in the Prince's time. I must be very careful not to get vain or silly.

It seems likely that Betsy had persuaded her susceptible father to allow her to pay a visit to London.

The following day her flyaway heart led her to ride to Norwich to hear the military band without her father's consent – and to regret it afterwards. In this volatile state of mind she went to London.

II

The Transformation

'My clothes I never had in such a droll state, I was quite shaking,' wrote Betsy after her journey to London in February 1798. Travelling in the dark, with the horses galloping, the horn blowing and the mail-coach swaying had unnerved her badly. The coach pulled up at a small alehouse past Newmarket and her father ordered strong brandy and water for her. She drank it down, with some laudanum and fortunately felt sleepy for the rest of the journey. Even in her youth, she was growing accustomed to taking laudanum and strong drink to soothe the frequent bouts of toothache, stomach-ache and 'nerves' that plagued her.

She and her father and her female companion spent the night with relatives in Brick Lane. The next day she was sad at having to part from her father. She had had him to herself on the journey and he had been 'truly kind' and paid her the particular attention she craved.

When he was gone, however, she revelled in her freedom. For the first time in her life she was her own mistress, able to make plans for herself. 'How I love being so independent,' she wrote.

Betsy decided to stay by herself in the big house in Brick Lane so that she could enjoy 'a little, nice quiet', when her relatives went away on a short visit. As usual her morbid imagination intruded. She had such a dread of thieves and footpads (ironically, in view of her future life) that every step or sound in the night disturbed her. She wrote in her diary: 'I am ready to jump out at my own shadow.

I will not be such a fool ... For what would people do with me ... I am not such a tempting morsel as for anybody to wish to run away with me.' At Earlham, she was always compared unfavourably with her vivacious sister Rachel. Yet Betsy, with her tall, comely figure, fair hair and graceful carriage, was more attractive than she realised.

Almost dutifully, she entered on her round of pleasure. On Monday 26 February, she went to Drury Lane. 'I must own I was extremely disappointed, it is true the house is grand and dazzling.' On Tuesday she went to the play at Covent Garden and continued not to like the theatre. By Wednesday she felt 'vain and proud and silly', and took a dancing lesson in the evening. Thursday saw her once again at the play, a double bill, *Hamlet* and *Bluebeard*. She did admit to a moderate interest in the 'grand Dramatic Romance of Bluebeard or Female Curiosity ... I suppose that nothing on the stage can exceed it ... There is acting, musick, scenery to perfection, but I was glad when it was over.' Upon *Hamlet* she did not comment.

'My hair was dressed and I felt like a monkey.' She was honest enough to admit that she would have enjoyed the London world more if she had someone of her own age to share the pleasures. Besides, she was used to Norwich society where a Gurney was a person of importance in the city. 'Being so insignificant a person, I am not of the consequence I am at Earlham, nor is [life in London] as gay as it is at Norwich.'

By Friday morning she was in a thoroughly bad mood and walked about the streets of London till she 'happened' to see 'the Rock [as she had come to regard him] of William Savery and that put me in a better state'.

Betsy, it seems clear, had agreed to taste all the pleasures of London so that she could meet the preacher who had made such an impression on her. She knew, of course, of all the wealthy Quaker households that offered him hospitality and of the Meetings which he was to attend. Whenever she could, she swooped eagerly to see him, despite the teasings of her cousins, who had been warned, no doubt, by Betsy's father, of her excessive fondness for Mr Savery. Very early one morning she got up and walked over to the house where William Savery was staying and waited till he came into the parlour. 'I always feel quite a palpitation at my heart at the sound of his voice,' she wrote. 'I walked to Meeting with him and he asked me if I was not rather ashamed to walk with so plain a friend.' William Savery wore the plain, loose-fitting coat of a Quaker, without collar or buttons. Betsy assured him that she felt honoured to be with him. Privately she noted that she behaved far more decorously than usual at Meeting.

London and its attractions hardly stood a chance. Nevertheless she called on Mrs Siddons, who had played at the Norwich Theatre, but the actress was out. She also visited the picture galleries. One evening did hold glamour for her. With her Norwich friends, the Opies, she visited the opera. To her delight, the Prince of Wales was there, already a gross and flamboyant figure but, for Betsy, enchanting. She confided to her diary: 'I do love grand company ... I own I felt more pleasure in looking at him than in seeing the rest of the company or hearing the music.' That evening, encouraged by Amelia Opie, her hair was dressed again and she was painted a little. 'I did look quite pretty for me.'

When she was away from Earlham she missed her sisters more than she had expected. To keep up her spirits, she asked her cousins to play all Rachel's favourite pieces on the pianoforte. She also sent a long letter full of advice and moral strictures to her younger sisters, urging them to be kind to one another.

She spent ten days of her holiday visiting other relatives, the Hoares, at Hampstead. They were an affectionate and amiable family who lived in high style, in a large house with a fine garden. They were, Betsy noted, 'quite struck' with her. These relatives, too, took her to the opera and, once again, it was the atmosphere – 'the house is rather dazzling and the company very fascinating' – rather than the music that impressed her. She was troubled by another bout of toothache and felt low, but through her journal in London runs the thread of William Savery and religion. She realised that the two were dangerously intertwined.

She went to Meeting and heard Mr Savery describe the secret of true religion and the nature of prayer. Once again she experienced a mystic glow. 'I really did cry with a sort of ecstasy.' Afterwards she felt ugly and disagreeable, doubtless annoyed that William Savery should see her tear-stained face. Savery was a married man of forty-eight at that time, Betsy not yet eighteen, and he seems to have, been completely unaware of her infatuation. On another occasion Betsy wrote, 'I could not withstand the temptation of going to see William Savery. I went but only stayed a few minutes, those few did me good, he is a wonderful man.' She noted in her journal that she felt jealous when he said that he liked Molly Knowles, a mutual acquaintance. She was in a dangerous state. In religion she had found an outlet for her highly emotional and hypersensitive nature but she had come to religion through a man. Only through Savery, she believed, could she realise herself. She used all her moral energy to understand her dilemma. 'I shall always love religion through him but must always love it away from him.' In her journal, which was to become more and more a spiritual biography rather than a record of daily life, she prayed to grow 'more and more virtuous, follow the path I should go in and not fear to acknowledge the God whom I worship'.

After seven weeks she was tired of London. 'I now long to be in the quiet of Earlham, for there I may see how good I can be.' In April her father came to fetch her. Together they went to a rout, and out to dinner and spent a pleasant, merry day with the poet Peter Pindar. But all the diversions, all the excitement could not touch the deep longing inside. On 21 April, back at Earlham, she wrote, 'All is forming within me … I do not doubt that this is the time of transformation.'

Richenda, for one, thought that Betsy had come back 'a good deal improved by her journey; she has seen a good deal of William Savery whose whole soul seems formed and made for true religion and perfect truth … Betsy seems to be changed from a complete sceptic to a person who has entire faith in a Supreme Being.'

For her father and the rest of her sisters, the change in Betsy was not only unwelcome but alarming. She seemed remote from the rest of the family as well as grave and preachy. Betsy herself was troubled by the change. Even with her favourite sister, Rachel, who was 'in a fright' lest Betsy turn Plain Quaker, she no longer felt the familiar, spontaneous surge of family feeling. What she described as her 'disgusting coolness' worried her: '… much as I am united to them all, I am, and always have been, separate from them … and yet I am not happy without them. I do love them. I cannot make myself out.'

At that time and for the next two years Betsy constantly found herself compromising in the outward expression of her religious feeling. She wanted to declare herself a Plain Friend by wearing the Quaker bonnet, going to Meeting twice on Sunday, refusing to join in dancing and singing, and using the Plain language, the 'thee' and 'thou' form, to everyone. But to do so meant defying and hurting the whole family. Her sisters, in particular, felt affronted 'that one of us seven should separate herself in principles, actions and appearance from the rest'. Young Louisa, the most spirited of the younger girls, refused to allow Betsy to give herself airs and thoroughly offended her. 'Louisa treats me as a person much below her, at times with disdain which is painful to receive from such a child,' Betsy noted crossly.

The girls suspected, rightly, that it was the encounter with William Savery that had caused the change in her. But when Rachel teased Betsy about being in love with him she replied, as truthfully as she could, that she did not think she was. She was hurt by the taunt. 'I think I may love a person as I love, him without being in love, but I doubt it. I first loved him for his religion but the feelings of human nature are very apt to join with the superior feelings of the heart … I think it a wrong suspicion to enter my mind, but I fear I shall never, no never, see him again.'

She was seriously considering her own religious position almost every day of her life. On a visit to drink tea in the family bank in Norwich, she wandered into the Cathedral. She was moved by the grandeur but felt reservations; 'I think worship which flows from the heart must be much finer than that produced by musick or a formal prayer.'

It was impossible at that stage for the other Gurney girls to understand the complex workings of Betsy's heart. She had always had a fevered imagination, always led a vivid inner life. For years she had had nightmares. Since the time she had heard William Savery preach and felt 'a little religion', the ending of her recurrent dream of being washed away by high waves in a wild sea had changed. Betsy was now always saved from the sea by a rock. Just before her conversion she had had another dream about William Savery, faithfully recorded in her journal. 'I dreamt that William Savery came and he was turned into a woman and that I did not love him as I do now, a good hint to myself.'

Quietly, but with remarkable courage for such a timid girl, she had begun to develop a life of her own at Earlham. One of the servants, 'Poor Bob', lay dangerously ill in a cottage in the grounds and Betsy took it upon herself to visit him every day and read to him from the Bible. Her visits irritated the family, and when she developed a cough her father was certain that she had caught it from the ailing man. She talked to Bob about his death, telling him 'that I felt such faith in the blessings of Immortality that I pitied not his state.' She did not relate how this crumb of comfort was received by the poor wretch, but had the grace to add that 'it was an odd speech to make to a dying man'.

She gave some of her clothes to the poor of the village 'not that I am particularly virtuous, I am only following my natural disposition', and drew up yet another set of rules of conduct for herself. She began to struggle against her inclination to lie in bed in the mornings – she was hardly ever down for the breakfast bell and sometimes it was ten or eleven before she appeared. In the warm summer days, when the garden was full of roses, she wrote wistfully in her journal, 'it would be delightful if I could spend a day in idleness. In both hot and cold weather, every thought and every action is recorded by our Father in Heaven.'

On her eighteenth birthday, her father, who was away from Earlham, wrote to her, offering her another visit to London, possibly with the idea of trying again to divert her from her obsession with religion. But Betsy preferred to stay in the countryside. She enjoyed it much more since her return from London.

She was making valiant efforts to acquire the habit of reading the Bible before an early breakfast. She preferred to read the Scriptures in the original rather than commentaries on them: 'My opinion of Christ is that he was most highly inspired by the spirit of the Almighty. I believe him to be an instrument sent from heaven but in a spiritual light … I do love the New Testament. It is *delightful* particularly to me.'

She had begun to read and interpret the Bible to one little boy from the village, Billy, and had plans for bringing in several other poor children to read to them on Sunday evenings. 'I hope to continue and increase one by one … It might increase morality among the lower classes if the Scriptures were oftener and better read to them. I believe I cannot exert myself too much, there is nothing that gives me such satisfaction as instructing the lower classes.' Betsy herself was a poor scholar, laughed at by her sisters for her eccentric spelling and her slowness with her lessons. In this entry one can detect not only her religious compassion but her obsessive need to surround herself with an admiring audience.

One asset she knew she possessed was a melodious and peculiarly attractive speaking voice, although no one else in the family seems to have noticed it. She never remarked on it herself but was critical of the delivery of others. Even at eighteen, before she had sensed that she might be called to preach, she felt 'quite vexed' at poor Bob's funeral when the parson read 'very badly'.

In other matters that concerned her vanity, she was trying earnestly to reform. On 29 June she rode into Norwich on her pony 'feeling rather worldly, thinking about dress and such trumpery'.

She annoyed her sisters by refusing to order a silk gown. 'I am determined to be economical,' she wrote sternly, 'I am to have £40 a year for washing and everything. I should wish not to spend more than £20 about my own person, but I fear that will be impossible. On average, washing comes to 9d a week and that only allows 3s 6d a week [for dress]. I don't like the thought that that might support a poor family ... it cannot be right to have such luxuries.' Yet she loved, she needed, the best in everything: linen, muslin, meat and wine. Entries such as this one – 'I have been luxurious in eating; I drank too much red wine' – appear frequently in her journals.

At this stage, Betsy had come to believe that she disliked the company of young men. After her unhappy love affair with James Lloyd two years earlier, she had 'given up the thought of marrying in this life'. When she recovered from the heartbreak, she looked at every young man as a prospective husband. Now, at the age of eighteen, she confessed herself sick at the thought of it. 'One day, no doubt when I least expect it, I may be married, if not, I do not doubt I shall be a happy old maid.'

Despite the tendency to probing self-criticism and the pious search for self-improvement, conventional in the journals of Friends of the time, hers held a note of common sense and real self-awareness. At the beginning of July she attended a funeral from the home of Uncle Joseph of The Grove, and confided to her diary: 'I was in the little room by Uncle Joseph ... the arrival of a corpse made me cry bitterly, if I'd encouraged it, I believe I should have gone into histericks.'

Kitty and her father in particular were anxious to distract Betsy from her alarming tendency to 'give way' to her religious feelings. Somewhat to her consternation, the family proposed to travel to Wales and the South-West of England at the end of July. Betsy feared she might become unwell on the journey and was unhappy about another matter: 'I am very sorry to say I am to leave this journal book behind me,' she wrote on 21 July 1798, 'for I think if I took it it would be a sort of support to me in doing right.'

Her elders obviously meant to wean her from her habit of pious introspection and make a more 'natural' girl of her.

She did persuade her father to allow the party to stop in London so that she could attend a farewell Meeting at Gracechurch Street for William Savery. She had bought him a pocket book as a parting present, but could not speak to him in private, since he was surrounded by other Friends. 'My dear, dear William Savery is, I think only five miles off me this night, it makes it difficult for me to sleep,' she wrote that night in a secret notebook, for she found it impossible to give up keeping a journal. For his part William Savery merely noted that 'a number of high Friends came ... and took the most affectionate leave of me. Dear E.G. was much affected.'

All through the journey Betsy battled with her scruples. Should she go to the play at Weymouth? Ought she to hear the fine marine band at Plymouth, even though she loved military music? Could she get out of attending the dance at Aberystwyth? How could she avoid attending the Assembly Rooms at Bath? The dilemma really tormented her. Sometimes she longed to enjoy 'the world'. But then she persuaded herself 'what real satisfaction is there in being stared at and thought pretty and genteel? Worst of all, she found that if she followed her own wishes, 'I shall have to contradict the will of all the others and most likely to disappoint my father by not going.'

She rarely swerved from her path. If she noticed the places of interest, castles, cathedrals, historic monuments – for they were the most diligent travellers – it was to moralise about them. When the family went to see a military review at Plymouth, Betsy stayed behind because 'I so highly disapprove of war'. In the port, she remarked that 'my mind felt deeply hurt on account of the poor sailors and bad women of whom I saw a great number'. It is easy to dismiss these as the highflown sentiments of a hysterical young girl, but within her lifetime Betsy was to make a contribution towards change in the circumstances of both sailors and 'bad' women. It comes almost as a relief to find her behaving badly in a small inn in rural Wales. 'A gentleman dined with us who I did not attend to till I discovered he was a Lord. Pride how it does creep in on me. I was rather flighty and worldly … Lord Burbrook breakfasted with us.'

Betsy's behaviour seems almost incomprehensibly priggish by today's standards. Yet for her it was a necessary means of asserting her religious conviction and individuality. For to defy convention in those rational and pleasure-loving times by a genuine concern for morality not only required courage but was also a sign of a deep need to express her own personality. To alienate her sisters was bad enough, but to stand apart from the father she adored suggests the urgency of her need.

On the journey her sisters found Betsy's reluctance to join in all the normal pleasures of a holiday thoroughly irritating. She, for her part, was hurt by their reluctance to attend Meetings but she tried to conceal her feelings. As always, her journal served as her confidant. From her personal point of view the expedition turned out to be far from worthless. The party paid a visit to the well-known Quaker colony at Coalbrookdale which grew up around the great Darby ironworks. They stayed at the home of Richard Reynolds, an elderly patriarch and philanthropist, who kept open house for family, friends and dependents. Betsy's cousin, Priscilla Hannah Gurney, a Minister and a Plain Friend lived there. She was a woman who had left her mother, her sister and all the gaieties of Bath in order to live a life of religious retreat. Stately and dignified in her plain, black hood, she made a great impression on Betsy, who felt peaceful and comfortable in this atmosphere for the first time since she had left home.

'It brings me into a sweet state, being with Plain Friends like these, a sort of humility,' she commented. With Priscilla she made a tour of the colony, peering at the Meeting Houses and model cottages for the workers, the furnaces and forges of the iron foundry. In cousin Priscilla's room she read an account of the life of a young woman called Rathbone. 'Shall I', Betsy asked herself, 'ever be sensible of deserving immortal glory?' She thrived amongst these sensible, pious women, who were capable of running a business as well as concerning themselves with religious matters. On Sunday she went to two Meetings and afterwards drank tea with Deborah Darby, an eminent and much loved preacher. Betsy was overjoyed to learn that her own name was known to the Coalbrookdale Quakers through a remark of William Savery's. It seemed to draw them all together. She became so excited that her father warned her later to behave more moderately.

The next day Deborah Darby came to breakfast and afterwards, as was the custom in intimate gatherings of this kind, she preached 'in a deep, clear and striking manner', addressing herself to Betsy and telling her that she was 'sick of the world' and that in future her life was to be dedicated to God. 'Could more satisfaction be given?' Betsy asked passionately. 'I really cried and I think I never felt such an inward encouragement.'

John Gurney was a fond father and seeing Betsy blossom in this atmosphere of pious affection, he allowed her to stay on for three days by herself. Before he left, he warned her to try to restrain her passion. The following day after tea, Betsy, Richard Reynolds and cousin Priscilla visited the Darby home and again that evening Deborah preached. She prophesied to the dumbstruck girl that she was to be 'a light to the blind; speech to the dumb and feet to the lame'. Staying among these confident and dignified women Friends, where religion was a natural part of daily living, increased Betsy's longing to become a Plain Quaker and give up the fripperies of dress and dance. Once again she experienced a mystical sense of God. 'Suddenly my mind felt clothed with light, as with a garment and I felt silenced before God. I cried with the heavenly feeling of humility and repentance.'

Once she was back at Earlham, this state of religious ecstasy faded quickly. In the autumn when they drank tea by candle-light she fell into 'a very flirting state'. And her journal is full of plaintive reminders of her distractions. 'They are all dancing and wanting me to join in.'

By October she had succumbed. She enjoyed a 'merry dance with my old favourites, the general, young H. and J.B ... I felt after dinner it was a pity to give up such pleasures for a false scruple ... today I blushed at the sight of a red coat – quite the old Betsy come once more upon the stage.' Her capacity to dramatise herself, to see her life as a spectacle lasted all her days. For once, it was a merry picture. The week of the dance, Betsy, her six sisters and their cousins, the Hanburys and the Barclays, set off on a donkey race, riding back to front. Three men followed the party to pick up those who fell off amid shrieks of laughter. 'We rode up the park with loud halloos,' wrote Louisa in her journal, 'and surrounding friends and neighbours were assembled to see us arrive.'

To counteract the distractions Betsy made herself yet another time-table: 'Rise at 8.15, quiet time, breakfast, little walk, 9.30 French, 12 walk for half an hour, attend to poor crazy woman, read chemistry till dinner, afterwards needlework or reading till tea.' Her efforts to concentrate and impose a discipline on herself, among all those carefree, pleasure-loving young people, were little short of heroic. She was only too well aware of her tendency to daydream: 'When I do my French I think of the poor, when I go to Meeting I am sure to let my thoughts wander on folly. True religion is what I seldom feel.' She was still reading the Gospels or some suitable book to her 'schollars' and her little school had grown. Through her conscious effort, she began to become aware of the misery and poverty around her.

Her concerns, at eighteen, were becoming less and less those of a normal young lady of her class. There were her school, her poor, her crazy woman. She also adopted Molly Norman, whom she met one day in the park carrying a bag of flour. The girl was about her own age, Betsy fell into conversation with her and asked her what it would cost to clothe her. About ten shillings, was the reply. Betsy begged her father to let her keep Molly out of her £40 a year allowance. Good-natured as ever, he agreed and she became Betsy's protégée, pupil and attendant.

Her religious fervour also led her to indulge in a dangerous form of excitement. 'I have been trying to overcome fear,' she wrote in her journal on 4 January 1799. 'My method has been to stay *in the dark* of a night, to go into those rooms that are not inhabited … considering that so far as I believed in ghosts, so far must I believe in the state after death and it must confirm my belief in the spirit of God … my most predominant fear is that of thieves … faith could cure that also.' By tormenting herself, seeking to conquer her faults and reach a more elevated spiritual plane, Betsy could also rise above the miseries of family life. A kind of martyrdom seemed necessary to sustain her belief in her own worth.

Her father and sisters still disapproved of her activities. Her father thought she was wasting money on books for her 'school' and, besides, it sometimes made her late for Sunday dinners. Her sisters made fun of Betsy as schoolmistress although, as she wrote sadly in her journal, she wished 'hartily … to write and spell English better'. She was attending to her lessons more carefully, trying to improve her needlework. By now she had girls attending her school as well and she showed them how to cut out a dress although she had never made one herself.

Above all there was her involvement with the Society of Friends. She was becoming more and more interested in Meetings and the business of the Society and tempted yet terrified to speak. Speaking at Meeting appeared to her like climbing an immense mountain. At Meeting on 12 March 1799 she almost spoke but 'shook from head to foot'.

'Even acting right will sometimes bring dissensions in a family,' she wrote in her journal and her resolve to become religious troubled her conscience. Her father appeared 'not to like all my present doings', Kitty begged her not to speak of her religious opinions to the younger girls and she offended her brother John by refusing to dance with him when he asked her very kindly. Looking back on her time at Coalbrookdale with the women preachers, Betsy regarded it as 'one of the happiest if not the happiest times in my life'.

In that atmosphere she had been able to explore her religious depths. At Earlham she felt obliged to compromise. 'I am', she wrote in her journal, 'much of a Friend in principle, yet do not outwardly appear much.' She was trying to force herself to say 'thee' and 'thou' in company but sometimes relapsed. She often found herself at houses where Quakers were laughed at and ridiculed. After a dance on 12 December 1799 she wrote, 'If I could make a rule never to give way to vanity, excitement, or flirting, I do not think I should object to dancing; but it always leads me into some one of these faults … But as my giving it up would hurt many, it should be one of those things I part with most carefully.'

She did not dress 'very gay' at that time but was probably still wearing a scarlet riding habit – her father had paid fifteen pounds for habits for the three eldest girls in 1798.[1] There is a description of her in the spring of 1799, wearing a plain, slate-coloured silk dress. Her hair was twisted into a turban of black veil, in the fashion of the day, with her long blonde hair hanging down one side.[2]

In March that year she travelled to London with her beloved sister Rachel. Both girls were discontented: Rachel was unhappy because she had been forced to separate from her suitor, Henry Enfield, whilst Betsy felt frustrated in the expression of her religious ideals. Perhaps the visit was intended as a diversion for both the sisters. As far as Betsy was concerned, the plan failed. Instead of succumbing to the worldly pleasures of London, she appeared for the first time in the Quaker cap which was to frame her face in history. She wore it at a party given by her cousins, with great trepidation, first trying it on and taking it off again. 'I felt it my duty deeply to consult the feelings of dear Rachel … finally, after much uncertainty, I felt most easy to appear like a Quaker and wore my cap.'

Back at Earlham, she was on guard for the smallest of backslidings. 'I rose just in time for breakfast … got down in time before the eight minutes had expired after the bell rang and therefore had butter for breakfast. I have sometimes observed the hurry

I am in when I dress for butter, but when there is no chance of that, how slow I am, though I should be reading in my Testament.' [Presumably Betsy was deprived of butter if she was late.] Life in the warm weather always seemed sweeter and her journal gives us a succession of charming vignettes: sitting snugly by the nursery fire reading *The Pilgrim's Progress* with Kitty; walking in the light evenings through the grounds of Earlham where the hedges were turning green and the primroses and violets bursting into flower; trying on a new bonnet and a new dress.

On 25 July 1799, she is full of 'a matter of consequence. Joseph Fry came here and I think is much in love with me. He has not yet made me an offer, perhaps he will not do it, but I own I feel a good deal agitated about it.' She had met 'young Fry' the previous summer when he came to visit her brother John, but now with his open interest in and admiration of Betsy, he became more interesting to her. The following day Joseph proposed. 'I discouraged the affair, but fixed not to give him a final answer till 6th day. It is difficult to behave really well in such a case, so much female vanity is likely to creep in.' But the day after, Betsy turned him down, conscious, as she wrote, that she might never have a chance of marrying so well again.

Part of the trouble was that the family had decided that he would not do for Betsy. Among the brilliant, cultivated young Gurneys, plain Joe Fry seemed a laughable fellow. He might be wealthy, but he was not worldly. He was clumsy; he could not sit a horse well; he was a poor shot and, what was worse, spoke with a lisp and had a loud laugh. Although his father's estate at Plashet in Essex was as extensive as Earlham and the family business of tea-importing a flourishing concern, the Frys mixed socially with Quaker merchants rather than with the quality. The sisters agreed that he was not the right suitor. Yet Betsy did not relinquish him entirely in her mind. She wrote about him in her journal from time to time and felt almost depressed when she left, after his visit, to journey north with her father and her youngest sister, Priscilla.

On this journey Betsy found much to interest her. The family visited the Quaker school at Ackworth, where at the age of nineteen, she was appointed to serve on a committee responsible for the school and household and for examining the children. She openly confessed that she had 'only a slight knowledge of grammar'. At that stage Betsy spelt went 'whent' and wrong 'rong', so it is difficult to imagine how she managed to supervise the girls' spelling with any confidence or accuracy. Yet she seems to have made a very satisfactory report to the Committee and was congratulated on doing so.

They travelled on to York and visited the Friends' retreat for the insane and York Minster. 'How much', Betsy commented, 'people would spend about a poor building. Would they spend as much time and trouble on their own souls?' At Sheepwash in Yorkshire, John Gurney and his daughters rode round the estate and Betsy tried to admire the scenery while sitting an unruly horse. Alnwick Castle, the Duke of Northumberland's seat, was, she noted, 'very magnificent, but seeing such places never leads me to wish for high life ... for after all are the possessors happier, if so happy as others? The only true and lasting source of happiness is an easy conscience.' For once, Betsy is less than honest in her journal. She revelled in grand company and luxurious living and was not unaware of the contradiction between her principles and her practice.

When they returned to Earlham in the autumn she recorded, on 2 October, that she had bought some very fine muslin for aprons. 'It appears hardly worthwhile to return it, and yet it seems inconsistent to dress plain from principle and economy and then have my things so fine and expensive.' This particular inconsistency was to remain part of her all her life. Her clothes were plain, simple, of sober colours, but they were made of the finest materials. The Quaker shawl of brown silk that she wore as a famous prison reformer was lined with ermine.

At home there were still trials of conscience when the others begged her to dance and she sometimes joined in, only to repent later.

She was troubled by nervous attacks, sometimes as frequently as once a fortnight, and suffered from stomach-ache and toothache. 'Weak and nervous,' she wrote in her journal on 26 September. 'It may be owing to laudanum.' At that time, of course, laudanum, the opium derivative now regarded as a dangerous and addictive drug, was prescribed as freely as we would take aspirin and, for a girl as highly strung as Betsy, the drug was a constant companion. Part of her restlessness was due to frustration. She could not enjoy playing the young lady, as the others did, practising, singing, learning French, reading and embroidering. 'I want some object besides the poor and French,' she wrote.

She set to work energetically to read Hume's *History of England* and Lindley Murray's *English Grammar*. She was also actively involved in Quaker affairs and had begun to attend Monthly Meetings where church business was transacted. On 10 December, at Norwich Monthly Meeting, she spoke – 'in real fear ... but in a manner so unconnected and trembling I believe they could but just understand me.'

Two days later her father received a letter from Joseph Fry saying he intended to visit Earlham. The news forced Betsy to clarify her views on marriage:

> I have ever since I have been a little under the influence of religion, thought marriage at this time was not a good thing for me as it might lead my interests and affections from that Source in which they should be centred ... Also if I have any active duties to perform in the church ... are they not rather incompatible with the duties of a wife and mother? And is it not safest to wait and see what is the probable course I shall take in this life, before I enter into any engagement that affects my future career ... but it is now at this time the prayer of my heart, that if I ever should be a mother I may rest with my children and really find my duties lead me to them and my husband; and if my duty ever leads me from my family, that it may be in single life. I must leave all to the wisdom of a superior power.

Betsy, however, did take a hand in her fate. Her father was about to write to Joseph Fry and ask him not to come, but to his surprise, she pleaded with him to let her suitor 'have one more fair chance'. Five days later Joseph Fry, shy and dogged, came again. Betsy was agitated, she liked him better than before – and enjoyed being the centre of attention – but she hesitated. 'I love and like so many far better.' And she had mixed views on being a wife.

'Marriage', she wrote in her journal, 'is a thing much to be liked … but when I bring it home to my mind it is almost shocking.' Again she turned him down, with some relief. Afterwards, when they went off together to visit her uncle, Richard Gurney, she was embarrassed to be seen with her clumsy suitor. 'That I might not be laughed at, I think I was next to unkind to Joe Fry,' she confessed.

Once again, after he had left, Betsy thought about Joe Fry and wrote about him in her journal. She was influenced by a changed attitude in the family. By now they were all convinced that Betsy's Quakerism was no passing whim. John Gurney had even grown quite proud of his daughter's 'school' held in the disused laundry at Earlham and had brought two of his friends to hear her read the Gospels there one Sunday. To marry a steady, Plain Quaker in a good position seemed to her father and even to her sisters the best solution for Betsy.

In the meantime Joe Fry, passionately in love with Betsy, had hoped to pay another visit to Earlham But on 16 March 1800 her father wrote to discourage the young man, this time without asking Betsy's opinion.

> I can do no less than recommend thee, at least for the present, to waive all thoughts of a visit to Earlham. I am of the opinion it is in no respect likely to further thy wishes, and if so, then it must have a contrary effect, because it must call upon Betsy, if she cannot return thy affection for her, to take a line of absolute prohibition as to casual intercourse.
>
> She will have to consider that young women suffer a disadvantage in character when there shall be any appearance of allowing a

young man to remain in the character of a suitor, when there is no inclination or intention to give him a future encouragement ...

The letter reads as if it were intended to be as much a lesson for Betsy as for Joseph. In the spring of 1800, she travelled to London dressed 'grey and plain' with a Quaker bonnet. And, of course, when she was up in the city Joseph called on her. Her entry for 5 April reads:

J. Fry called in the morning and stayed to dinner. I felt very changeable towards him, but I now always feel emotion, either like or dislike. The remembrance of him is very pleasant to me, the other day it was truly disagreeable.

That April, almost every entry in her diary mentions Joe Fry. For the only time in her life, the spiritual outpourings of psalms, prayers, passages from the Bible ceased. She wavered and hesitated: 'I like him as a friend and dislike him as my lover,' she wrote, but later added, 'dreamed pleasantly about him ... I should not be surprised if I was to be his before very long.' On 25 April, Joseph's birthday, he spent the day with Betsy. She told him, when they were out walking, that she had 'half a mind to throw myself into his power and make the effort of thinking myself in a measure engaged to him – he behaved in the handsomest manner and said if I felt uneasy with the engagement, even an hour before the time of marriage, I was free to give it up. He kissed me which agitated me so much I went upstairs and cryed.'

On her way home to Earlham she met her father with her two elder sisters Kitty and Rachel. They had paid a visit to the Frys at Plashet, no doubt to discuss marriage settlements, and were delighted with the hospitality and kindness they had met from the family and with their beautiful home. Joseph accompanied the party on several stages of the journey and gave Betsy a bunch of spring flowers. She felt the old misgivings at parting, but by the time the coach arrived at Clare in Suffolk, she wrote, 'I love J.F. this morning.'

Her journal was full of the anticipation of a young girl in love. 'I was most of the morning on the watch for a letter from Joseph. I felt surprised to think I should feel so much about a letter from Joe Fry.'

When Joseph arrived at Earlham in May, Betsy felt very undecided again, although she had longed for him to come. According to family legend, Joe Fry determined to settle the affair by a dramatic gesture. He bought a handsome gold watch and chain for her and placed it on the white garden seat in the Earlham grounds. He warned Betsy that if she picked up the watch, it was to be a sign that she had agreed to be his wife; if she left it, then they must part for ever. The six sisters hid themselves behind the laurel bushes in the garden, stifling their giggles, to watch.

Her own account is more sober:

26th May before breakfast. I went down to breakfast – my heart was full. I could hardly keep from crying before them all … he gave me the watch last night with this engagement: if I give it back to him by nine o'clock this morning, he never more would renew the affair. If I kept it after that hour, he never would receive it back. I found inclination, reasoning and imagination so fickle that I saw the best plan was to leave them all, and in humility try to do the will of God … I did not feel at liberty to return the watch. I cryed heartily. Joseph felt much for me.

At last the engagement was irrevocable. But her feelings were still far from overflowing. 'I think', she wrote three months before they were married, 'I have felt the least dislike of anything in him today I ever remembered and certainly much pleasure in his company.' After a week of courtship Betsy was restive, anxious to get on with her work, her poor and her school. 'I had an idle afternoon with Joseph which was not pleasant. He seems to me to have stayed long enough this time.'

By June she was busy putting her affairs in order, bundling up clothes for the poor and cutting out linen for herself. She felt a want of confidence in practical things and was slow in her work. But yet it was pleasantly diverting. 'I have thought rather seriously upon becoming mistress of a house, the preparation of clothing etc., leads me into the little things for which I have a taste. If I do not take care they may hurt me and yet they are both pleasant and interesting to me.'

Betsy was busy preparing her trousseau. To her annoyance Kitty, jealous perhaps of her younger sister's marriage, commented tartly on her 'fine and nice' wedding clothes. It was, she remarked, inconsistent with Betsy's principles. 'I have not felt an objection,' she wrote, 'as I have not lately had a silk gown.' Her father provided for her handsomely with 'a full assortment of clothes of every best and wearing linen' which came to the considerable sum of £250.[3] When Joseph arrived again in July it became clear that she was to be the dominant partner in the marriage. 'Joseph', she noted primly in her journal, 'was not so compliant to me as he should have been.' (They had disagreed about a place to drink tea.) Kitty noticed her attitude and reprimanded her for being so 'dictatorial' to her fiancé!

Yet she was in love with Joseph as far as her nature would permit her. 'I almost follow him about,' she wrote. Moreover, she was a passionate young woman and very attracted to him. She wondered to herself 'how far personal attentions should be admitted before marriage, for I think it appears necessary to fix limits and adhere to them.' She still felt cool now and then, but in her dreams he triumphed: 'It is droll how much fonder I am of Joseph sleeping than waking, for I dream very lovingly of him of a night.'

By now Betsy was beginning to gain confidence in speaking in public. At Women's Monthly Meeting she had to read answers to queries about religious discipline and recognised that she read better than anyone else. Even at this stage, a month before her marriage, Betsy felt pressed to settle plans for her schoolchildren and longed for the wedding preparations to be over 'as they have a weakening effect upon the mind'. However, the Fry family arrived and she had to entertain them dutifully and discuss housekeeping with her future mother-in-law.

Joseph was planning more romantically: 'I have been thinking that we ought to contrive a few days after the wedding alone,' he wrote to her on 25 July. 'I do not know when we shall have the opportunity, because we expect Kitty with us when we first settle ... do, my sweet love, think of some pleasant plan of that kind.' It was typical of their relationship that Betsy was left to make the arrangements. She liked the idea and mentioned it to her father who suggested that the young couple should stay at Uncle Richard's shooting-box, overlooking a large pond at Hempstead in Norfolk, 'within three miles of the sea and sweet country surrounding ... free of expense'.

The wedding was fixed for Sunday 19 August. The week before, Betsy 'spoke very well in both Meetings'. Joseph, she wrote, was delighted with her. The following day, eighty-six of the 'poor imps' from her school came to say goodbye. 'Many of them wept ... when they went away I shed my tears also.'

On 19 August 1800 the Meeting House in Goats Lane was crowded for the wedding. Betsy was outwardly calm. Joseph made his declaration to her and then she hers to him:

> In the presence of the Lord and of this assembly I take this, my Friend Joseph Fry to be my husband, promising by Divine assistance to be unto him a loving and faithful wife, until it shall please the Lord by death to separate us.

'I felt every word,' she wrote later, 'and not only felt it but in my manner of speaking expressed how I felt ... Joseph also spoke well.' Despite cold hands and a beating heart, Betsy remained calm and dignified, though tearful, whilst John Gurney was overcome at losing the first of his girls.

Even on her wedding day, she did not relax her self-conscious analysis of her feelings. 'I did not much feel a bride all day,' she wrote. Four days after her marriage she obviously found Joseph's company day and night somewhat stifling. 'It seems as if I had hardly anything alone ... not even my mind.'

Yet instinctively she realised that the marriage was important to her. She was a passionate young woman and Joseph knew how to arouse her by his tender, ardent love-making. With Joseph she felt more secure than with any other human being. No matter how she tried him, she knew that he would remain loving. Throughout her youth, throughout her life, she felt threatened by close human relationships. Her fragile sense of her own identity and worth, coupled with the enormous power within her, made her genuinely fearful of revealing herself, hence the intimate journals. With her husband she felt safe, sure of space in which to develop.

By marrying Joseph she was also able to live as a Plain Friend, without the constant strain she had felt at Earlham. Since he adored her, and was patently the weaker character, she became her own mistress, free to follow her destiny.

III

'A Careworn Wife and Mother'

From the very beginning marriage proved a strain. Betsy wept at leaving Norwich, and Earlham, where she had so often been unhappy, now seemed indescribably dear to her. Throughout her married life she hankered for a Norfolk face and employed servants from her home county whenever she could.

Clearly the stress of settling to a new life was difficult for such an insecure and introspective girl and living at first with Joseph's parents in their large country house at Plashet (now overrun by urban East Ham) only added to her discomfort. According to their standards, they treated her hospitably and with great kindness. 'Mother Fry' was always pressing food on the young couple and fussing about their health and comfort. Betsy had the pretty flower gardens to explore and the park with its fish-ponds and woods, but within three weeks of her marriage she was restless, yearning for 'useful employment'. By then, she had already grown tired of gossiping about ailments and cures or clothes with her mother- and sister-in-law and longed for the stimulating discussions on philosophy and world affairs heard at the Earlham dinner table. Although she tried to smother her feelings, she found her new relations coarse-grained and narrow-minded.

For their part, they disapproved of Betsy's lofty manner and thought the young lady with her clever talk and her low melodious voice was altogether too exquisite. The very qualities that Joseph had admired in her were regarded as suspect by the Fry family.

Doubtless he was reflecting family feeling when he reprimanded his young bride on the extraordinary grounds that 'her manners had too much of the courtier'. She did not speak her mind, he complained. Her innate timidity and her gentle upbringing prevented her from expressing plainly what she felt. The Frys were blunt, if well-meaning, and sometimes downright hurtful. Her father-in-law told her, with the loud laugh that grated so, that he would never have given his consent to her marriage to Joseph if she had remained as worldly as her sisters, which naturally upset her. 'You would have been very wrong,' she replied.

For her part, after a month of marriage she was finding weaknesses in Joseph's character which seriously disturbed her. On 22 September 1800, she wrote in her journal: 'This morning I rose early and went to town with my husband ... partly to, please him and, I believe, partly to please myself and to get him to town in good time.' For she had discovered, to her horror, that Joseph was slack about business. As a Gurney and a banker's daughter, she was accustomed to regard time-keeping and devotion to daily work almost as a sacred trust. In many ways Joseph resembled her father – he was indulgent, affectionate and essentially simple – so Betsy had perhaps expected him to be a diligent businessman as well. Two months later she wrote, 'soon after waking, I hurt my dear Joseph by begging him to get up on account of business. He did not like my interfering ... and spoke rather sharply to me .:. I mentioned I thought him not active in business.'

They differed radically in attitudes towards money too. Joseph was generous and a spendthrift. Betsy planned every detail of her expenditure and this caused a quarrel. One day Joseph, who had more appreciation of fine art than his wife, brought her home a caricature which had cost him two shillings, well pleased with himself. Betsy scolded him for 'throwing away his money' and the despondent young bridegroom tore the cartoon in half and threw it into the fire. On another occasion, when Joseph had attended an auction and bought a drawing, she reproved him publicly for wasting money and then repented for her outburst in private in her journal.

Yet although careful about money, she expected to have the best in everything, so that when they went to choose beds for their new home in Mildred's Court, in the heart of the City, she wanted them plain, 'yet I do not wish for very plain but handsome'. She was quite put out when she had to make do with ordinary plate rather than silver. Since the house would not be ready for them to occupy until the end of the month, Betsy decided to escape to Norfolk for a few days. 'I never was so glad at the thought of seeing any place.'

Safe in the music room at Earlham, she sat once again writing her journal, plagued by a 'stupid' backache. She suspected herself of being pregnant, 'in the way' as she called it. The prospect made her anxious not sentimental. 'Children, more particularly babies, are often such trials as well as pleasing.' She was not in fact to be free of childbearing for twenty-two years. Her symptoms frequently interrupted her concentration at Meeting. 'I went to Meeting and am sorry to say … owing to being a little sickish, I thought of little else,' she wrote on 3 December.

At the beginning of November, on Betsy's return to London the Frys moved into their new home. The young couple were to live 'over the shop' in Mildred's Court, with the Frys' warehouse for tea, coffee and spices on one side of the large house and the counting-house on the ground floor. Several clerks from the business lodged in the house.

Poor Betsy found confusion everywhere when she moved in. She felt uncomfortable about replacing Eliza, her sister-in-law, and imagined that 'the servants looked at her as if she were turning out a mistress they loved'. (William and his wife Eliza were to live in the house at Plashet.) She had a bedroom turned into a sitting-room, busied herself with shopping for the new home and wrote down in some detail 'my footmen's business'. They were to 'rise at six, to clear everything remaining after midday dinner, brush up the hearth, rake up the fire and leave the room neat'.

Her position as mistress of Mildred's Court was made uncomfortable because the whole family looked on the house as their own, since it was part of the business. They had always eaten Sunday dinner after Meeting there and took it for granted that they would continue to do so. 'I think they could not be freer if it were their own,' she wrote. William Fry, who worked in the counting-house, ate dinner with them even on the day they moved in. This was perhaps understandable, but he also gossiped to Jane King, the housekeeper, about Betsy's management.

Moreover, the house was conveniently situated both for Gracechurch Street Meeting House and Devonshire House, where Yearly Meetings of the Society of Friends were held. As leading members of the Society, the Frys had established a tradition of hospitality and open house, so that Mildred's Court was regarded as a natural stopping point for any prominent Quaker who came to stay in London. A week after they had settled in, George Dilwyn, a Friend and Minister of the Gospel from America, came to stay. He was a plain and rather blunt Friend, lacking the polish and charm of William Savery, and he made the sensitive girl feel 'ashamed of the handsome things I have'. Often he would be 'led' to spend the evening by the fire in the young couple's comfortable parlour. Other Friends would drop in and soon the gathering would hold a long and tedious Meeting so frequently that she feared that such Meetings 'begin to lose their solemnity'.

What disappointed Betsy most of all in her newly married state was that although she was living as a Plain Friend, in an atmosphere of strict religious observance, she felt curiously dead to religion. 'I do not wish for the company of religious people. I do not like religious books, even the Bible and Testament are rather a cross to me.' The reason, it seems, that religion had lost its relish was that, for the Fry family, Quakerism was more a well-tried and comfortable pattern of life than the deeply spiritual experience that Betsy cherished.

At Meeting she found her mind burdened with 'worldly thoughts' and usually came away feeling dispirited and let down. Her life seemed full of muddle and tumult. So earnest was her desire to find some peace during the day that she suggested to her husband that they should read the Bible after breakfast. She felt awkward about it, because it meant imposing her will on people older than herself. At that time, the practice of reading the Bible aloud daily with the family was very rare, particularly among Friends.

On the morning of 11 November, after breakfast, she began to read the Forty-sixth Psalm, 'God is our refuge and strength, a very present help in trouble …' but broke off 'so overcome that I could hardly read, and gave it to Joseph to finish'. Four days later George Dilwyn told his young hostess that he thought her notion of reading the Bible after breakfast a good beginning for the day.

Such encouragement was rare. Her sense of religious inspiration had left her and her time, she felt, was frittered away 'in much ado about nothing'. 'My life', she wrote at the end of the year, 'appears to be spent to little more purpose than eating, drinking, sleeping and clothing myself. But if we analyse the employment of most, what do they do more, than in some way attend to the bodily wants of themselves or others … for in men of business, what else is their time spent in?' Even at this stage in her life Betsy had a sense of a frightening power that would not let her rest. She knew that a materialistic way of life would never satisfy her. 'I believe I have so much faith as never to be a happy woman without endeavouring to do the will of a Superior being … although my belief in religion may lead me in paths that are strange and appear ridiculous.'

Family Christmas at the Frys was not a success. On Christmas Eve her in-laws arrived bringing with them a present of a turkey. Since Betsy already had a fine Norfolk turkey, which in her eyes was superior, 'I drew a comparison between them'. The Frys did not appear to appreciate her speaking her mind bluntly and, it must be said, tactlessly. Christmas day with the large family party at Plashet she found 'rather bustling … I do not think such family parties often answer.'

For the first year of her marriage Betsy struggled to find a way out of her 'muddled and uncomfortable state'. Again and again she records in her journal her sense of frustration and time wasted with their continual outings and visitors. 'I do not think since we are married we have had a quarter of our meals alone.' She found it hard to manage the servants, even on days when there was little company. At Earlham, she was used to a household run like clockwork where, although guests were entertained lavishly and frequently, the visits were planned well in advance. Her servants may have played the young matron up. At any rate, she found that William the footman often served meals late, which she detested and yet she could not quite bring herself to reprimand him.

Even for an experienced housewife, it would have been hard to take over the household at Mildred's Court. Whenever there were large meetings of Friends it was taken for granted that the house would offer hospitality. In May, Friends from all over the country assembled for a fortnight at Yearly Meeting. The house was virtually taken over by them. Every day dinner was prepared for sixty or more in her home. The tables were laid with huge joints of roasted meats, fine dishes of the first salmon of the season, mighty plum puddings and jellies and bowls of fresh fruit. Friends would swarm into the house, eat their fill and then the first shift would stroll upstairs to lie down on beds, sofas and chairs. At that time of the year the house was one teeming throng. In addition to supervising her household, Betsy attended two of the women's sessions a day.

Well before Yearly Meeting took place, Betsy knew for certain that she was pregnant. Despite her constant struggle against the 'body's domination' she was a hypochondriac, morbidly anxious about every ache and pain, and aware of her failing. 'I have been foolishly anxious for some time past,' she wrote on 28 March 'because I thought I felt the child, which has made me very watchful about my body and foolishly talkative about it.' Five months before the baby was due, she was cutting out baby linen and making preparations.

In the spring of 1801 she took another trip home to Norfolk by herself and was surprised how much she missed Joseph. 'I felt the want of him in the night as I was but poorly with a pain I suppose to be the cramp, and my cough, and nobody minds me like him.' Despite his irritating habits, his continual humming and his worldly tastes for chess and non-religious books, she found in him a tender husband, always ready with the sympathy she craved. He came to fetch her and she was looking forward to their meeting, but had built up unrealistic expectations which were inevitably disappointed.

When they came home another annoyance upset her. Joseph's father and his brother William had drawn up articles of partnership in the business which gave them the legal right to enter the parlour at Mildred's Court, which was, after all, the young couple's home. Her mother-in-law called Betsy into the room and said she was sure that her daughter-in-law would approve the arrangement, knowing that her son would never stand up against the rest of the family. Betsy retorted that the subject had never been mentioned to her and that she took it as a tacit reproof for the Frys to have needed legal reassurance of her hospitality and kindness. There *had* been criticism when they were first married of Betsy and Joseph's lack of hospitality to the customers but the difficulty was that, since their home was also the business, their privacy was constantly invaded.

That year Betsy spent very little time on her poor or even in Meetings. Joseph, like her father, was not keen for her to attend more than once a day and was inclined to be sceptical about the duties and obligations she imposed on herself. However, she did visit Joseph Lancaster, a young man just beginning to make a name for himself for his educational methods. Lancaster was a Quaker who kept a school for poor children of all denominations. By dividing his boys into groups of twelve, with a monitor to help the schoolmaster, he was able to teach much larger classes than usual. Betsy found the visit extremely interesting and was to remember the method.

Throughout June and July she was fussing over linen for the baby and baby caps. With her two sisters, Hannah and Rachel, who had come to stay with her for the birth, she made a little cradle. 'How anxiously I wish … that everything is done that I can do before I am brought to bed, it would be a great relief – in proportion to our indulgencies, so come our cares – having too many clothes, household linen etc., are troubles, they take so much to keep them in order, so are servants etc.' In the days before anaesthetics or chloroform, Betsy naturally found childbirth frightening and her mother-in-law's alarming stories about the subject increased her fears. 'Should I recover my lying-in,' she wrote three days before the baby was born, '… I believe there is nothing in the world I wish for so much as to 'obtain good.'

On 22 August, a year after her marriage almost to the day, her daughter Katharine was born. Her labour was intensely painful and she felt exhausted and guilty after it. 'I did not experience that joy some women describe,' Betsy recalled a fortnight later. 'My husband brought me my little babe … I hardly knew what I felt, but my body and spirits were so extremely weak I could only bear just to look at those I love, my husband, Rachel and Hannah.'

She was an over-anxious mother and fretted about every little ailment. 'I gave my dear babe a little opening medicine in the night as her food began to come up … as her bowels have been long without relief … I was happily much relieved by her medicine operating.' Her baby's inoculation against the smallpox, her baby's rash, baby's whooping cough and crying in the night preoccupied her for almost a year so that her journals are sparse and 'worldly'. As always, she worried intensely about her lack of religion. 'When I hear spiritual things mentioned I appear to have lost all, or nearly all, of my understanding about them.' She did, however, find a rare peace of mind in feeding her baby, 'the child feels so like myself'. Curiously her old dream of being washed away by the sea reappeared at this time, only now little Katharine was in it and they both escaped the waves.

As a young matron, bickering politely with her mother-in-law over the care of her baby, fussing over the child's or her own health, queening it over her unmarried sisters on a visit to Earlham, Betsy seems to have lost her inspiration. She was not suited to domesticity and Joseph, at that time, showed little sympathy with her religious aspirations.

By October 1801 the long war with France had apparently come to an end and crowds in London roared with delight and let off rockets. Oil lamps lit up the streets all over town. Mrs Fry of Mildred's Court sat in her own room with her 'dearest babe' sleeping beside her. Joseph and her sister had gone to the west end of the town to look at the illuminations. But the buzz and noise of the mob from the streets made her head ache. Besides, she noted, 'it does not appear to me the right means to express gratitude, as it appears to me to lead to much drunkenness and vice.'

Betsy was firmly convinced that for herself drink was a necessity for health. 'I sometimes think of leaving off malt liquor and wine … but it appears almost impossible if I do that to be well,' she wrote in April 1802. She knew drink made her feel heavy, languid and stupid but apparently did not connect her own 'medicinal' intake with the cheap gin or beer that gave temporary oblivion to the labouring poor.

She also liked 'her poor' to be recognisably pigeonholed in the lower classes. In the autumn of 1801 she had taken a boat to Vauxhall in answer to a begging letter. 'To my surprise I found this person's dress, house and furniture almost like a gentlewoman – these sort of beggars I cannot understand … they want so large an amount … The woman had asked for £30 to clear her debt but Mrs Fry apparently refused. 'I have other reasons for not wanting to have much to do with her, they live so far off.'

Discontented herself, Betsy always seemed to disapprove of other people's pleasures. 'I think I spoke rather improperly because my husband would not leave his fishing to come home … Afterwards I felt particular love for Joseph.'

Later that autumn Mrs Fry took a journey with her husband through the Midlands to the Lake District. She contrived to find almost everything displeasing. On 30 September she was in Oxford, 'a beautiful city. I continued very flat and my husband, appeared rather vexed with me for being so.' In Stratford she visited Shakespeare's monument and Warwick Castle but was disappointed by an 'unpleasant dark and dirty' inn. Arriving at a large inn in Coventry displeased her because, she said, 'it creates improper feelings'. When they came to Westmorland, after what she acknowledged to be a beautiful ride, 'my Joseph was so exhiliarated to be at the Lakes as to try my patience.' She could not bear Joseph in a boisterous mood, it jarred on her sensibility. It made him appear thoughtless and childish and heightened her own sense of frustration. She was upset because they spent their Sunday riding in the country instead of attending Meeting. The following day they rode in the rain to look at a waterfall, 'a grand and beautiful sight, but I do not much like this country at this time of year, it looks so barren and dreary ... there is too much water in this place ... too much lake and too much barren mountain, too little snugness and too few fine trees' – an independent judgement for the time; the Romantics were soon to make the Lakes into a place of pilgrimage. She had found the long stages of the coach-ride tiring and the inns were sometimes dull and dirty. The toothache was troubling her again, but it came almost as a relief; 'pain has sometimes a rather comfortable effect on the mind, as it now and then appears ... to lead us to the spiritual for enjoyment.' It also led her to take laudanum, and, at this stage in her life, Betsy felt no misgivings about using the drug. She even gave it to her cat who 'settled poorly and took laudanum'.[1]

At the beginning of 1803 her young brother Samuel, then sixteen, came up to Mildred's Court to live with the family and to be apprenticed to Joseph Fry as a bookkeeper. Betsy was pleased to have him, and her father paid her £30 a year for his keep, but it did of course restrict her privacy. However, she was fond of Sam, a sturdy independent lad, not bookish but shrewd, and the family were extraordinarily close. Later he became a famous banker and philanthropist in his own right and was a great help to Betsy in her many causes. At the time he settled in quite happily and worked hard.

In her early twenties Betsy Fry's personality was at its least attractive; she was ill at ease with herself, frustrated in her religious aspirations, unable to use her powerful intelligence for the social work in which she was to excel. Also, she was pregnant again and terrified at the prospect. 'I believe women's labours are the hardest trials … human nature has to go through,' she wrote. 'Suffer we must in this world and the less we kick against it the happier for us.'

Her second daughter Rachel was born on 25 March 1803. A fortnight after the birth Betsy recorded her thankfulness. 'My heart abounded with joy and gratitude when my dear little girl was born, perfect and lovely.' This time the birth had not been too difficult. 'Words are not equal to express my feelings, for I was most mercifully dealt with, my soul was so quiet and so much supported.' Shortly afterwards, however, she was surprised by a severe attack of 'indisposition' and what would today almost certainly be diagnosed as post-puerperal depression, a depressive illness that occurs in about one in ten pregnancies more than a month after birth, and that requires medical treatment. Betsy described her symptoms as 'real bodily weakness and also the trials of a nervous imagination: no one knows but those who have felt them, how hard they are to bear, for they lead the mind to look for trouble … nothing I believe allays them so much as the quieting influence of religion … But they are a regular disorder that I believe no mental exertion can cure or overcome.'

Betsy always showed extraordinary insight about her 'nerves'. She was to tell her daughters when they grew up that worrying about nervous diseases only made them worse. She rested and by June was gradually recovering; 'still not in usual health; my nerves are in an irritable state, I am soon overcome and overdone'.

In the summer the whole family, Betsy, Joseph and the two tiny girls, paid a visit to Earlham. Betsy was still in a downcast frame of mind and the continual playing of the pianoforte, particularly when Joseph took his turn, annoyed her. Their holiday in Norfolk was interrupted dramatically by the scare of invasion that swept the country, when the uneasy peace with France was ended. All over England hasty defences were erected, Martello towers were built along the coast and volunteers, including John Gurney, Elizabeth's brother, who defied the Quaker prohibition against military service, swelled the ranks of the regular army. The Gurneys had four carriages ready and plans were made for the girls to set off in the coach-and-four for Ely – a marshy place regarded as safe from invading craft – should the French land.

William Fry wrote to his brother in July asking him to return immediately 'to be at his post'. Preparations had been made to flood the marshes of the river Lea and the bridges on the Essex road were broken down. Betsy only remarked on the interruption to her holiday.

Back in London, Betsy found her mother-in-law seriously ill. She set off with the doctor to visit her. But the Frys believed in 'animal magnetism', a form of faith-healing by hypnotism, of which Betsy disapproved strongly. From time to time, particularly when she was ill, Betsy tried to overcome her disdain for her mother-in-law, whose conversation was centred on 'common subjects'. She felt a kind of love for anyone who suffered but 'Mother Fry' preferred William's wife, Eliza, to nurse her and Betsy was jealous. She received so many 'put offs' from Plashet, that she concluded that 'they appeared to wish us (me and the children) to keep away'.

In the autumn, somewhat to her chagrin, for she had a great need of his love for her and felt keenly the slightest sign of inattention, Joseph went on a brief shooting trip to Norfolk. During his absence, Betsy traipsed the narrow, dirty streets 'in one of the disagreeable parts of London' looking for a poor woman who had begged from her in the street. She could not find her, but gave money to two other destitute women and came home that day more satisfied than she had felt for a long time. That such a nervous and well-dressed young woman dared venture into the seamier alleys of London may seem surprising, but Betsy never shrank from the poor. Her reputation soon spread and a stream of wretched women, some with sickly babies in their arms, pulled the iron bell outside Mildred's Court to ask for Mrs Fry. She tried to follow them up and visit them in their hovels. Sometimes they were heartbreaking cases. Others, like the baby-farmer who came holding two crying babies, were charlatans and she gradually learnt to distinguish between them.

She was, even in her Quaker dress, a very elegant and personable young woman. Mother Fry accused her of wearing her hair in a fashionable style. 'I cannot bear to be reproved,' Betsy complained to her journal, '… partly owing to not being used to it.' The Frys were very critical. She supped that night at her brother-in-law's and the conversation turned on Betsy and her 'coldness'. 'What I believe they want in me is freedom and vivacity,' she observed, 'but merriment is not in my nature and I cannot bear to affect what I do not feel.' It is almost impossible to imagine her joking or laughing with the Frys and no evidence of a sense of humour breaks through in her journals. Only rarely, with her small children or with one of her 'poor', would she permit herself to be playful.

A month later in March 1804, her mother-in-law died. Betsy stayed with her the day before 'and although I have every reason to believe she died happily, I did not experience those awful sweet feelings I should have looked for at so serious a time … I have been surprised how little this event has led me into a serious state of mind, I fear it has not had so profitable an effect upon me as it might.' Betsy could have acknowledged that although both women wished to keep the families together, they had never been close, yet, as always, she looked for spiritual profit in every event.

Her own father came to town for the funeral and some time later confided to Betsy his anxieties about the Gurney business. He was by now a partner in the Bank as well as having his own profitable woollen business. He told Betsy that he stood to lose £60,000 if an action brought against him succeeded. Presumably it did not, since there is no subsequent record of a sharp decline in the Gurney fortune. She was flattered to be taken into his confidence, a sign, she felt, that she had really become independent. 'I never remember taking so active a part in advice about my father ... and felt the difference of understanding between men and women – men have clearer ideas than women and yet I think the judgement of a woman equal to that of men, in most if not in all cases.'

Six months later, after she had given birth to her third child, John, she again suffered from depression and wondered whether she would ever have the opportunity to exercise her judgement outside the home. On 29 October 1804 she wrote in her journal:

> I think perhaps my pride is a little concerned in some of my dis-
> couraging feelings, for it does appear to me as if I might become
> the careworn and oppressed mother ... many sink under the duties
> of wife and mother and particularly young mothers like myself
> and my constitution appears delicate.

She was twenty-four with three children under five.

To her sisters who visited her at Mildred's Court, but indulged in concerts, visits to the west end of the town, and parties, Betsy's routine seemed incredibly dull: 'poor people coming one after another 'till twelve o'clock and then no quiet; and each day I have been here we have had the Frys or my uncle or someone else at dinner.'[2] Hovering over the scene was Betsy in her 'pink acorn gown' attending to the flock in the dining-room, the draw-ing-room and the parlour, alternately running after her servants, children and poor. Her brother Joseph, however, always found her activities stimulating. In February 1805, on his way to Oxford, where he was studying with a private tutor, he called at Mildred's Court but found Betsy out. She had driven off in a post-chaise with her sister-in-law to free 'a little negro boy from a ... captain who intended to sell him after leaving the country.[3]

Betsy by now realised that she was not suited to a humdrum domestic life. With her servants she was either too timid or over indulgent and the children too easily upset her, so that a year later, she was relieved to be given a definite interest outside the home. She was appointed Visitor to the Friends' School and Workhouse in Islington. 'My Joseph does not object,' she remarked, 'my fears are whether I may not get too many outdoor duties and so leave the first duties of my own home too much.'

There was still plenty to occupy her at Mildred's Court. Her three small children all had the measles and there were sisters to visit and Meetings to attend. She was rather taken aback, in the spring of 1806, when a Friend from her Meeting came to visit her home to ensure that her children and servants were being brought up suitably, with frequent reading of the Holy Scriptures and in 'plainness of speech, behaviour and apparrel'. That she could be suspected of what Friends called 'delinquency' was a blow to her pride but, she reflected piously, 'a poor child like me ought to rejoice in being cared for'.

She felt much more comfortable in caring for others. Two days later, in her capacity as Visitor, she went to the Islington Workhouse and took the children some cakes for tea. She also brought along a little pamphlet of a religious nature written for children, and she first read it and then began to explain it to them. She appears to have had an extraordinary effect, the children and the governess wept and Betsy herself was overcome. 'It is marvellous how I got courage to do it ... that which I said seemed rather to flow naturally from my heart and understanding than anything really deep from the living fountain. I have a desire that this little event may not encourage me too much, for hard things seemed made quite easy. Oh! that in anything like a religious duty I may never go beyond the right Guide, nor ever give self the praise.'

The prayer was obviously sincere. Yet Betsy had glimpsed for the first time her extraordinary power over an audience at that little gathering and felt the exhilaration of it. Her performance was even more remarkable, considering that she was more than eight months pregnant. Two weeks later, on 1 June, her fourth child William Storrs Fry (named, this time, after her father-in-law) was born. The conflict between home duties and her longing to play a part as a Quaker occurs again and again in her journal. After the baby was born she wrote, 'How much do I desire that I may more earnestly endeavour to do my duty towards my beloved husband, for I sometimes doubt whether enough time is devoted to him and his interests.'

In August she took little five-year-old Katharine to Meeting for the first time. To her pleasure she found herself able to speak during the Meeting 'without great pain'. She was appointed Representative to her Monthly Meeting which also gratified her.

The affairs of her own sisters took up a great deal of her time. Louisa, now a good-looking young woman of twenty-two was to marry Sam Hoare of the wealthy banking family where Betsy had once stayed. They were relatives of the Gurneys but not strict Quakers and Betsy was impatient of young Sam's 'high manners'. On 'dear Louisa's account', however, she behaved easily with the Hoares, and in fact Sam, like so many of her family connections, was to prove a valuable ally in the future. The wedding was held in the country close to Norwich, at Tasburgh Meeting House and all the family were present. It was, Betsy remarked, 'rather remarkable to see so large a family, all so nearly sympathising and closely united'.

Then in January 1807 her brother John married his first cousin Elizabeth Gurney. This wedding Betsy did not attend. Since marriages between first cousins were strictly forbidden by Quakers, Richard Gurney, the father of the bride, had to walk away in an opposite direction during the ceremony, so as to be seen to disapprove of the match. Betsy wrote a long, sermonising letter to the couple:

My very dear John and Elizabeth

I leave off writing my journal to write to you; for whilst I was expressing in it my feelings, the love I then felt ... for thee dear John came so perfectly before me, that instead of writing it in my journal, I wish to express [it] to you both ... my desire [is] sincere that in your union you may indeed obtain the Divine blessing. What is the Divine blessing but in the first place to be cleansed from our sins and weakness ... And secondly to live under the protection of Him who is able to save us from every hurtful thing, and turn all the circumstances of our lives to good account ...

It is hardly likely that I shall see you before or soon after you marry; you have, you know, my good wishes for your prosperity in every way, but you must expect some bitter mixed with the sweet cup; for without it we should rest too much in the enjoyments of life. I think you will be a very devoted couple to each other; therefore I advise you to be on your guard, and to remember that all natural things, and natural affections among the rest are corruptible. That there is something better that must be loved first, and that we must hold all things in subjection to this Power ... that alone can sanctify all other things to us ...

She made a journey in the spring of 1807 to the North of England where Joseph was travelling on business. The youngest child, William, was just weaned and she left the small children at Earlham to be cared for by their adoring aunts and old Nanny Norman.

By May she was back in Earlham again for another family wedding. This time it was another younger sister, Hannah, who was to marry Thomas Fowell Buxton. Tall (he was over six foot-four), ponderous Fowell, affectionately nicknamed 'the elephant' in the family, had been brought up in the Church of England. He had recently become a Quaker although neither he nor Hannah were to remain in the Society for long. The wedding was the most colourful that Earlham had seen.

The house was overrun with bridesmaids in muslin cloaks and chip hats. We led our sweet bride to the stairs where our men joined us ... To me the Meeting was solemn in its beginning and striking from such a circle of brothers and sisters so united in affection ... our dear couple spoke with much feeling and Fowell with usual dignity ... nothing could be prettier than the train of bridesmaids dressed alike in white, with small nosegays, except the bride ... who was still more white and was distinguished by one beautiful rose ... I think there was scarcely ever such a brother admitted to a family.

Fowell Buxton was to become as close as a brother to the family. For Elizabeth Fry, the connection was more important than she realised at that time, since Fowell Buxton was to become a Member of Parliament, Wilberforce's successor in the anti-slavery campaign, and her most important ally in the prison cause. Family connections were to play a significant part in her initiative; her in-laws, Buxton and Samuel Hoare, and her own brothers supported all her public work.

In September 1807 Priscilla Gurney wrote to Hannah, Mrs Buxton, from Mildred's Court: 'Thee knows how dull Mildred's Court can be ... The children have been my only comfort, little Rachel, Johnny and I have been drinking tea together and they have made me quite cheerful and happy.' In a later letter Priscilla wrote to Hannah that she had managed to see Betsy at intervals between her preoccupation with the household, her husband, relatives and poor, and had snatched some private conversation about Hannah and Fowell. 'She was so interested about you, but she is never as warm about people as we are, which arises from her very superior principle and yet is perhaps a little damping where your feelings are highly interested. She is, to be sure, a most uncommon person, and one is almost surprised to find anyone so exemplary in conduct, so entirely under the right subjection as she is.' In other words Priscilla found her sister cold and priggish but she added, 'I can hardly say how sweet I think her conduct is to all of us.'

Betsy, meanwhile, was suffering from another period of depression. She was 'in the way' again, nervous and irritable. She was worried by toothache and felt 'in that sort of insensible state when reading the Bible etc., etc., is truly flat to me'. Had she, she asked herself at the end of the year, performed her duty to God and her fellow creatures? Had she been 'a tender, loving, yielding wife ... a tender yet steady mother to my children, a kind yet honest mistress, telling the servants of their faults but never worrying them about unnecessary trifles?'

In January 1808, a month before her fifth child was born, the Frys engaged a governess to teach the children and live in. Betsy felt very uneasy about the appointment. Her children were lively and unruly and she sensed that neither she nor Joseph knew how to manage them, nevertheless was loath to give them up. February came and the 'great nervous shaking' in her stomach. She was taking brandy and water to relieve the pain. 'Oh that faith fail not, but that I may be enabled to look to the right place for support.' On 18 February the child was born, and her prayers were answered. 'I called on the Lord for mercy and it seemed as if my cry was heard for suffering was cut short indeed ... my beloved Joseph is a great comfort to me.' The baby was a girl and named, after another Gurney aunt, Richenda.

The after-effects of the birth were painful and distressing. By the end of March Betsy was still taking brandy and water 'in moderation' to relieve her pains. But her sense of vocation was as urgent as ever; 'I am convinced', she wrote on 27 March, 'that the real work of religion is in the heart and what I desire is a heart fully, simply and singly dedicated to its creator and to be always ready to wait as a servant ought for orders, and not, in my own activity, come forward. For a true, deep inward waiting on the Lord that I may always be ready to do the work committed to me of whatever kind it may be ...'

Her depression lasted almost all that year. Although she was 'poorly all night', she did manage to attend the wedding of her brother Samuel, now twenty-one years old and launched in business with a prosperous firm of bill-brokers in Lombard Street. 'I did feel deeply for Sam and Liz,' she wrote.

In May the whole Gurney family were shocked by news that her brother John's wife, Elizabeth, who had been a bride the year before, had died in childbirth. The Frys travelled to Lynn for the funeral, but to Betsy's shame she was too painfully nervous and depressed to comfort her brother. At the funeral she was 'almost entirely devoted to my own nervous feelings'. Other people wallow in this form of self-indulgence at funerals, but Betsy longed desperately to be able to set a good example. When she visited her sisters Louisa Hoare and Hannah Buxton, whose husband had now entered his uncle's brewery business, Truman Hanbury, as a clerk with prospects, Betsy felt her inadequacy keenly. They managed to be contented and cheerful and to run their households with ease.

In August Betsy was back again at Earlham with her family. 'I have been married eight years yesterday,' she wrote in a passionate outburst, the day after her anniversary. 'Various trials of faith and patience have been permitted me; my course has been very different from what I expected, and instead of being, as I had hoped, a useful instrument in the Church militant, here I am a careworn wife and mother, outwardly nearly devoted to the things of this life!'

Even at Earlham, she was distressed to find her sisters strongly drawn towards the Church of England. They had made friends with a prominent and personable evangelical parson, Edward Edwards, of King's Lynn, who had proved a great comfort to young John Gurney when his wife died. Later, Edwards had spent a week at Earlham and the sisters found him 'truly comforting and encouraging'.

Catherine, her eldest sister, in particular, was attracted to the Church of England and searching earnestly for religious inspiration (she was baptised the following year). Betsy and Joseph discussed the matter together and decided, from their standpoint as strict Quakers, that Catherine 'was studying religious subjects too much for her own good'. It would be safer, they argued, if Catherine trusted her own feelings. Betsy showed Catherine a letter from Joseph in which he expressed his misgivings about her religious doubts. She found it easier perhaps than broaching the subject directly. Catherine was upset and outraged. That Betsy, who had always flouted her authority, who had caused the whole family such distress by her religious extremism, should criticise *her* seemed the height of indignity. 'She told me', Betsy recorded, 'that nobody gave her such pain as I did.' Never before had she fully realised how much her older sister resented her.

When she returned to Mildred's Court that autumn, her father-in-law, William Storrs Fry, now a widower and relying far more on his children, came to her 'very ill indeed'. The sight of suffering never failed to excite her compassion. It sprang principally from a religious impulse, a desire to save the sinner from eternal damnation before it was too late, but for anyone ailing she had infinite practical kindness, too, and she spent a great deal of time with him. At first he was afraid of dying, but Betsy was certain that once he had been confined to his bed, he began to develop an interest in 'that Power which can alone do all things for us'. One morning when the old man thought he was dying, he sent for his son and daughter-in-law and told them they need not be afraid for him for he was 'comfortable, comfortable, comfortable'. She took it to mean that he had come to terms with his death and looked forward to it.

'It does not much signify what talent is committed to us if we but be faithful with it,' she wrote in an unconsciously patronising manner. 'My dear father-in-law was not one that had great things required of him, apparently, but being faithful in the little, we need not doubt he now possesses more … the awful sight of death was very affecting to me, never having witnessed such a scene before.'

Scarcely had the family settled down after the funeral, when Betsy was sent for urgently by the Buxtons to nurse her sister Hannah.

Hannah's illness turned out to be scarlet fever and Betsy, as the mother of five young children, with a baby only ten months old, realised the gravity of the risk. Fortunately none of her family contracted the disease.

There was to be a new upheaval in the spring of 1809, but one she looked forward to. Her father-in-law had left Plashet, the house and the estate, to Joseph and Betsy. She had never enjoyed living in London or the bustling atmosphere of the counting-house. A country house for her and her children seemed ideal. She had grown up as the daughter of a big estate; to be the lady and mistress of the manor suited her admirably. At the time she was extremely concerned about her servants. They were expected to be present when she read the Bible and she found 'sweet satisfaction' in the exercise. (One can only guess what the servants made of it.) A true banker's daughter, she was careful, yet wistful, about the salary she paid them; 'how much pleasanter it is to be liked and loved by our servants than perhaps to have a few more pounds in our pockets.' The good employer, she believed, had a duty to make them happy in their station in life and 'be truly their friends, though not their familiars or equals'. She rightly felt that most employers dismissed them as creatures of another race with different feelings and instincts from their superiors. Betsy would, one suspects, improve them whether they wanted her to or not. But her attitude was enlightened for her time and her experience with them was to prove valuable to her later.

She revelled in the role of lady of the manor. She found the change from the smoke and noise of the city to the tranquil pleasures of country life entirely delightful. With her four small children in tow, each holding a trowel and a trug, she spent hours in the park, filling the flower-beds with primroses from the woods. Nurse Barns and the Irish gardener, Denis Regan, followed respectfully. She was pregnant for the sixth time, and suffering from feverishness and agitation in her stomach. She was trying, in that pleasant home, to ignore the pains as she was convinced that they were 'principally nervous'. She was extremely relieved to receive a kind message from Dr Sims, on 19 September 1809, the day before the baby was born, 'saying he would give almost anything up rather than miss attending me'. Her labour was easier this time and, as always, when she needed him, 'beloved Joseph' proved a 'sweet companion'. She only wished that he would show more signs of spiritual growth.

News from Earlham that their faithful old nurse Williman, who had tended her youngest brother Daniel, now nineteen and in Gurneys Bank at King's Lynn, through scarlet fever, had caught the disease herself and died, came as a severe shock. Nurse Williman had been with the family for over twenty years and was a link with her childhood. Betsy was recuperating at Tunbridge Wells from the birth of little Joseph when more bad news arrived in a letter from Earlham. Now it was her youngest sister, Priscilla, who had caught scarlet fever and her father lay dangerously ill after an operation. Her sister Richenda, who had been staying with them, left for Earlham. 'On the 26th as we were sitting quietly together an express coach arrived bringing Chenda back saying our most dear father was so ill, they did not expect his life would be spared.'

Despite scarlet fever at Earlham, the Frys and their month-old baby set off at a gallop in their carriage. Richenda went straight on to Earlham; the Frys spent the night at Mildred's Court. They left early the next morning and, hearing at different stages on the road that John Gurney was still alive, hurried on and reached Earlham by midnight. 'We got out of the carriage and once more saw him who has been so inexpressibly dear to me through life, since I knew what love was; he was asleep, but death was strongly marked on his sweet, and to me, beautiful face.' John Gurney was only fifty-nine on his deathbed.

Through the night Betsy had time to talk with her father. His acceptance of death and his kind and loving words allowed her to accept the loss. 'He encouraged us, his children to hold on our way; and sweetly expressed his belief, that our love of good had been a stimulus and help to him.'

This vindication by her father of the path she had taken had an extraordinary effect on Betsy. When he died the following morning, she went into his room and fell on her knees overwhelmed, 'so that I could hardly help uttering my thankfulness and praise … the power given was wonderful to myself and the cross none; my heart was so full that I could hardly hinder utterance.'

At the funeral her state of charged feeling was marked outwardly by 'solemn quietness'. As she walked to the graveyard where generations of Gurneys lay, the sense of love for her family and gratitude for the manner of her father's death swelled within her.

> I remained silent till dearest John began to move to go away …
> I fell on my knees and began, not knowing how I should go on
> with these words 'Great and marvellous are Thy Works, Lord God
> Almighty, just and true are all Thy Ways, Thou King of Saints; be
> pleased to receive our thanksgiving' … There I seemed stopped,
> though I thought that I should have had to express thanks on my
> beloved father's account. But not feeling the power continue, I arose
> directly; a quiet, calm and invigorated state were my portion.

The rest of her family were dumbfounded. They had never seen Betsy fall to her knees in such an extraordinary demonstration. John and Daniel, the two banker brothers who shared a house in King's Lynn, found her public testimony tasteless and embarrassing. 'The exhibition … of the family … and the preaching of men and women … contributed – perhaps not rightly – to estrange me from the Society of Friends,' Dan wrote later.

But for Betsy her father's death had acted as a psychological release. Whether she was prevented from preaching during his lifetime through fear of his disapproval or whether from some other more deep-rooted sense of shame cannot be known. What is certain is that from the day of his funeral Elizabeth Fry began to speak at Meetings. Twice before she had experienced a state of religious ecstasy, once through the preach-ings of William Savery and once from Deborah Darby's prophecy. This time she was exalted through her own words. She felt 'like a bottle that has been corked up and pressed down and now there is an opening inside, there is much to run out.'

'I think', she wrote that day, 'this will make way for me in some things that have been long on my mind.'

IV

'Laudable Persuits'

Elizabeth Fry's marriage must have been one of the first in which role reversal took place. From 1810 onwards, as her religious duties took her further afield, it was her husband who stayed at home to watch over the household. 'My dearest Joseph was kind enough to stay at home to nurse to let me go to afternoon Meeting,' she noted in February of that year. Later, he was to remain at home while his wife travelled all over Great Britain and on the Continent. He admired her so much that it hardly seems to have occurred to him to question her movements; he only complained, rather sadly, that he felt widowed when she stayed away too long. He had no illusions about his own ability to take part in public work and a generous opinion of hers – this at a time when wives, even women Quaker Ministers, were naturally expected to take second place to their husbands.

Betsy was not yet thirty, a handsome young woman, rather severe in her expression but with kind, penetrating blue eyes. Although the effect of bearing so many children had begun to thicken her figure, she held herself regally and outwardly radiated graciousness and composure. Gradually Mrs Fry was gaining confidence, beginning to speak at Meetings so frequently that she prayed that she should only utter if she felt real inspiration. Grave self-doubts still troubled her. She could not quite believe that 'such a one as I should have such concerns'. A sense of sin possessed her. Often she was convinced that what she described as 'the enemy',

Satan, lurked at Meeting, waiting to invade her mind and terrify her so that she could not speak or, more rarely, lead her on to foolishness. Even though so many of her ideas were years ahead of her time and full of common sense, she lived in constant fear of damnation.

In February 1811, a month before she was formally acknowledged as a Minister by Barking Monthly Meeting, her seventh child, Elizabeth, was born. Her journals at that time have frequent references to the difficulties of running a household and complaints of the servants' slackness and the older children's rudeness. In her heart, although she would no longer admit it, even to herself, she disliked and despised household duties. The servants, of course, sensed it and it was only when they skimped their work obviously that she noticed. Her journal had now become a refuge again as it had been in her girlhood and not even Joseph was allowed to read it. Only occasionally would she insert a scribbled laundry list in the middle of her prayers, pious thoughts and soul-searching.

To her children 'dearest Mama' seemed somewhat ludicrous, always dashing off to Meeting or to visit the comical poor people. They saw her irritated, or wracked with pain because of toothache. Sometimes she was too timid to visit the dentist to have a tooth drawn. They could not really understand why people admired her. Since she herself could not comprehend the power that came to her when she spoke in public, her children could hardly be expected to. With them, she was either doting and sentimental in the manner of the day, for ever teaching them little prayers and hymns, or else barely able to conceal her impatience. It was only when they were babies and she was nursing them that she felt warm and motherly and close, although all her life she tried hard to be a good mother.

They were too young to witness an extraordinary transformation of 'Poor Betsy' when she visited Earlham in September 1811. She had come to attend an inaugural Meeting of the British and Foreign Bible Society held in Norwich. The assembly was addressed by the Bishop of Norwich and £700 raised for the purpose of spreading the Scriptures. Members of all denominations of the Christian faith were present in that tolerant gathering and her younger brother, Joseph, one of the founders, invited thirty-four of them back to dinner at Earlham Hall. Six Church of England clergymen, a German Lutheran Minister, a Baptist and several Quakers sat down to a splendid meal in the large dining-room.

After dinner Elizabeth Fry experienced an unusual state of ecstasy. 'Such a power came over me of love, I believe I may say of life, that I thought I must ask for silence.' Just before the tablecloth was removed, Richard Phillips, another Friend, called for quiet on her behalf. She knelt down 'in a most sweet and impressive manner, imploring the Divine blessing upon the present company, upon the peculiar labours of the day and for the … promotion of truth upon earth … the wine and dessert were kept back and the servants dismissed for half an hour that nothing might interrupt the soul-refreshing current, the like was never witnessed by most of us before.'[1]

As always, she spoke simply and to the point, but such was her power over her audience that all the reverend gentlemen were genuinely impressed, if somewhat stunned. Today it would be a noteworthy occasion for a woman preacher to speak publicly at an ecumenical gathering. One hundred and seventy years ago it caused a sensation. The clerics muttered among themselves seeking to gain their assurance. The Secretary of the new Society, Joseph Hughes, was heard to observe that 'God is no respecter of persons', while another astonished clergyman blurted out that the Almighty had visited the gathering, and neither sex nor anything else stood in the way of his grace.

When the wine was brought in, a Church of England clergyman remarked that no wine was needed 'for there is that among us that does instead'. This story sounds somewhat apocryphal and it is difficult to imagine the Gurneys sending back the wine. Nevertheless all the accounts of her preaching, when she was in full flood, do suggest that she possessed a kind of magic.

Among her brothers and sisters at that time, with the exception of Joseph and perhaps Priscilla, both 'decided' Quakers, her brilliance merely seems to have aroused an acute sense of embarrassment, disapproval, perhaps even envy. Her brothers John and Daniel disliked her public speaking extremely. Her sisters criticised her on the grounds that she neglected her own family and was too indulgent a mother. Betsy's brood ('Betsy's brats' Louisa called them) were lively, untidy and noisy.

While she was still staying at Earlham, after that extraordinary Bible Society Meeting, she told Rachel and Priscilla, not without misgivings, that she intended to travel to Ipswich for the Suffolk Quarterly Meeting. Rachel disapproved and when Priscilla, who was shortly to become a Minister herself, replied that her own faith was shaken by Betsy so often leaving her own family, she was extremely upset. She had helped her youngest sister, been a source of inspiration to her. Now, apparently, she was a threat. Yet none of them was able to realise that she had a self to fulfil. Their objections seemed to have been based more on the conventional conception of a woman's role rather than on personal concern. For when Betsy left her own household for weeks at a time to nurse an ailing aunt or a sister in labour, the family thought it only right and natural. It was only when she was concerned with her 'career' that they grew critical.

In a curious way, the criticism seemed to spur her on to almost frenetic activity. For two weeks in mid-winter she travelled about two hundred miles visiting Meetings around London. She was back home in January 1812, Joseph had also returned from a business trip, and her journal was full of elevating thoughts about the comfort of being together as a harmonious family. She was yet again with child. But within two weeks of her homecoming, this pregnant mother of seven was planning a journey to Norfolk for religious reasons during March.

It is no doubt a sacrifice of natural feeling to leave the comforts of home and my beloved husband and children; and to my weak, nervous habits, the going about and alone (for so I feel it in one sense without my husband) is a greater trial than I imagined; and my health suffers much … 'What I desire to consider most deeply is this: Have I authority for leaving my home and evident duties? What leads me to believe I have? For I need not doubt that when away, and at times greatly tried, this query is likely to arise.

She could, of course, claim the Supreme authority for her ministry but whether she was asking the question of herself or seeking a means of fending off criticism is not clear.

In this extract Betsy shows herself forced into self-deception by the convention of the time. She had far too much insight not to realise that staying at Earlham, where she was to be based on this particular journey, free from the responsibilities of Mildred's Court, would be at least as comfortable and pleasant as staying at home.

She *would* have to face criticism for neglecting her 'evident duties' but the one thing that Betsy would have found unbearably painful was to stunt her own spiritual growth. Nothing, neither her health, nor her family, nor public opinion, was allowed to stand in its way.

She could not, however, escape the burden of bearing children. In the autumn of 1812 she gave birth to her eighth child, Hannah, 'a fine, sweet girl'. This time her lying-in was almost free of nervous feelings and she suffered very little reaction. It was fortunate, for she had to face an unexpected anxiety shortly afterwards. Her husband's tea business had expanded into banking shortly after her marriage, probably due to Gurney influence. But 1812 was a bad year for business. The Napoleonic Wars and the blockade which had prevented Britain from selling her goods to North America, her best customer, resulted in hardship and economic depression. In October, the news of Napoleon's retreat from Moscow had an unsettling effect on the City. Many banks failed. Their own bank was dangerously short of funds. William Fry, Joseph's brother, had lent considerable sums of money to his wife's family, which in those critical times had imperilled the bank. 'Without help', Betsy wrote at the end of October, 'the banking house must stop payment.'

The situation seemed grim. Bankruptcy and the ensuing disgrace would surely finish her career. The Society of Friends prided themselves on their business integrity, and members who failed were usually disowned. Besides, she had been brought up to expensive tastes and liberal habits. Her sense of wealth and social position was extremely important to her, for on it rested much of her fragile sense of security. She could not bear the thought that she would be publicly humiliated. However, she held a firm and rather touching belief that the affluence of her family was divinely ordained. 'I do not think faith has ever left me to believe that we should not have prosperity granted, though we may not have the same abundance.'

In the event it was not divine intervention but the Gurney connection that saved their bank. Her brother John, her brother-in-law Sam Hoare and cousin Hudson Gurney went to visit the business at Mildred's Court with Betsy to study the accounts. Her business judgement was obviously respected. According to Betsy the affairs were in such good order and the state of the business so satisfactory that there was no doubt that the Gurneys would do 'what is needful for us', which meant, presumably, putting money into the bank.

Economies led the Frys to move from Plashet and spend the winter at Mildred's Court. Elizabeth Fry was loath to make the move but it turned out to be the most timely event in her life.

The distress in the London slums, where Dr Johnson had calculated a thousand starved to death every day, had increased appallingly. The unemployment brought about by the new machines, the swelling urban population, the shortage of corn and resulting high price of bread in the war years caused a vast increase in disease, crime and prostitution. The wretchedly poor lived in teeming hovels with overflowing privies, cesspools and drains. A bad harvest in 1811 sent the price of corn soaring to its highest ever level of 150 shillings a quarter in 1812, 50 shillings more than the previous year. Mrs Fry had made it her business to get to know the poor in her parish in Essex. She kept a store of calico and flannel petticoats always ready for them and in hard winters she had soup boiled up in an outhouse. But the rootless flotsam of the London streets, many of them ragged and barefooted, posed an entirely different problem.

In town that winter was Stephen Grellet, a French aristocrat, who had settled in the United States and become converted to the Society of Friends. He was travelling in the Ministry in Europe, with a deep concern for the social as well as the spiritual conditions of the people. In the pleasant and comfortable home where he was staying, he was haunted by the spectacle of the poor wretches of London. He held a religious meeting for the Spitalfields weavers, thrown out of work by the powerlooms, and thousands turned up. But he was particularly moved by the plight of the 'vicious and degraded' of the city. After careful consultation with Ministers and Elders of the Society of Friends, Stephen Grellet arranged to hold a religious meeting for them at the Meeting House in St Martin's Lane. Notices were sent out to pickpockets, thieves and abandoned women and the meeting was arranged at the late hour of seven o'clock in the evening, since most of the guests spent their nights revelling and did not go out much before dark. A huge crowd gathered, far greater than Stephen Grellet had anticipated, and the solemn prayers and tears of the preacher produced a sobering effect on the mainly young people who attended. The chief police magistrate in London came to hear of the event and offered to gather together all the city's reprobates so that Grellet could use his influence for good. He asked instead to visit the city's prisons.

He went first to the Compters – committal prisons – found in every district of the town, and then visited Newgate, built by George Dance between 1768 and 1778 on the site where the Old Bailey now stands. The crowd knew it for the wild excitement of the hanging days. Outside the debtors' door, until 1790, women had been hanged and then burnt on piles of faggots while the crowd roared and shrieked. By 1813, they were hanged on the scaffold. The executions usually took place at eight o'clock on Monday morning and by Sunday night young pickpockets and their girls began to swagger about the narrow street. During the night, drunkards would stumble out of the taverns in Newgate Street and Smithfield to watch the workmen build the temporary scaffold, hung with black. By seven in the morning a riotous mob collected, pushing and elbowing to get a good view. A seat at one of the windows overlooking the gallows could cost up to ten pounds. The funeral bell in the prison began to toll and church bells were muffled but for the mob, and for some of the gentry, the event was a great fair. One of the governors at the gaol would offer a 'hanging breakfast' to his friends. The guests would watch the prisoner mounting the scaffold and the 'drop' as the victim fell down the trap door suddenly, to the roars and stampede of the crowd. The Governor and his party would then go in and take a leisurely breakfast while the corpse was left to swing for an hour. When they had eaten their fill, they would stroll out to watch the body being cut down.

It was a brutal age, frank in its obscene callousness and indifference to suffering. Small children worked fourteen hours a day and an eight-year-old chimney-sweep was burnt to death, when sent down a chimney to put out a fire.[2]

Perhaps because men and women like Grellet and Elizabeth Fry were Dissenters, members of the new middle classes, classless in some sense, they could see the horrors with a fresh eye.

Grellet went inside Newgate and first visited the prisoners waiting for the gallows. He and his companion were disturbed to find a great number of poor boys in a kind of thieves' kitchen within the prison, lured to crime by Fagin-like figures. In prison they were mixing with old lags, likely to draw them further into depravity. They succeeded in persuading the authorities to separate these boys from the hardened criminals. However, when Stephen Grellet applied to visit the women's yard, the gaoler tried to frighten him off.

He warned Grellet that the female convicts were 'so unruly and desperate a set, that they would surely do me some mischief ... the very least I might expect was to have my clothes torn off'.[3]

The women occupied two long rooms in the yard. On that dark January morning some of them were still asleep. They were sleeping in three tiers, one row of bodies on the floor, the rest in hammocks in two tiers without any bedding. Grellet began to speak to them, despite the fearful stench of unwashed bodies. At his words, a handful of the prisoners began to soften. He asked them if there were any other females in the prison and was told that the sick ones were housed upstairs. Here he found some very ill women, lying on the bare floor with old straw scattered on it and only a scanty covering over them, although it was January and cold. There were also several newborn babies in the prison, lying almost naked and crying.

Appalled by the suffering he had seen, Stephen Grellet hurried round to Elizabeth Fry at Mildred's Court to describe to her the state of the women in Newgate. She could picture the scene as he talked; her pity and imagination were fired immediately. She sent out that morning for several pieces of flannel and gathered together a number of young women Friends. The party worked all afternoon to make up a bundle of garments for the Newgate babies. The morning following Grellet's visit they were ready. With Anna Buxton, she took the baby clothes to the prison and persuaded the Governor to let her go inside to visit the women. He was astonished and apprehensive at the idea of allowing ladies to go in among the convicts – he did not like visiting the female section himself. Mrs Fry swept him aside, although she did consent to leave her watch behind, on his advice. What she saw was a scene straight out of *The Rake's Progress*. There were nearly three hundred women in the two rooms, some sentenced to death, some untried, young girls and old hags, cooking, eating, cursing and tearing each other's hair. One sight that moved her more than anything else was of two prisoners stripping off the clothes from a dead baby to clothe a live one.

The two women worked hard, dressing every baby in flannel, comforting every mother. The next day they returned with more comforts and clean thick straw for the sick. This time the gaunt, grey prison walls seemed even more sinister and Elizabeth Fry had to nerve herself to go inside. It was undoubtedly the most striking scene that she had ever witnessed in her life. She came home, took a bath and changed all her clothes. In a letter written on 13 February to her three small children, John aged nine, William aged seven and 'Chenda aged five, she wrote:

I have lately been twice to Newgate to see after the poor prisoners who had poor little infants without clothing, or with very little and I think if you saw how small a piece of bread they are each allowed a day you would be very sorry … how would you like to go all day with nothing but a piece of bread, and some water? We should feel it very sad and I could not help thinking, when there, what sorrow and trouble those have who do wrong and they have not the satisfaction and comfort of feeling among all their trials, that they have endeavoured to do their duty. Yet people are no doubt often much try'd but they have so much to comfort them when they remember that the Almighty is their friend and will care for them and we may also hope that if the poor wicked people are really sorry for their faults that He will pardon them for His mercy is very great.

I hope, if you should live to grow up, you will endeavour to be very useful and not spend all your time in pleasing yourselves …

Farewell my darling children and remember the way to be happy is to be good …[4]

Clearly Betsy wanted to inculcate the importance of being good into her children's small heads, but the letter also reads as if she herself were trying to reduce a horrifying experience to manageable terms. In her journal on 15 February she is preoccupied by fears of undue pride, 'being engaged in some laudable persuits, more particularly seeing after the prisoners of Newgate. How deeply, how very deeply I fear the temptation of ever being exalted or self-conceited.'

It is hard to escape the impression that Mrs Fry was more concerned in her prayers to subdue the tip of a monstrous ego than in the spiritual or physical welfare of the prisoners. Events were to disprove that view; but she knew herself well enough to realise that the limelight she apparently shrank from was, in fact, the greatest need of her nature. Her fears were partly owing to the inevitable censure that a woman who meddled in public life would provoke.

The following day she visited Newgate with Anna Buxton again. The latter said a few quiet prayers and Betsy 'very unexpectedly to myself, did so also. I heard weeping and thought they appeared much tendered; a very solemn quiet was observed; it was a striking scene, the poor people on their knees around in their deplorable condition.' When Mrs Fry spoke she was transported, serene, confident, infinitely consoling. Her audience listened, as if hypnotised, to her lilting voice with its message of hope and love; as she prayed, there seems no doubt that they too felt momentarily lifted above themselves and relieved of their burdens. The power she possessed was not yet fully appreciated by her family. From Earlham her brother Joseph wrote, more concerned about Betsy's welfare than the comfort of the prisoners, '… dear sister, do not trudge about in this expedition of thine and do not omit proper nourishment for the sake of appearance [evidently, she had been slimming] … on second thoughts I mean to make thee a present … of six pairs of Thortle's thick shoes.[5]

On her spring visit to Earlham, Mrs Fry once again had to face the criticism and disapproving looks of her brothers and sisters. That a matron and mother of eight should stand up in public and preach to grave men seemed to them intolerable. Her brother John, who had proved so helpful to her when business was bad, particularly disliked her public utterances. How could she hurt him? Yet how could she deny her true self? There was really never any question about it. She was accorded a reluctant measure of respect at Earlham when Ministers of other denominations called to see her. By now she was no longer poor Betsy, but Mrs Elizabeth Fry, a person of some standing, even at Earlham.

Back at Plashet that winter the cold was unusually severe. A hard frost covered the ground, vegetables were blighted and buried in the frozen earth and the distress among the poor was acute. Her impulse to help them, to relieve suffering, was spontaneous and generous; but she was no longer the green girl of Earlham days. She knew that there were those who took advantage of her as well as the many needy cases. Her name had spread for miles around and there were always poor women knocking at her door and a host of pallid, seedy-looking children from nearby Bow playing in the grounds. Even when she did her best, they were not always grateful. In February 1814 she ordered gallons of the same broth and dumplings that her own family ate to be made. 'I find great fault has been found with them and one woman was seen to throw them to the pigs.' With great restraint she persevered.

The winter always depressed her and that year the frost did not break until nearly the end of April. Pregnant again, she was suffering from one of her inexplicable 'shaking fits'. Doctor Sims reassured her that her fits sprang from a nervous origin. She knew this herself and must have written to confide in her brother Joseph at Earlham too, for he replied on 26 May with advice that might have been more helpful:[6]

My dearest Betsy,

I am truly sorry at thy continuing so poorly ... pray do not suffer thy thoughts to run in too gloomy a channel. But cheer up and endeavour to believe thyself in tolerable trim, as I am much disposed to think thou are in reality however sinking thy feelings may be. ...

The Lord will not forget his obedient servants in the day of their trouble and of this number I believe that thou, through grace, mayst well be reckoned.

At the same time, my dear sister I would recommend thee to meet the animal tendency to a low state by endeavouring to make things a little lightsome about thee and by rousing thyself, if possible, to cheerfulness – also by freely taking wine and porter. ... Have no scruples about the fourth glass being a little inconsistent with the expected proceedings of public friends!

Tell Joseph also to pay thee more attention than he generally does. Tell him thou art in want of it, and that he owes it to thee and much more with it ... I charge thee to send me a better account of thyself.

> Thy loving brother,
> J. J. G.

The implied reprimand of Joseph Fry by his brother-in-law was less than fair, but ever since the business lapses, Joe Fry had been regarded with slight patronage by the Gurneys.

In the family, from adolescence onwards, Betsy's tendency to nervousness and depression had always been treated with glasses of brandy and water, porter, wine and laudanum. Earlham had its own brewery. By now she was a drinker, by no means an alcoholic, but it was almost an article of faith within the family that the Gurneys needed liquor more than other people. Many years later when Joseph Gurney was recovering from a serious illness she wrote to him to warn him that his ailment had been aggravated by giving up malt liquor and wine. 'Medical men', she wrote, 'say they have never known such a case as ours for requiring good living.'

Even with the help of a liberal intake of drink Betsy could not banish the 'horrors' at the thought of yet another childbirth. Stephen Grellet and her sister Rachel came to visit but for a month before the child was born, her thoughts and prayers were preoccupied with the trial to come. Her ninth child, named Louisa, was born on 14 June 1814.

Once again she was trapped by household duties. She had

now, besides her newborn baby, five girls and three boys, aged from two to thirteen. She was mistress of a large and hospitable household with more than a dozen servants – the girls' governess, the boys' tutor, the eight indoor servants and numerous gardeners. She was thirty-four and oppressed by the feeling that her life was slipping -away. A typical day that summer is recorded in her journal:

> Rose a little past 7, dressed, read [the Bible] with household; breakfasted; nursed children, ordered dinner till near 10; went to meeting till half past one; called on widow, home, nursed, rested and walked till 3. Dinner, rested, dressed, attended to children till 5.30. Went to see Aunt Shepperd and J. Dinsdale till near 8. Attended to husband and children till nine. Then up to bed.

In the village she was admired, gossiped about and loved by some. She had made close friends with the vicar, Mr Angelzaark, and his wife. In consultation with him, she had opened a school for girls in the district, renting a large room in a local house and hiring a school mistress. The school was run on Lancastrian lines and Mrs Fry kept a watchful eye on it. She noted the girls' projects and awarded Bibles to the best scholars. There was a gipsy encampment close by and she visited the caravans and lectured the startled gipsies on cleanliness and child care, handing out Bibles. Most of them would not, of course, have been able to read but they were shrewd enough to recognise that Mrs Fry was a soft touch and to enjoy listening to her musical tones.

Her favourites were the Irish cottagers. She liked their singsong voices and their stories and she could be found, some afternoons, sitting on an upturned bucket listening to them. For her the Irish families were fun and that was rare.

Life was always presenting her with duties, apart from those she chose to adopt. Not only did her own and her extended family have claims on her, but she also felt tied to the Earlham clan. Her brother John, who had so much opposed her allegiance to the Society of Friends and her Ministry, lay dangerously ill. Since his wife's death six years earlier, he had suffered from physical and mental decline. Although her baby girl was only two months old, Betsy set off in the coach to visit him in August and again in September. On the second visit he died within a few hours of her arrival. Family, old servants, uncles and aunts, gathered around the bedside; Betsy described the scene vividly to her husband and children in a letter written 'by the remains of my beloved brother'.

By January 1815, the Frys were once again living at Mildred's Court, trying to make discreet economies since business was again worrying. At the same time they had to maintain a certain standard and keep up appearances in order to create confidence. Her servants, who did not, of course, understand the family position, accused Mrs Fry of meanness. As her children grew older, they became more and more unmanageable. Rachel, her second daughter, now eleven, was rebelling against the piety imposed on her and had turned into quite a tomboy. She was not entirely happy with Mary Ann, the governess, either. There were the sick, the poor, her relatives to visit, plenty to distract her but never enough time for her real calling.

In March 1815, she travelled to Earlham for her spring visit and in the summer accompanied Joseph to Liverpool and Manchester. He went to visit customers in the north, while she attended several Meetings on the way. In the autumn she was in Surrey, visiting Quaker families as part of her duties. Although she travelled in comparative comfort, and by then some of the main highroads were smooth-metalled, so that coaches could travel up to ten or even twelve miles an hour, the journeys were still long and fatiguing. She usually had with her a young baby whom she was feeding and a nurse and maid to attend her. Yet she bore the journeys extremely well. It was when she came home to household troubles that she wilted.

Late in November that year tragedy struck her family. Betsy, her seventh child, not yet five years old, died after a short, feverish illness. Heartbroken, her mother wrote in her diary, 'It has pleased the Almighty in his infinite wisdom to take our most dear and beloved child, little Betsy.' To modern readers her journal is full of sickeningly sentimental stories about the child's goodness, kindness to servants, poor people and animals, devotion to her Mama and extraordinary piety. But a moving note of simplicity creeps in: 'she had so sweet and easy a life, followed by so sweet and easy a death.' At her funeral, Mrs Fry rallied impressively and prayed for the child's salvation, but she was deeply shaken. She found it a great effort to attend Meeting and could hardly bring herself to visit the sick and bereaved.

Almost unbelievably, just two weeks later she was journeying to Shaftesbury for the Dorset & Hants Quarterly Meeting, an engagement she had undertaken before the sorrow. She was pregnant and with great resilience even looked forward to having the child. Her brother, Joseph, sent her an encouraging letter and a present of wild ducks and shrimps from Yarmouth to cheer her. 'My dearest husband is very tender of a night,' she confided to her journal a month before the child was due. The baby boy was born on 18 April 1816 'after a long labour'.

Once again the Frys had nine children, and once again, business was disturbingly bad throughout the country. A year after the defeat of Napoleon, the victorious nation was facing a slump. Thousands of returned heroes, ex-soldiers and seamen came home to find themselves jobless. That year the harvest was again poor and distress and discontent grew. In the North, the radicals were rallying at meetings, burning factories and smashing the machines which put men out of work. War-time contracts had ceased abruptly and industry was not yet geared to peace. After over twenty years of war, the national debt stood at £800 million and the cost of the interest was heavy. The impact of the recession was felt everywhere.

Gurneys Bank was able to draw on liquid assets in London and an unassailable reputation in Norfolk to carry them through. The Frys' bank was on a much more shaky basis. Once again they had to turn to the Gurney brothers for assistance and advice.

Betsy felt apprehensive and rather cynical about the effect on their relationship with the Gurney family: 'We have seen how little connections are kept up with poor relations ... I think poverty is seldom so painfully felt as by those who have been rich and are surrounded by rich relatives.' She added the pious thought, carrying perhaps less conviction, that if righteousness and the pure riches of the Kingdom belonged to her family, she cared little for anything else.

Although she disliked this dependence on her brothers and sisters, she realised that she could not manage without it. Her elder children, Katharine and Rachel, were to stay at Runcton with their Aunt Rachel and Uncle Dan (both unmarried) while the older boys, John and William, would live at Earlham until after the Christmas holidays and then go to boarding-school. Richenda and Joseph were to be brought up in the schoolroom with her brother Samuel's children. This left her with only three small children, Hannah, aged four, two-year-old Louisa and the new baby, Samuel, who was always called Gurney, so as not to confuse him with his uncle. She was grateful for the saving, of course, but worried about the arrangements, particularly for the eldest girls. Rachel was already wayward and liked to make fun of Quaker 'peculiarities'. Under the influence of brother Dan, who was himself disaffected, she was likely to grow further away from her mother's religious convictions. They would also be near a new uncle they had taken to, Francis Cunningham, a Church of England clergyman, married to Betsy's sister Richenda.

The house at Plashet seemed deserted to her and she wrote to her eldest daughters, Kate and Rachel:

My dearest Girls,

After drinking tea alone in your father's little dressing-room and taking a solitary walk and sitting in the rustic portico at the end of the green walk, I am come to write to you as I cannot have your company. Only think! this evening I have neither husband nor children to speak to, little Hannah being gone to tea at the cottage. I found it even pleasant to go and stand by poor old Isaac and the horse and the cows and the sheep in the field, that I might see some living thing to enliven poor Plashet. The grounds look sweetly, but the dining-room window is cut down which I think quite a loss. The poor little school children when I see them look very smiling at me and, I suppose, fancy that they will soon see you home. Poor Jones' little boy is still living; such an object of skin and bone I have hardly ever seen ... Our house looks charmingly, as far I think as a house can – so clean, neat and lively, but it wants its' inhabitants very much.

> Your most nearly attached mother
> E.F.

By October 1816 she was urging her girls in a letter to study hard:

> ... not only on your own account but for our sake. I look forward to your return with much comfort as useful and valuable helpers to me ... I mean that you should have a certain department to fill in the house amongst the children and the poor, as well as your own studies and enjoyments. I think there was not often a brighter opening for two girls ... I shall be glad to have the day come when I may introduce you into prisons and hospitals ... It appears to me to be your present business to give all diligence to your studies and then I cannot help hoping that the day will come when you will be brought into much usefulness ... Read Peter 1 from verse 13.

However emphatically Mrs Fry denied feminist ideals throughout her life, she equipped her daughters to expect to work in the public interest almost half a century before such an idea gained acceptance. Later, Katharine, her eldest daughter, was to act as housekeeper and amanuensis to her mother.

In November the Frys again moved from the country estate at Plashet to live over the counting-house at Mildred's Court in order to reduce expenses. Mrs Fry disliked the move, but there seemed to be no alternative. Another family funeral, of a Gurney cousin, sent her travelling into Norfolk and while she was there she visited her daughters Katharine and Rachel, coming away disturbed at the influence of 'those not Friends' on her girls.

She was anxious about sending her boys to boarding-school and had drawn up a set of rules for them, advising them not to reprove their school-mates or cheat their schoolmasters. Her hope for herself at thirty-six, mother of ten, with one child dead, was that she might 'live to a better purpose'. Within a year, Mrs Fry and her purpose were to be the sensation of London.

V

'Quite a Show'

'Scenes of horror, filth and cruelty which would have disgraced even the interior of a slave ship'[1] met visitors who ventured inside London's prisons in Regency England. Throughout the country prison conditions for women were even worse. Herded into small, dark rooms, where they cooked by day and slept on straw at night, women prisoners served 'often as a mere brothel for the turnkey'. At Newgate, half-naked, drunken women clawed through the iron railings with wooden spoons tied to sticks to beg the public for pennies for porter or for 'garnish money', to be paid to their fellow prisoners to buy them a sight of the fire. Shrieking curses, brawling, spitting and tearing each other's hair, they aroused an almost superstitious horror in spectators.

Victory over Napoleon had brought in an era of distress and discontent. Half a million soldiers and sailors, discharged from the services, came home to compete for jobs with pauper children and civilians who had been engaged in war work. In the Midlands, starvation was driving men to riot and to wreck the machines which they believed to be the cause of their misery. Poverty-stricken, half-criminal men in the capital swarmed to the west end of the town and gangs of very young children roamed the streets, ragged and barefoot. As the Prince Regent drove to open Parliament in January 1817, a mob of hunger-marchers tried to serve him with a petition protesting about the price of bread. The crowd was rudely dispersed, but a missile from a marcher broke his carriage windows and grazed him on the forehead. By 1818, 107,000 persons were committed to the gaols of the United Kingdom, 'a number supposed to be greater than that of all the other kingdoms of Europe put together'.[2]

For four years Mrs Fry had lived a peaceful life in her country home at Plashet fully occupied with her own home, her ministry and 'her poor'. Since her visit to Newgate in January 1813, she had given birth to two children and grieved over the death of another, but nothing that she wrote in her journal during those years suggests that she particularly recalled the plight of those wretched mothers she had seen in Newgate. It is true that she had interested herself, when she could, in prison conditions. Members of her extended family – her own brothers, Joseph and Samuel, and her brothers-in-law Fowell Buxton and Samuel Hoare – were committed to the prison cause; with them she had visited Norwich prison and the women's section of the Cold Bath Fields House of Correction in London. Her relations and friends intended to form an association to reform the delinquents and they had discussed their plans with her.

At Christmas in 1816, after returning to Mildred's Court for the sake of economy, Elizabeth Fry went to Newgate. Once again the turnkey shook his head as she showed him her permit to enter. Once again the massive bolts of those huge doors were unlocked as she entered and locked after her again. In the dark prison, with its smell of damp and decay, she found the women begging at the grate, fighting for money, playing cards with a filthy pack and reading 'bad books'. She was moved, as she had been before, by the sight of the small children, pale and in rags. It was religious compassion, she was to explain later, that prompted her to action. She was dismayed 'to see children exposed among those very wicked women. … I understand that the first language they began to lisp was generally oaths or very bad expressions.'[3] Thinking, perhaps, of her own small children, taught to recite prayers and hymns from the moment they could speak, she appealed to the women. She told them that she was a mother (she was still breast-feeding her eight-month-old son at the time), that she was distressed for their children. 'Is there not something we can do for these innocent little children? Are they to learn to become thieves and worse?'

The prisoners – coiners, forgers, thieves and prostitutes – listened to her with tears in their eyes. She was immensely dignified, with her snowy white clothes, her coal-scuttle Quaker bonnet and her stern, direct gaze. They were not accustomed to being asked for their opinion. The public and the other prisoners jeered or leered at them. The authorities sniffed with disapproval. Even Dr Cotton, the Ordinary (chaplain) did not address them personally, as individuals. Every male seemed to shrink from them or ill-treat them, as creatures who had defied their laws and transgressed against their natural femininity. Until Elizabeth Fry came to Newgate, it had not occurred to anyone to focus so much attention on them. They were overwhelmed.

The curious thing was that delicate Mrs Fry, who had been terrified all her life of thieves and who shrank from violence – she could not bear her sons to be whipped – seemed to thrive in that grim and squalid place. Newgate, the most notorious prison in England, appears to have held a curious fascination for her. Filled with evangelical religiosity, awed by stories of hell-fire and damnation, she found, among the fetters and blunderbusses and in the condemned cells, a release for her spirit. She knew, with the certainty of her religious faith, that the prisoners were lost souls in deadly peril. Painful experience as mistress of a household had taught her to understand the servant mentality, (and the women, she noted, were nearly all from the lower orders), how to temper authority with gentleness and command respect by a look.

The first entry in her journal about her new work occurs on 24 February 1817:

I have lately been much occupied in forming a school in Newgate for the children of the poor prisoners as well as the young criminals, which has brought much peace and satisfaction with it; but my mind has also been deeply affected in attending a poor woman who was executed this morning. I visited her twice; this event has brought me into much feeling by some distressingly nervous sensations in the night, so that this has been a time of deep humiliation to me, this witnessing the effect of the consequences of sin. The poor creature murdered her baby; and how inexpressibly awful now to have her life taken away.

Evidently news of her sensational activities had reached Earlham, for three days later, on 27 February, her brother Joseph sent her a word of caution:

My dearest Betsy

When I heard of thy visiting that poor woman at Newgate I felt anxious about thee, knowing how racking such things are to the spirits and how exhausting to the frame. I believe it is scarcely prudent, my love, for thee so to expose thyself and though I would check none of thy duties, nor prevent thy pouring of thy balm into any wounded heart, I think it right to suggest the consideration whether that wisdom which dwells with prudence justifies thy entering at Newgate into that most trying line of service.[4]

It would have been impossible to explain, even to such an understanding brother, that at last Mrs Fry had found an outlet for her genius for leadership in great moral issues. At last she had discovered an activity that drew on all her talents. In the prisoners' response, she had found the admiration and respect that she had hungered for all her life.

Once she had persuaded all the prisoners that a school for their children was desirable, she had to convince the authorities of her plan. Her social position as a well-known banker's wife and a Quaker Minister, as well as her influential friends and relatives, made it possible for her to gain a hearing. She met the Governor of Newgate prison at his house, with the two Sheriffs of London and the Ordinary of the gaol present. The gentlemen listened politely to her plan. The idea, they agreed, was admirable. It did Mrs Fry credit. But she simply did not understand the nature of the problem. The women prisoners and even their children were vicious and incorrigible. They would turn the school into a roughhouse. Gently, humbly, but with relentless persistence, she asked the authorities to permit her at least to try the experiment. It was hard to refuse Mrs Fry. The gentlemen prevaricated and promised to grant her another inter view. At the second meeting they told her triumphantly that her scheme was impossible: a thorough examination of the prison had revealed that there was not a single room or cell available. Was it then, Mrs Fry asked innocently, only the lack of space that prevented the experiment? They agreed reluctantly that that was the case. She took her leave courteously and went down to the cells to consult the prisoners themselves.

Since her first visit to Newgate in 1813, the seventy or more women prisoners were somewhat better off. Then they occupied two rooms and a part of the prison yard. Now, owing to the pressure of reformers, they had six rooms, two cells and the whole yard. Through the delay Mrs Fry had gained a valuable advantage. She was working with the women and, in their minds at least, against the authorities. Together they decided that one of the smaller cells could be used as a schoolroom. When Mrs Fry returned to the authorities and told them that she had found a room for her school, they agreed, wearily, to allow her to try her 'benevolent, but almost hopeless experiment'. The very next day school started. Mary O'Connor, an educated young woman imprisoned for stealing a watch, voted for by the prisoners themselves, gave the young children their first lessons. Most of the thirty 'pupils' in the cell were children under seven, born in prison, but there was a handful of convicted children attending as well. Outside stood prisoners in their teens and twenties, clamouring to be taught to read and sew. Mary Sanderson, who accompanied Mrs Fry, told Fowell Buxton that she 'felt as she were going into a den of wild beasts'[5] and recollected 'quite shuddering' when the door closed upon her. Mrs Fry, however, appears to have felt quite at her ease. After all, she had, as a mere schoolgirl, taught poor boys to read at her Earlham home; and at her own home, Plashet, she and the vicar's wife had founded and supervised a school for poor girls. This school, in the grim chaos of prison life, was a novelty for the women. Mrs Fry and her ladies sometimes gave little gifts of Bibles, tracts, small articles of clothing or occasionally a dinner to the prisoners. There is no doubt that they found Elizabeth Fry, with her low, musical chanting and her stern love, a very remarkable person.

She and her helpers came to the school nearly every day. As they processed through the prison with baskets bearing Bibles, sewing materials and their own food, they saw women begging, swearing, swigging beer, singing lewd songs, chewing tobacco and spitting it out and cavorting about in men's clothes. Sometimes the scenes they witnessed were 'too bad to describe'.[6]

Mrs Fry intended keeping her experiment at Newgate a secret at first. But when she saw despair and depravity around her and the adult prisoners' longing for occupation, she determined on a course that could not be kept quiet.

'Until I make some attempt at amendment in the plans for the women I shall not feel easy,' she wrote to her sister Rachel, '… in taking care of my dearest girls, thou art helping me to get on with these important objects.'

But how could she change the system? She turned to her brothers-in-law, Fowell Buxton and Samuel Hoare, both solid men of affairs, deeply concerned with penal reform, and outlined her ideas for employment and instruction for women prisoners. To her distress, they dismissed her plan out of hand. The prisoners, they argued, would steal the materials and turn her school into a mockery. These women were the scum of London, thieves and prostitutes, very different from the hardworking country girls Betsy had been accustomed to teach. The flogging of women prisoners was not abolished until 1820. For a number of ladies to dream of ruling women who could not be governed by sheriffs and turnkeys and all the awful punishment of prison was sheer folly. Her sentiments, of course, and her intentions did her credit.

At this point Mrs Fry showed extraordinary courage. Since men would not help her, she decided to enlist her own sex. She set up a Committee composed of eleven Quakers and her friend and neighbour from Plashet, Mrs Angelzaark, the clergyman's wife. 'The Association for the Improvement of the Female Prisoners in Newgate' pledged themselves to take turns in visiting Newgate daily; to pay the salary of a resident matron; to provide funds for the necessary work materials; to arrange for the sale of work; to clothe the women and 'introduce them to a knowledge of Holy Scriptures and to form in them, as much as possible, habits of order, sobriety and industry which may render them docile and peaceable while in prison, and respectable when they leave it'.

Very early on Mrs Fry became convinced that women understood their own sex better than any man could and, a year later, in her evidence to a House of Commons Committee, she informed the Aldermen of the City of London that women should have no male attendants other than medical men or ministers of religion.

In the meantime, she had to find a way of persuading the male authorities to allow her to embark on her experiment. Before she was married, her husband had promised her that he would allow her to follow her spiritual vocation. He supported her work publicly all his life. Together the couple decided that they would invite the prison authorities to Mildred's Court, with Joseph present as host. Governor Newman, the Ordinary, Dr Cotton, and Mr Bridges, the Sheriff, accepted the invitation. The authorities were, once again, sceptical about her plan. Dr Cotton, who had reduced his Sunday services from two to one in the past year, was extremely doubtful. After a prolonged discussion, in which Joseph stolidly backed his wife, the Governor agreed to attend a meeting the following Sunday afternoon where, Mrs Fry promised him, he would see for himself the mood of the prisoners.

Mrs Fry's convicts were well prepared for the event, unique in prison history. More than seventy women were assembled in the presence of the prison authorities and the ladies. Mrs Fry opened the proceedings by addressing the women. She reminded them of the misery of their present existence and asked them if they would agree to a change of system which would introduce occupation, instruction, religion and cleanliness into their lives. Quite unconsciously, she used all the advantages of her position as a wealthy, well-educated, beautifully-spoken woman and a Minister of religion, to subdue the female felons. Already friendless prisoners had benefited from extra food to supplement their meagre rations and extra clothing brought by the ladies. Quiet, clean, almost demure, they listened to Mrs Fry and gave her their assurance that they would obey any rules which would have to be made.

The Governor, who had watched the performance with some amazement, spoke briefly to the prisoners. He warned them that the new system was on trial and would continue only if they behaved themselves and obeyed the rules strictly. Then Governor Newman turned to Mrs Fry and her Committee with a little shrug, saying: 'Well ladies, you see your materials.' A member of the Committee closed the meeting by reading the parable of the Prodigal Son.

In her journal Mrs Fry confessed that she found working in a group a great strain: 'In getting helpers, I must be subject to their various opinions and being obliged to confer with strangers and men in authority ... is a very unpleasant necessity.'

The first meeting with the Governor, the prisoners and the Committee, took place early in April 1817. Mrs Fry's worries and prayers about Newgate occupied much of her journal the month before: 'My mind too much tryed by a variety of interests and duties,' she wrote on 10 and 11 March, 'children; household, accounts, meetings, the church, near relations, friends and Newgate ... I hope I am not undertaking too much, but it is a little like being in the whirlwind ... may I not be hurt in it, but enabled quietly to perform that which ought to be done;

and may it all be done so heartily unto the Lord and through the assistance of His grace … and if ever any good be done, that glory of the whole work be given where it is alone due.' However hard she struggled for spiritual purification, she found herself 'ruffled and confused' and 'a little angry' at the gossip and censure her Newgate plans had excited.

Before her 'school' could be opened on 10 April there was a lot of preparation to be done. The Governor, evidently more impressed than he cared to admit, agreed to adapt the former laundry at Newgate into a workroom for the prisoners. The room was also cleansed and whitewashed.

One of the Committee (except for Mrs Fry, the names of Committee members were rarely recorded) called upon Messrs Richard Dixon and Co., contractors to Botany Bay, and 'candidly told them that she would like to deprive them' of the contract to supply the convict settlement with clothing and other articles. The prisoners, she explained, needed the work. So powerful was her appeal that the firm guaranteed to buy all the prisoners' output. Quaker merchants in the drapery trade, approached by the ladies, supplied scraps of materials free and the first work that the Newgate women began was a patchwork quilt, easy for beginners to stitch and colourful in the prison.

Within a week of the preliminary meeting, the school was ready. Once again the prisoners were assembled and once again Mrs Fry addressed them.[7] She pointed out their 'distressful, uncomfortable' plight. Most of them, she said, were poorly clad, hungry, unable to earn anything and without employment. By spending their time in loitering, begging and gambling, they often became worse through being in prison. ('Ah, that we do', chimed in several prisoners.) If they could be employed in some useful needlework they would be able to earn some money for themselves, added Mrs Fry, and if they were very careful and industrious, they could save a little of their earnings for the day when they left the prison.

Their lives were wretched and sinful, she reminded the women, while the ladies of the Committee led happy, virtuous, useful lives.

But the ladies were anxious to share their advantages with them and to help them – women from whom other ladies fled.

By twentieth-century standards, Mrs Fry was appallingly patronising. In her view, the ranks of society were divinely ordained. She treated them as feckless servants, not inhuman wretches, and the prisoners responded. She did not, however, consider that their poverty was a mitigating circumstance or indeed the root cause of much crime. But she did promise the women more than anyone else had ever done, practical help and a means of earning money.

To encourage their efforts, she remarked significantly, the Committee would add a shilling to every five a prisoner earned. A matron had already been appointed and was present. Mrs Fry introduced her to the prisoners and explained that she was 'a respectable person' who would keep account of their work and do her best to promote their comfort.

She explained earnestly to the women seated in front of her that the Sheriff had fully approved the Committee's plan but that the final result depended on them. The ladies had not come to Newgate to rule over the prisoners and expect them to obey. They wanted to work with the prisoners, in concert. Not a rule was to be made, nor a monitor appointed, without their full and unanimous consent. Her initiative in enlisting the prisoners' co-operation and her insistence on it was astonishingly enlightened for her time.

When Mrs Fry read out her rules, each one was voted on separately, by a show of hands. Every prisoner in the room voted for every rule. It was a total triumph.

RULES

1   That a matron be appointed for the general superintendence of the women.

2   That the women be engaged in needlework, knitting, or any other suitable employment.

3   That there be no begging, swearing, gaming, card-playing, quar-relling, or immoral conversation. That all novels, plays, and other improper books be excluded; and that all bad words be avoided; and any default in these particulars be reported to the matron.

4   That there be a yard-keeper, chosen from among the women, to inform them when their friends came; to see that they leave their work with a monitor, when they go to the grating, and that they do not spend any time there, except with their friends. If any woman be found disobedient, in these respects, the yard-keeper is to report the case to the matron.

5   That the women be divided into classes, of not more than twelve; and that a monitor be appointed to each class.

6   That monitors be chosen from amongst the most orderly of the women that can read, to superintend the work and conduct of the others.

7   That the monitors not only overlook the women in their own classes, but if they observe any others disobeying the rules, that they inform the monitor of the class to which such persons may belong, who is immediately to repeat to the matron, and the deviations to be set down on a slate.

8   That any monitor breaking the rules, shall be dismissed from her office, and the most suitable in the class selected to take her place.

9   That the monitors be particularly careful to see that the women come with clean hands and face to their work, and that they are quiet during their employment.

10   That at the ringing of the bell, at nine o'clock in the morn-ing, the women collect in the work-room to hear a portion of

Scripture read by one of the visitors, or the matron; and that the monitors afterwards conduct the classes from thence to their respective wards in an orderly manner.

11   That the women be again collected for reading at six o'clock in the evening, when the work shall be given in charge to the matron by the monitors.

12   That the matron keep an exact account of the work done by the women, and of their conduct.

These rules, which introduced order and hope into Newgate, were later to be adapted for women prisoners all over Europe on Mrs Fry's recommendation. With due formality, the names of the monitors were proposed one by one, and again the prisoners agreed to every nominee. To close the meeting, a member of the Committee read aloud, from the Thirteenth Chapter of St Luke, the parable of the fig tree, and Elizabeth Fry 'knelt down in solemn supplication'.

Contemporary accounts of the 'miracles' at Newgate dwell on Mrs Fry's sensational readings of the Bible and the instant transformation they produced in the hearts of the prisoners. Whether it was through her religious inspiration or the material improvements in their lives, a remarkable change soon became apparent.

Only a fortnight after the new rules were adopted, a male visitor to the prison was taken to the women's side of the prison

… where stillness and propriety reigned. I was conducted by a decently-dressed person … to the doors of a ward where at the head of a long table sat a lady belonging to the Society of Friends. She was reading aloud to about sixteen women prisoners who were engaged in needlework … each wore a clean-looking blue apron and bib, with a ticket, having a number on it suspended from her neck by a red tape. They all rose on my entrance, curtsied respectfully, and then, at a signal resumed their seats and their employment.[8]

In her own journal, Elizabeth Fry recorded the 'peace and prosperity' she had found in her new venture. '... those in power are so very willing to help us ... already from being like wild beasts, the prisoners appear harmless and kind.'

With the system working so well, Mrs Fry decided to apply to the Corporation of London for permission to establish her school as part of the prison system. Then her work would not depend on the charity of individuals. By now the authorities were eager to see the work. The Lord Mayor of London, accompanied by several sheriffs and aldermen, asked to visit on a typical day. They heard one of the Committee read a chapter from the Bible and then they visited the classes where the prisoners sat quietly with their monitors, sewing and knitting. The visitors could scarcely take in the change. This 'hell on earth' where only a few months ago abandoned and shameless women affronted their eyes now appeared more like 'a well-regulated family'.

All Mrs Fry's rules were adopted as part of the prison system and the Corporation agreed to pay the matron a salary of a guinea a week, supplemented by an additional £20 a year contributed by the Committee. They were so impressed by the demure new look of the prisoners that they donated £80 towards their dress. Sometimes women arrived in Newgate so scantily clad that a member of the Committee had to stand between her and any male visitors to preserve propriety. At the ladies' request the Corporation dismissed the soldiers guarding the inside of the prison who overlooked the women's yard because 'they rendered the women disorderly'.

They were more cautious about promising reforms in arrangements for cooking, washing and dining because, they explained, in the current economic depression any measures that incurred expense to the City would have to be deferred. Perhaps the most important change that Mrs Fry brought about in the officials was a change of attitude. She forced them to consider the women prisoners as human beings. As a member of her committee put it, she helped them to see 'the individual value of these poor creatures'.[9]

A month after she began to work officially in Newgate, Mrs Fry had herself undergone an important change. She was no longer a voluntary Christian welfare worker but a prison reformer. To widen her knowledge, she set herself a number of tasks: 'Read Howard, consult with clever and charitable men and endeavour to learn about the management of the best conducted prisons.'

In Regency London, she was a unique figure, a woman in public life, consulted by men for her professional knowledge and advice. Her fame brought with it an attack on her feminity. The charge that she was neglecting her own home and family pursued her throughout her life. Gossips whispered that she had packed off six of her nine children to leave herself free for her prison work. The children had been sent away to relatives to help the Frys to economise but as they were bankers, and therefore obliged to keep up appearances, she could not refute the accusations.

At the Yearly Meeting Ministers and Elders of the Society of Friends were quick to point out the dangers of neglecting her home duties. The question became almost a matter of national importance. Was it womanly, was it fitting, for a mother of nine to play such an important part in national life? In *The Gentleman's Magazine* of August 1820, 'Cryptos' ardently defended her:

> The numerous family and large domestic establishment of Mrs Fry are properly conducted with the utmost propriety ... nor does her zeal in the holy cause of humanity ever lead her to infringe on those domestic duties which every female is called upon conscientiously to fulfil.

Despite the legend of saintly domesticity, so necessary at this time, Elizabeth Fry did not relish home duties, nor had she any special aptitude for them. As soon as her eldest daughter Katharine was old enough to supervise the household, she was recruited to the task.

Nor was she a woman who took to motherhood with any great enthusiasm. She found the endless childbearing a strain on her constitution and a curb on her activities. Even before her marriage she had suspected that she was not really suited to family life. Now that she had found her true vocation she had to outwit the system. With tact and much protestation about her devotion to husband and home and her reluctance to 'expose herself' in public, she managed.

One method she used was to recruit as many of her relatives as she could to help her. When her two daughters Katharine and Rachel, who were sixteen and fourteen respectively in 1817, were about to come home for the summer, she wrote to remind them that they must help her:

> You must, my loved girls, industriously do your part … you must rise early; remember there is no governess. Then I shall expect your diligence in your own education and in some other things I may want you to do; we must none of us be idle and as you are now come to an age of some understanding, I hope to find you real helpers.

The girls were set to work to help with the vast correspondence pouring in from all over the country asking for advice on setting up local prison associations, for permission to attend her readings at Newgate, for opinions on prison discipline. Requests poured in, too, from hundreds of poor people 'humbly praying for assistance'. The poor were rarely turned away. Her brothers and brothers-in-law contributed money, advice, support, and her sisters in Norfolk watched over her children.

That summer the public interest in Newgate rose to a peak. With a soaring crime rate, and a Tory government frightened by the decline in law and order, the subject was of great news value. Predictably, Mrs Fry felt uneasy at 'being publicly brought forward in the newspapers' but despite her misgivings, she very quickly learnt how to behave as a personality and seems to have rather enjoyed the sensation. On 28 August 1817, she wrote in her journal: 'I fear I make the most of myself and carry myself rather like a somebody amongst people in power in the city; a degree of this sort of conduct appears almost necessary – yet oh! the watchfulness required not to bow to man, not to seek to gratify self-love.'

Her almost obsessive craving for spiritual purification, her desire to do God's work, undoubtedly unleashed her drive to right wrongs. It was necessary for her to see her work as divinely inspired, for it was only through her religion, through her status as a Minister, that she could emancipate herself and leave the domestic sphere with any peace of mind.

In September she paid her annual visit to Norfolk, this time to attend her brother Joseph's wedding to Jane Birkbeck, a Plain Friend. The following year this brother, eight years her junior, 'with his sensitive and tender mind', was to be acknowledged as a Minister himself. Increasingly he was to become her ally in religious and philanthropic concerns.

In the winter the family moved from their country home to Mildred's Court, close by the prison. This time her two eldest daughters, Katharine and Rachel, stayed at home as well as the nursery party. By now her Newgate experiment was regarded as a brilliant success, 'perhaps the greatest blessing on my deeds that ever attended me'. Ministers of religion of all denominations, politicians, philanthropists, diplomats and, not least, members of high society came to see the spectacle and Mrs Fry was gloriously busy.

The post-war crime wave reached its peak during 1817–1819, the years of Mrs Fry's most original work as a prison reformer. In February 1818, only ten months after she had introduced her new system at Newgate, she was invited to give evidence to a House of Commons Committee on London Prisons. For a woman it was an unprecedented honour, and she asked her brother Joseph to accompany her.

Elizabeth Fry's evidence evokes a vivid picture of Newgate at that time. All the women prisoners – the number fluctuated between seventy and eighty – were confined together, 'old and young, hardened offenders with those who have committed only a minor offence or their first crime; the lowest of women with respectable married women and maid-servants.' Thirty women slept in a room, each with a space of about six feet by two to herself. 'It is almost like a slave-ship I have sometimes thought,' she commented.

As to the food, it was quite insufficient for most of the prisoners. Three quarters of them survived on the prison allowance of two pounds of meat and one pound of bread a week. Some looked 'very pale, very thin, frequently dropsical'. Prisoners with wealthy friends, by contrast, fed on luxuries. They even had poultry sent in: 'That we think very improper,' Mrs Fry said primly, 'for prisons should not be made palaces.'

She had no quarrel with the quality of meat provided: 'mouse-buttock, a nice, nourishing part. I have bought some similar to it, at threepence or fourpence a pound, when I have wished to give some of the poor prisoners a dinner – but I give eightpence for that which I use for my own table.' Although gin was no longer so easy to get inside prison, beer and wine would be sent in from a nearby public house. Mrs Fry told the aldermen on the Committee of one girl 'kept by a gentleman' who had bought ten shillings worth of beer for her. 'The girl, of course, threw a great deal of it away – she was so terribly intoxicated she was almost mad.'

No prison dress was provided by the authorities and the poorest women came into prison in rags. Recently, she told the committee, a pregnant woman had come into gaol: 'she had hardly a covering, no stockings and only a thin gown'. A few hours after her admission the prisoner gave birth and 'we provided clothing immediate for her and her baby'.

Keeping clean was difficult for the prisoners since the supply of soap depended on the 'Sheriff's charity', sometimes out of funds. Even when soap was available, the prisoners were not provided with either basins or towels.

Since the prisoners had started to work ten months previously, they had produced about twenty thousand articles of clothing and earned approximately one shilling and sixpence each a week. Their contracts for work were running out and Mrs Fry was of the opinion (and here, too, she was years ahead in her thinking) that Government should provide the prisoners with employment and pay them for it. In the meantime, the ladies had set up a little shop 'between the gates' where women prisoners could buy tea, sugar and haberdashery with their earnings.

Employment, she stressed, was vital to the success of her scheme. 'We may instruct as we will, but if we allow them their time and they have nothing to do, they naturally must return to their evil passions.'

Mrs Fry tactfully underestimated what she saw as the reforming power of the Scripture readings and, since the Parliamentary Committee was mainly concerned to discover whether she and her ladies were teaching a sectarian form of Christianity, she was able to reassure them.

They were curious to know how she maintained discipline. One of the prisoners had been overheard to say 'that it was more terrible to be brought up before Mrs Fry than before the judge'. 'I have never proposed a punishment,' she replied, sitting up even more erect in her chair, 'and I think it is impossible in a well-regulated house to have rules more strictly attended to.' It emerged in her evidence that 'about four times' offenders had been placed in solitary confinement for two to three days. This power of punishment the Corporation had granted to the ladies when their rules were adopted. One can imagine, however, that a word of reproof and a look from Mrs Fry might well be more terrible than the sternest punishment.

For good conduct she liked to reward the prisoners with small articles of clothing, Bibles or Testaments. They were also aware of the remote possibility of a pardon, 'if their conduct was very good and we could bring Lord Sidmouth [the Home Secretary] an account of it'. She could even report a modestly successful rehabilitation effort. One poor woman had been granted a pardon through Mrs Fry's intervention. 'We taught her to knit in the prison,' she explained, 'she is now living respectably out of it and in part gains her livelihood by knitting.' Another woman to whom the Committee had lent money 'comes every week to my house and pays two shillings. We give part and lend part to accustom them to habits of punctuality and honesty.'

The Committee reported perceptively on the ladies' achievements in their summing up:

> The benevolent exertions of Mrs Fry and her friends in the female departments of the prison have indeed, by the establishment of a school, by providing work and encouraging industrious habits, produced the most gratifying change. But much must be ascribed to unremitting personal attention and influence.'[10]

In another paragraph which must have caused even the stern and virtuous Mrs Fry to smile, they remarked: 'on the male side, attempts to give employment have been baffled by the dishonest practice of those on whom the experiment has been made.'

By now Mrs Fry was a household word; the curious and the pious flocked to see her. William Wilberforce, who had become a friend, first of her brother Joseph, and now of the extended family, visited Newgate in February 1818 with her brothers-in-law and her sister Priscilla, the Minister, and he recorded in his staccato style[11]: 'Went with our party to meet Mrs Fry at Newgate. The order she has produced is wonderful ... much talk with the governor and chaplain – Mrs Fry prayed in recitative – the place from its construction bad.' And later: 'What lessons are taught by Mrs Fry's success.'

In April she was thankful to move back to her country house.

> Since I last wrote I have led rather a remarkable life, so surprisingly followed after by the great and others in my Newgate concerns ... the prison and myself are becoming quite a show, which is a

very serious thing. I believe that it certainly does much good to the cause in spreading amongst all ranks of society a considerable interest in the subject, also a knowledge of Friends and of their principle, but my own standing appears critical.

She prayed, as she had always prayed, to live 'in the fear of God, rather than of man and that neither good report nor evil report … should move me in the least.'

By that time she had made her first serious but understandable blunder in her role as a penal reformer. From the time that she began her work in prison and met her first condemned prisoner, she had hated the death penalty. The more she saw of it – and she visited male prisoners and their families in the condemned cells as well as women, and stayed to be with them to the last on the scaffold – the more convinced she grew that capital punishment was evil and produced evil results. Criminals could be sent to the gallows at that time for over two hundred offences, such as stealing a pair of stockings or a teaspoon, or passing a forged banknote.

By using her unique position, she soon began to direct public attention to the horror of it. Very often condemned prisoners had to wait for six weeks or more for their appeals to be heard. Mrs Fry reserved the front bench at Newgate for these condemned prisoners and their appearance always caused comment and curiosity. Politicians found it harder to take an abstract view of capital punishment when they were praying with condemned women and facing them.

On 17 February 1817, Charlotte Newman and Mary Ann James were executed for forgery. At six o'clock on the morning she was to be hanged, Charlotte Newman wrote to Elizabeth Fry:

Honoured Madam:

As the only way of expressing my gratitude to you for your very great attention to the care of my poor soul, I feel I may have appeared more silent than perhaps some would have been on so melancholy an event, believe me dear Madam, I have felt most acutely the most awful situation I have been in ... I have much to be thankful for. I feel much serenity of mind and fortitude. God of his infinite mercy, grant I may feel as I do now in the last moments! ... It is now past six o'clock. I have not one moment to spare. I must devote the remainder to the service of my offended God.

> With respect,
> Your humble servant,
> Charlotte Newman.

Mary Ann James wrote a similar letter, equally calm and submissive in tone and the two letters from the condemned cells 'found their way into the public prints'.[12] Stories about condemned prisoners, paragraphs in the newspapers and pamphlets on capital punishment combined to produce a climate of opinion, both inside and outside Parliament, that was opposed to the death penalty for relatively trivial offences.

In March 1818, one of Mrs Fry's favourite prisoners, Harriett Skelton, a maidservant to a solicitor, a quiet, well-behaved girl, with 'an open, confiding countenance', was sentenced to death. Harriett had passed forged banknotes 'under the influence of the man she loved', her husband. She was a popular girl, both with fellow prisoners and with the Committee and, when her appeal was dismissed, one of her cellmates was heard to remark that Harriett had been chosen to die because she was so much better than the rest of them. The remark was hardly a boost to good conduct. Urged on by her Committee, Mrs Fry decided to appeal to Lord Sidmouth. By now she had grown more confident of her power. Indeed she had somewhat rashly told the House of Commons Committee that Lord Sidmouth had been 'very kind to us whenever we have applied for the mitigation of punishment'.

With her brother she went to plead for Harriett Skelton's life. To her distress she failed. Lord Sidmouth was losing patience with the reformers. 'They were removing the dread of punishment in the criminal classes,' he told the House.[13] Perhaps privately he felt that Elizabeth Fry was becoming too much of a nuisance. She, however, would not let the matter rest. At that time so many forgers were liable to the death penalty that the Directors of the Bank of England were empowered by Act of Parliament to allow a number to be transported rather than hanged.[14] If certain forgers pleaded 'guilty to the lesser count', discreet arrangements between the Bank's solicitors and Old Bailey officials ensured that the prisoner would escape with a sentence of transportation. Mrs Fry believed that Harriett Skelton had been given that option but had staked her life on a 'Not Guilty' plea, and so thrown away her chance of a reprieve.

Whatever the truth of the matter, Mrs Fry thoroughly upset Lord Sidmouth. She criticised the Bank Directors to him and, when that proved futile, persuaded her old friend the Duke of Gloucester to intervene on Skelton's behalf. (He was Prince William Frederick, the gallant army officer who had dined and danced with the Gurney sisters in her girlhood at Earlham twenty years before.) The Duke was known to be sympathetic to the campaign against capital punishment and under the force of her bustling indignation agreed to visit Skelton himself. He spent over an hour in the condemned cell with Harriett, shook her by the hand on leaving and went himself to Lord Sidmouth to beg for a reprieve. But Elizabeth Fry, according to her own account, 'had tryed Lord Sidmouth exceedingly'. He obviously resented her attempt to use influence and turned down the Duke's appeal.

Even then she persisted, persuading the Duke to accompany her to the Bank Directors to see if he could not induce them to spare Harriett Skelton. She succeeded merely in affronting their dignity. By now Mrs Fry had gone too far and the male oligarchy closed its ranks on the outsider. Lord Sidmouth wrote her a reproving letter, casting doubt on her truthfulness.

Mrs Fry, offended in her turn, refused to have any further personal dealings with him. *The Times* criticised the Home Secretary for this 'dreadful example of severity' but Harriett Skelton was hanged.

Mrs Fry realised that she should not allow personal pride to interfere with her work in Newgate. Soon after the hanging she went to see Lord Sidmouth, accompanied this time by Lady Harcourt, an old friend and sympathiser in the prison cause. The move was, apparently, tactless. Sidmouth reproved her again for speaking 'unadvisedly' to the Bank Directors.

'Nothing but pain', she noted in her journal, came out of the interview. On 2 May 1818, she wrote to him again, regretting that she had acted contrary to his wishes and adding, rather pathetically, that the Ladies Association of Newgate would like to send Lord Sidmouth a specimen of 'the poor prisoners' work'. He never really forgave her.

Part of the trouble was that Betsy was new to the situation. She was immensely perceptive about human conduct but inexperienced in the world of politics and intrigue. She behaved in government circles as she was accustomed to behaving in her own religious Society. Reform was discussed in an atmosphere of affection and support in well-appointed Quaker households. Her status among friends as a recorded minister tended to make her feel that she was in a unique position, as indeed she was. What she did not appreciate was that this made her conduct an object of suspicion in the eyes of the establishment. To maintain her influence she had to respect and understand their code. She learnt the lesson well, but at a price.

It was not easy, however, for Betsy to realise the vulnerability of her position. The very afternoon that she had been so summarily dismissed by Lord Sidmouth, Lady Harcourt persuaded her that she must visit the Mansion House. Queen Charlotte would be there, presiding over the public examination of over a thousand schoolchildren, and she had intimated a desire to meet Mrs Fry. 'The Queen', reported *The Gentleman's Magazine* of May 1818, 'conversed with the benevolent Mrs Fry.' And Betsy, cock-a-hoop, wrote in her journal: 'I think that no-one had the same attention paid to them … there was quite a buzz when I went into the room.'

Such moments of elation were rare. Most of her days were spent in Newgate, in committees and in correspondence and conversation about the prison cause. She did not neglect her duties as a Minister. Rather, she saw her reading at Newgate as an extension of them, a means of influencing not only the 'poor prisoners' but the 'ton', the fine ladies and gentlemen who came to see the show. In the summer of 1818, she faced the danger of a riot in her well-ordered female section. Transportation was the alternative to hanging for serious offences, a useful means for the government to thin out the overcrowded prisons and get rid of disturbing elements. A group of her prisoners were due to be shipped off to the settlement in New South Wales and the turnkeys confided their fears of the consequences to Mrs Fry. On the night before a transport, the women usually smashed up the furniture, broke windows and drank whatever they could lay their hands on as a last protest. In the morning, still rebellious and surly, they were clapped in irons, loaded on to open waggons and driven to the waterside, followed by a jeering crowd who pelted them all the way to the river.

When she went to the workroom and cells the women poured out their horror of the future and of the tales they had heard of life in the harsh, primitive colony. 'Women prisoners', a House of Commons Committee reported, 'were received rather as prostitutes than servants'.[15] She went straight to the Governor. She realised that she could not alter their sentences but surely she could make parting easier for them. She persuaded Governor Newman that the prospect of their ignominious journey, shackled together in an open cart, was at the root of the trouble. If he would permit them to travel in closed hackney-coaches, with turnkeys escorting them, she would be on hand to supervise. If he would only listen to her, Mrs Fry entreated, the women would leave prison quietly without any disturbance or damage to property.

She proved her point admirably. The following day the women transports left Newgate quietly and sadly, in closed coaches. Bringing up the rear of the convoy in her own carriage was the portly figure of Mrs Fry, armed with her Bible and the box of tracts which she carried everywhere. At Deptford where the convict ship, the *Maria* was anchored, the women prisoners were soon herded below. Distressed by their cramped quarters, the ladies, with Mrs Fry at the helm, set about dividing the 128 convicts into classes of twelve, based on the Newgate system.

Women prisoners from other gaols arrived by the cheapest routes. A group, chained together with clanking bunch of irons, with hoops around their waists and legs, clambered down awkwardly from the outside of a coach. Sometimes women convicts were bundled aboard a fishing smack, to arrive chilled and seasick after a voyage of great discomfort.

As far as possible the women convicts aboard the *Maria* were given an ordered routine. They were classified according to their age and the nature of their crime and placed in a class. A small space in the stern of the ship was set aside for a 'schoolroom' for fourteen of the prisoners' children who were old enough to learn to read and sew, and a schoolmistress was appointed. If she worked well, she was to be paid by the captain at the end of the journey. Voluntary classes for adult illiterates were also arranged. The Newgate prisoners were used to work and eager to earn money, so the Ladies Association brought scraps of material to the ship and set them to sew patchwork quilts, known to be popular in New South Wales. Of course the ladies provided for all the prisoners on board, not only those from Newgate. They bought work materials, aprons and extra clothing for women in need and visited the ship daily for the five weeks that it lay at anchor. Altogether they spent £72 10s on the convicts.[16]

The last time that Mrs Fry boarded the *Maria* before she sailed, all the women prisoners assembled on the quarter-deck to hear her and sailors climbed high into the rigging to get a view of the strange scene. Crews of vessels lying alongside leant over their ships as she opened her Bible and read in a clear voice to the prisoners.

She was privately apprehensive about the maintenance of discipline. For the next twenty years, whenever she could, Mrs Fry personally inspected the female convict ships that left London, to make sure that the women would live as decently and piously as possible on board. With her usual energy she set herself to find out about conditions for women in the colony. She never objected on principle to the harsh punishment of transportation but was opposed to capital punishment, mainly on religious grounds, and despite the setbacks continued to speak and write against it with great courage all her life.

Throughout that eventful year of 1818, as her fame spread, not only in Britain but abroad, doubts and misgivings as a wife and mother continued to fill her journal. Now that she was not only a Minister of the Society of Friends but their most famous representative, Elders watched unceasingly over her conduct and she felt forced to justify herself and to pray that she was doing the right thing.

'Oh! that I could prosper at home in my labours as I appear to do abroad,' she had written in December 1817 after almost a year's work in Newgate. 'Others appear to fear for me that I am too much divided, but alas! What can I do but follow the openings. I think that I do labour at home ... but my humble trust and strong confidence is that He who hears and answers prayers, listens to my cry, hearkens to my deep inward supplications for myself, my husband, children, brothers, sisters and household, my poor prisoners and all things upon which I crave a blessing.'

Both her children and her husband made easy targets for her critics. The children had spent many happy months under the influence of aunts and uncles who were not Quakers. Uncle Dan was sceptical and Aunt Richenda was married to a Church of England clergyman. The young Frys did not like going to Meetings any more than their mother had done at their age and they were fidgety and restless. Their language was not always the simple language of Friends. The boys liked to hunt and fish and the girls, particularly Rachel, were rebellious. As for their father, he too loved the sporting life, he liked to play chess and read non-religious books. He even went out occasionally to listen to a concert, for he loved music. To Betsy he seemed 'more devoted to the world than ever'.

She was of course hurt by the constant censure and gossip about her private life. Members of her Society disapproved of her children's lack of piety. But 'their natures are not easy', Mrs Fry confided to her journal, 'and all their faults appear to be laid to my charge.' Her prison concerns were going well, she wrote in July 1818, and 'many flock after me' but at the Yearly Meeting of the Society she had met many Friends who 'have great fears for me and mine'. Outside her own religious Society she was a source of scandal: 'some people outside the Society do not scruple to spread evil reports as if vanity or political motives led me to neglect a large family.'

Nevertheless the sheer excitement of her new life carried her along with it. On 8 July she spent 'a very interesting day at Newgate with the Chancellor of the Exchequer and many other people of consequence'. She read well, she noted, and afterwards felt peaceful and comforted. Peace, comfort, were words she rarely used about herself except in the context of her prison work. There she could combine the strict Quakerism she had chosen to practise with her pull towards high society; there she was admired and made much of. She never doubted that her cause was divinely inspired.

Earlier in the year she had intended to journey to Scotland with her brother Joseph, now a Minister, and his new wife. Together they would combine religious duties with an inspection of the prisons en route. Barking Monthly Meeting had recorded on 18 June 1818 her 'weighty concern' to attend the General Meeting of the Society in Scotland and were preparing a certificate to release her for the journey. Once again it meant splitting up the family. Members of her Society were censorious.

All the children except her second daughter Rachel were sent off to ever-welcoming aunts and uncles in different parts of the country. It seems likely that she took Rachel, who was at her most troublesome stage, on the journey so that she could keep a watchful eye on her.

By 29 August Mrs Fry was in Aberdeen, 'five hundred miles from my beloved husband and children', feeling rather homesick. She consoled herself with the thought that her journey was a duty, 'not of my choice or my ordering'.

VI

The National Crusade

When Elizabeth Fry began her work in the prisons, no government inspectors were required to visit them and no central authority controlled them. The local authorities assumed responsibility for their own gaols in each borough and county and paid for their upkeep. Naturally, they resented outside interference.

Mrs Fry's ambition was to create a local Ladies Association in every area, so that women prisoners, at least, should live according to standards set by her. The visits with her brother Joseph to prisons between London and Glasgow served to alert public opinion to the national scandal of life 'inside'. She prepared as carefully as she could for her task by carrying letters of introduction to local magistrates and gentry.

Despite the comfortably upholstered Gurney coach, the journey itself was a strain on her. There was danger on the roads, although by that time not from highwaymen. The horses often kicked or stumbled and could easily overturn a coach – Elizabeth herself had fallen onto her head when her gig overturned on a journey near her home – and even for the wealthy travelling was uncomfortable. The new macadamised surfaces threw up clouds of dust and when the windows were open passengers found themselves covered with grime. Mrs Fry was a nervous traveller and always took a dressing-box full of medicines. Her sisters and her daughter Kate between them combined to make sure that she had stout walking shoes, warm shawls and kneecaps in her boxes.

For both brother and sister the expedition had a serious religious purpose. At their many stops on the way up to Glasgow, they held Meetings. Although her exceptional reputation, even then, had transformed her in the public mind into a prison reformer, she considered herself all her life as a Minister first and foremost. Without that position she could never have entered public life.

But it was the prisons that brought her satisfaction, fame and authority. During her visits she worked hard and systematically, insisting on peering into every corner of the gaol and asking innumerable questions. The pair visited both the men's and the women's cells and made careful notes on accommodation, diet, clothing, gaolers' fees and, of course, the medical and spiritual care of the prisoners. Employment she considered vital and praised those prisons that provided it. To the surprise and disapproval of the authorities, it was the prisoners that she listened to with particular attention. After their visit to a prison, they would send a tactfully worded letter of thanks to the magistrate – Joseph's help here was invaluable, since Betsy's spelling and grammar were still eccentric – and include a list of recommendations for improvement. Mrs Fry usually managed to persuade a lady of leading social position locally to serve as president of a Visiting Committee and she tried energetically to organise associations run on the lines of her successful model at Newgate.

As they journeyed north, the picture they uncovered of prison life was depressing in the extreme. In the country districts they found small, dirty prisons such as the one at Durham, where the sleeping-cells, down thirty steps, were 'perfectly dark and without any ventilation except for a hole in the ceiling'. At Doncaster they visited a four-roomed gaol on two levels, thirteen feet square. As many as fifteen prisoners were locked up in these poky rooms, with irons on their feet. The convicts were allowed eightpence a day to buy food, but neither clothing nor soap was distributed. Debtors, criminals, vagrants and women prisoners of all ages were confined in this dark and smelly lock-up. At Aberdeen, the county gaol was housed in an ancient, square tower. In the women's room, which measured fifteen feet by eight, they found five people and a sickly-looking child. The husband of one of the women lay ill in one of the two beds, an elderly woman in the other. Often prisoners were in irons. At Berwick they found men chained to the wall. And at Newcastle-upon-Tyne, prisoners were penned in a tower built over a gateway with no space to exercise. The two rooms of Dunbar prison, one for debtors, the other for criminals, were filthy, 'furnished with a little straw and a tub for every different purpose'.

The bigger, purpose-built prisons in the new industrial towns were not much better, for although more modern in design, they were just as badly overcrowded as London's prisons. Wakefield prison had been built to hold 110 prisoners. When Elizabeth Fry inspected it there were nearly 1,700 prisoners, about a sixth of them women. Curiosity and compassion combined to make her persevere in these dreary and depressing visits – and, of course, the public acclaim. Everywhere she went, she was now a celebrity.

In Glasgow Mrs Fry had arranged an appointment with several of the magistrates and a number of philanthropically-minded ladies at Bridewell prison. She explained to them with her usual clarity what had been done at Newgate and suggested that a similar experiment might be tried in Glasgow. When she offered to speak to the prisoners herself, the party was delighted, though the keeper of Bridewell cautioned her against it. He told her that it was a dangerous experiment – at best the women would ridicule her. She agreed in her most disarming manner that this might be so. Nevertheless she felt her address could give pleasure to some of the women.

A Scottish woman wrote an account of her visit:[1]

The women, about one hundred, were assembled in a large room and when we went in … were misdoubting and lowering. Mrs Fry took off her little bonnet and sat down on a low seat fronting the women. She looked round with a kind, conciliating manner, but with an eye that met everyone there. She said, 'I had better tell you what we are come about'. She described how she had had to do with a great many poor women – sadly wicked, more wicked than any one present and how they had recovered from evil. Her language was often Biblical ... 'Would you like to turn from that which is wrong; would you like it', she said, 'if ladies were to visit and speak comfort to you and try to help you to be better? You could tell them your grief for they who have done wrong have many sorrows.' As she read them the rules, asking them if they approved, she asked them to hold up their hands ... The hands were now almost all ready to ride at every pause ... In this moment she took the Bible and read the parables of the lost sheep and the piece of silver and of the prodigal son ... She often paused and looked at the 'poor women' with such sweetness as won all their confidence ... The reading was succeeded by a solemn pause, and then, resting her large Bible upon the ground we suddenly saw Mrs Fry kneeling before the women. Her prayer was beyond words – soothing and elevating and I felt her musical voice in the peculiar recitative of the Quakers to be like a mother's song to a suffering child.

In such moments, Elizabeth Fry herself was deeply affected, absorbed and compassionate and lacking in self-consciousness. Afterwards she felt completely drained. It is hard to reconcile this sublime Mrs Fry with the simpering and smug image which she often draws of herself in her journals. 'We have been so sought after,' she noted after a visit to Liverpool in September, 'I hardly dared to raise my eyes because of the feathers and ribbons before me.' Plain Quakers, of course, disapproved of outward ornament.

The party received a warm invitation from the Earl of Derby to visit his nearby country seat. Mrs Fry was captivated by her reception. 'I was made far too much of,' she wrote in her journal, 'if a duchess in the land, I think that more would not have been made of me ... my internal feeling was humiliation and self-abasement, yet the surface of my mind; light, vain and foolish, rather enjoyed the novelty and cheerfulness of the scene.'

Here one can find traces of that mercurial girl of seventeen, hovering between heaven and high society. For, as she revealed in her journals, mercilessly and in detail, she was infatuated by the nobility. At Knowsley, the home of the Derbys, she found herself feted and honoured. After breakfast she called on the company to pray. 'I was summoned into the grand dining room ... the servants were open-mouthed. Lady Derby and I walked in first, arm in arm, the rest followed – I should think that there were in all about a hundred assembled.'

Joseph's account was a little more restrained. He estimated that there were about seventy people present at prayers and noticed that a crowd of the large, patriarchal family thronged around his sister and 'thoroughly relished' her tales.

Fortunately Joseph felt a wholehearted, if uncritical, admiration for his famous sister, her example, her conversation, her deportment and her ministry. Throughout the journey Elizabeth Fry 'exhibited a perfect tact and propriety in her transactions', her devoted brother commented, but what struck him most was her 'deep humility amidst love and applause'.[2] She seems to have disguised her appetite for admiration completely. Their relationship was mutually supportive. He was immensely useful to her, since he was a scholar and a banker, able to draft her letters and ease her way with officialdom. She appreciated his practical help, his sympathy, his financial generosity. He, in his turn, recognised that she had a touch of genius in her personality, an ability to move the heart of a crowd. Wherever he went, he found that his own reputation rested almost entirely on being the 'brother of the benevolent Mrs Fry'. The book they produced, *Notes of a Visit made to some of the Prisons in Scotland and the North of England in company with Elizabeth Fry*, was published in his name and written by him, using her notes.

Nothing affected Mrs Fry more on the journey than the plight of the lunatics in prison. In the early nineteenth century they were mocked and baited. The 'luckier ones' in asylums were purged, bled, blistered, made to vomit, knocked down and plunged into cold baths. In prison the poor wretches were chained in dark, dank cells where many of them lingered for life. In a cell in Haddington county gaol she found a lunatic who had been arrested for loitering in the grounds of the home of the local squire. The madman had apparently damaged some garden seats. Nobody knew who he was, where he came from or anything about him. He was kept in solitary confinement for 'being mischievous'. When Elizabeth Fry saw him, he had lived in his solitary cell for over eighteen months, without once receiving a visit from a doctor or a chaplain. She protested about his treatment and, whenever she could, drew public attention to the most wretched and misunderstood creatures.

By now she had been away from home for almost two months. Although Joseph Fry enjoyed reading newspaper reports about his famous wife, he was growing distinctly sorry for himself. He had had a fall and was confined to the sofa. In a letter to their cousins, the Backhouses, in Darlington, thanking them for their hospitality to his wife, he wrote: 'My Betsy was truly sensible of the kind attention she experienced with you, I should have much enjoyed being a partaker, but home duties must not be neglected …'[3]

Joseph Fry was too unsophisticated to have intended any irony to be attached to his words. However, when Betsy did arrive home in October she felt genuinely baffled to find that even her own family were 'almost jealous over me and ready to mistrust my various callings'. It sometimes seemed to her as if they saved up their ailments until she came home. Katharine was seriously ill, Louisa was very poorly and Joseph was mending. She hurriedly took on as many of her burdens as she could and carried off home to Plashet her Aunt Hanbury, who had a bad cough, to nurse as well. Within two weeks of her return she was journeying up and down to Newgate for her readings, still a star attraction. Then there were the accounts to look into – they always seemed to need attention when she had been away – her Quaker duties and, of course, the poor.

1 Joseph Fry in 1823, by
C. R. Leslie.

2 Betsy (Elizabeth) Fry
in 1818. Joseph made an
awkward suitor but their
marriage in 1800 was vital
to Betsy's development;
he was a devoted and
obedient husband, allowing
her free rein to pursue her
outstanding career.

3 Earlham Hall, near Norwich, the home of the Gurney family and now part of the University of East Anglia.

IOUR IN NEWGATE *Exhibiting* M.^{rs} FRY *and her friends, as published by the* QUAKER

4 A satirical aquatint published in the 1820s. Mrs Fry's 'unwomanly' public role evoked censure and hostile gossip as well as admiration.

Above: 5 Mrs Fry reading to the prisoners in Newgate, 'a den of wild beasts' in the opinion of the terrified general public. Mrs Fry's most original work as a prison reformer took place during the years of a mounting post-war crime wave, 1817–1819, and for the rest of her life she continued to travel throughout Britain and the Continent, implementing her enlightened reforms.

Right: 6 Pencil drawing by Amelia Opie of Betsy Gurney at the age of nineteen.

7 Pencil drawing by Amelia Opie of Rachel Gurney, the second of the ele... Gurney children, and Betsy's favourite sister.

8 George Richmond's portrait of Joseph John Gurney. J.J., Elizabeth's cultured and devoted younger brother prominent Quaker in his own right, w... an invaluable aid to her and a frequent companion on her travels.

9 George Richmond's portrait of Elizabeth Fry.

10 J.J. Gurney, with his third wife Eliza and, from left to right, son John, daughter Anna, sister Elizabeth Fry, one of her daughters (probably Katharine) and Josiah Forster, circa 1842, three years before Mrs Fry's death. Anna Gurney and Josiah Forster accompanied Mrs Fry on journeys to France and the Continent in 1838 and 1839.

11 A family portrait of Joseph and Elizabeth Fry's children who were living at home in February 1830, from a drawing by Charlotte Giberne.

She was harried by the unctuous advice of pious Friends, so worried about her welfare and the welfare of her family. 'The prudent fears that the *good* have for me try me more than most things,' Betsy exclaimed bitterly, 'I know by myself what it is to be overbusy.' She preferred, of course, to be the giver rather than receiver of improving advice.

Yet she was overtaxing her strength. She felt pressed when she was at home to put more effort than ever into trying to fulfil her Quaker role and to discipline her family. John and William, now aged fourteen and twelve, had been to a school she disapproved of and she blamed their bad manners and language on its influence. In January she decided to take them to Darlington to a schoolmaster recommended by the Backhouses After the long journey in the cold weather she felt in low spirits and exhausted when she returned. For once she was almost grateful to give in to her depression. At the age of thirty-eight, she was pregnant for the eleventh time. 'Here I am,' she wrote from her home in Plashet in February 1819, 'surrounded with everything that this poor body can wish for its comfort … perhaps this state of bodily infirmity is permitted … that I may retire a little from the world and its business.'

Her husband and her children were only too ready to indulge her. Distressed to see her so weak, they tiptoed into her room to read to her and tried to ease her suffering. Her brother Joseph sent her £500 which he had 'spare', so that she could draw money whenever she needed it. He urged her never to walk when she could take the stage nor to deny herself any comfort. She was so weak and wrapped up in bodily miseries during February and March that she did not even fret about the prisons or her poor but was content to lie on the sofa in her room. By 19 March she was about four months pregnant, but whether the baby had died in the illness or not, even the doctors could not tell. She needed a change, they pronounced, and a little travel was advised. She journeyed by gentle stages on a bed in the family carriage to Brighton with her husband, Kate, 'Chenda, and some of the servants.

Even as an invalid she missed the limelight almost unbearably. 'Last winter what was not said of me, what was not thought of me ... this winter instead of being the helper of others I am ready to lean upon all, glad to be diverted by a child's book.'

Joseph's book on their visit to prisons in the North had been attacked by the Yorkshire magistrates who were angered by the public denunciation. Betsy always took criticism of her work personally and at that time, when she was feeling low, it seemed to her insupportable. Yet Joseph had been able to refute the magistrates' main criticism, which was that he and his sister had exaggerated the defects in their prisons, and that the improvements, made since the Friends' visit, had been there all the time.

Still, she rightly feared that the reaction to reform was growing. In a letter to the prisoners at Newgate from Brighton, she voiced her fears. There had been a disturbance among the women and the offenders had written to beg her pardon. Pressure had almost certainly been brought to bear on the rebels by the Committee and the other prisoners as well as the prison officers. She was pleased with their repentance but uneasy at the consequences of the upset. 'Let me entreat you,' she wrote to the women at Newgate, 'whatever trying or provoking things may happen to you to [offend] no more, for you so sadly hurt the cause of poor prisoners by doing so all over the kingdom; and you thus enable your enemies to say that our plans of kindness do not answer.'

She came home to Plashet in May 1819, the cause of her mysterious illness finally resolved. 'Regular symptoms of labour very overcoming,' she recorded, 'the miscarriage finally got through.'

In the summer she was quite content to spend a month at Broadstairs nursing Kate, whose health was delicate, collecting seashells and seaweed and carefully sorting and labelling the treasures with her small children. It brought back happy memories of sunny days on the Norfolk coast with her mother when she was a small girl. Her brother wrote to tell her that two prison committees in Paris had been formed as a result of 'le bon exemple de Mme Fry',[4] and this helped to raise her spirits.

About this time she began a correspondence with Walter Venning, an Englishman in Russia concerned with the welfare of the prisoners there. Inspired by reports they had read of Elizabeth Fry's work, the ladies of the Russian Court, headed by Princess Sophia Mestchersky, had formed themselves into a committee to visit women prisoners in five of St Petersburg's prisons. John Venning succeeded his brother in the work and when he became governor of a new lunatic asylum, to be run on reformed lines, he sent Mrs Fry a plan of the building bought for the purpose, asking for her comments and recommendations. She advised that two wings be added to the house for dormitories and that iron window frames be installed instead of the bars that the lunatics disliked. Over £18,000 was spent on her suggestions.

As soon as the Empress had read Elizabeth Fry's letters of advice, she ordered them to be translated into Russian and entered into the journal of the asylum for immediate adoption. In one letter she drew up a list of rules for the institution. They included: 'treating the inmates, as far as possible, as sane persons, both in conversation and manners towards them; to allow them as much liberty as possible; to engage them daily to take exercise in the open air; to allow them to wear their own clothes and no prison dress; most strictly to fulfil whatever was promised them; to exercise patience, gentleness and kindness and love towards them; and to be exceedingly careful as to the characters of the keepers appointed to watch over them.' This enlightened counsel was immediately adopted. Thanks to Elizabeth Fry, the lunatics also enjoyed more dignified mealtimes. They were now seated together at a table, covered with a cloth, and furnished with plates and spoons. The Empress herself came to visit their table and was delighted with the result.

At home that year, the year of Peterloo, the harvest had failed again and the winter was exceptionally severe. When she was settled in Mildred's Court, Mrs Fry was drawn into relief work by a vivid reminder of the distress. One morning a small boy was found standing on a doorstep in the City, frozen to death. The family felt impelled to act quickly. Fowell Buxton and Sam Hoare called a meeting, collected a large sum of money and organised committees. Mr Hicks, a Friend, lent his large warehouse in London Wall as a nightly shelter for the homeless. Elizabeth Fry headed the Ladies Committee to supervise the female homeless. A bed and hot soup, night and morning, were provided and a nightly average of two hundred men and women found shelter there that winter. Mrs Fry also organised classes for the women and children and, where possible, work was found for the men with the merchant navy. Through their action the lives of hundreds of paupers were saved.

Once again her life was 'like living in a market or a fair'. A missionary from India visited her and told her horrifying tales of a province in which seven hundred widows had thrown themselves on the funeral pyre after the deaths of their husbands. Through the family network, wrongs could be righted, and causes launched. Ten years later a bill forbidding the practice of suttee, introduced into Parliament by Fowell Buxton, became law.

The families – the Frys, Gurneys, Buxtons and Hoares – shared exceptionally close ties. Political and philanthropic causes as well as personal joys and sorrows bound them together. When Buxton's ten-year-old boy came home from school with inflammation of the lungs, Elizabeth Fry hurried to Hampstead to nurse him. Within five weeks four of the Buxton children were dead, Thomas Fowell the eldest, Rachel, aged five, Louisa, aged three, and Hannah, nearly two. Betsy had been present most of the time, reading to the children and praying for them and their parents. She was stricken by the loss.

Her occupation brought her into daily contact with suffering, grief, death. She had sought it out and yet in many ways she was unsuited to the constant drain on her emotions. With invalids in the family she was fussy and over-anxious, rarely able to conquer her own terror of death. Yet to the condemned prisoners she could bring a unique quality of sweetness and comfort.

That winter in 1819 her sister Priscilla was dangerously ill, spitting blood and Rachel, her daughter, had the same symptoms.

The sorrows of the year found her cast down at Yearly Meeting but for her there was no tonic like admiration. Again she wrote a cloying account of the attention and deference paid to her inside and outside the Society, 'from princes and archbishops to people of almost every rank'.

Her life see-sawed from heights to depths. In the public eye she was exalted and admired, triumphant. Yet at home her husband seemed almost indifferent to religion, her two eldest girls treated her insolently and she felt completely at a loss. It was only when she was playing with Samuel, her four-year-old, or teaching prayers to Louisa, her six-year-old, that she enjoyed home life. Rather surprisingly, at the age of forty she felt saddened that there would be no more babies to nurse. She was convinced that the horrors of childbirth were over, 'yet I think my pleasures are certainly reduced'.

That summer Elizabeth Fry had been married for twenty years. Although her husband seemed more worldy than ever and she believed their religious differences had a harmful effect upon the whole family, she realised that she was fortunate. Joseph was a kind and liberal husband and, she said, 'I believe [he] really loves and highly esteems me and is always willing to make my way and give me up for any religious duties.'

In the autumn the Frys, with Kate and Rachel, went on a journey that combined Joseph's business interests with Betsy's prison work. While Joseph paid visits to customers in the grocery trade concerning his tea business, his wife interviewed local magistrates and the girls went sightseeing. At Nottingham, Lincoln, Wakefield, Sheffield, Leeds, York, Durham, Newcastle, Lancaster and Liverpool, Mrs Fry followed her normal routine of inspecting prisons and founding Ladies Associations to visit prisoners. Occasionally she would take a day off to look at a castle or museum with her daughters who were amused to notice how she asked questions and 'investigated' in her sightseeing as thoroughly as if she were visiting a prison.

The journey was a success, almost a second honeymoon. 'My Joseph and I have had a very uniting journey,' she noted. 'I desire to make pleasing him one of my first objects.' How often had that sentiment been repeated in her journal. Yet somehow, when they were back home it seemed more difficult. Joseph still liked to slip out to a concert in the evenings, sometimes leaving off his Quaker coat. She particularly disapproved of his keeping late nights. 'My dearest husband and Rachel went to a party and did not return till past twelve,' she noted sadly in her diary on 17 January 1821. 'I spent a long evening in accounts. Very low.'

In February her family life was disrupted yet again by illness at Earlham. Her brother Sam travelled to Cromer with her to be at Priscilla's deathbed. The invalid was staying at Cromer Hall, now the home of the Buxton family, who had moved to the seaside after the tragic death of their four children. At first Betsy enjoyed being with her brothers and sisters by the sea, despite the sadness. She found Priscilla in a gentle and resigned frame of mind that helped her family to accept her death. But as the days turned into weeks, Betsy grew restive: 'I was certainly impatient at my darling sister being so long passing through the valley of the shadow of death, but how did I perceive my folly when I saw how gently she was led through it.'

Even when Priscilla was close to death, Betsy told her sister briskly that she was so certain of her reaching heaven, it was as if she could see it with her own eyes. She put her oratory down to the 'power' that came and went beyond her control. It sounds, from her own description, as if there was more in it of Mrs Fry's desire to get back to her 'real life', Newgate, than of religious inspiration.

Once again the devoted Gurney clan gathered close in a deathbed scene, so pious, so genuinely affectionate, despite the tensions, so remote from our own time. After commending Priscilla's body to the Lord, Joseph recited these words:

One gentle sigh the fetter breaks
We scarce can say they're gone
Before the willing spirit takes
Its station near the throne.

The funeral was held on 2 April. 'It was generally thought to be a satisfactory day', Betsy wrote in her diary.

A busy season awaited her in town. There were her Friday Newgate readings, and in mid-April she was caught up in forming a new society which reflected the national and international character of her work. 'The British Society for Promoting Reformation of Female Prisoners' was founded to advise and encourage local and foreign associations on the welfare of women prisoners, to deal with the vast correspondence on the subject and to take charge of the convict ships. To Betsy's delight, the Duchess of Gloucester consented to be President.

'Found my Joseph in town, after having met with a serious accident', she noted tersely on 14 May. She, however, had pressing business at Newgate with the Prison Committee. Five days later Joseph was resting comfortably at home and they spent a pleasant day together. Relations were always easier between them when one or the other was unwell and dependent.

23 May 1821 was an important day for Mrs Fry. Her friend Sir James Mackintosh was to put his motion 'for mitigating the severity of punishment in certain cases of forgery and the crimes connected therewith', to the House of Commons. As a woman, Elizabeth Fry could only be on the fringe of political activity. Yet her influence in the campaign against capital punishment has never been fully acknowledged. She was the only member of the lobby with constant contact with the criminals, and she mounted a campaign to save their lives. Her example of compassion towards them, her belief in the possibility of their redemption and her firm public denunciation of the evil effects of the death sentence, had an incalculable influence. On display at Newgate every Friday was the example of her work.

'Dined at Devonshire House,' Sir James Mackintosh had written in a note to his wife three years earlier, on 3 June 1818, 'the company consisted of the Duke of Norfolk, Lords Lansdowne, Lauderdale, Albermarle, Cowper, Hardwicke, Carnarvon, Sefton, Ossulston, Milton and Duncannon etc. The subject was Mrs Fry's exhortation to forty-five female convicts … Lord – could hardly refrain from tears in speaking of it. He called it the deepest tragedy he had ever witnessed.'

The afternoon of the debate, Mrs Fry hurried to Meeting and then on to the House of Commons. She was in time to hear Fowell Buxton deliver an excellent speech advocating the abolition of the death penalty for all but major crimes. 'I do believe', he told the House, 'there never was a law so harsh as British law or so merciful and humane a people as the British people … and yet to this mild and merciful people is left the execution of that rigid and cruel law.'

In practice the law was not only savage but inefficient. For the more trivial crimes which carried the death penalty – cutting down a tree or a hop bine – the majority of offenders were reprieved.

Although Mackintosh's motion was defeated in the Commons, the majority was a narrow one and the reforming lobby, Elizabeth Fry among them, was heartened by the increased support for a more humane system of justice.

A few days later she met many of the same speakers at a large public meeting of The Society for the Improvement of Prison Discipline and the Reformation of Juvenile Delinquents. The meeting was held in Freemasons Hall with the Duke of Gloucester in the chair. Many of the speakers, including Sir James Mackintosh, paid tribute to Mrs Fry and as she left the meeting, the crowd clapped and cheered. 'Greatly flattered … by the people,' she wrote of that meeting on 2 June. 'Attended in a marked way by the Duke of Gloucester.'

For some extraordinary reason Elizabeth Fry's daughter Rachel, who edited her journals after her death, commented specifically on the fact that no allusion to the meeting was found in her mother's journal or in any letters after her death. The edited version of the journals seeks to sanctify Elizabeth Fry, to remove any suggestion of human failing from her writings. Since at that precise time, Mrs Fry's journals were taken up with her distress about Rachel's wayward courtship, it is tempting to suppose that her daughter was seeking to atone for the hurts inflicted so long before. The same day that Elizabeth Fry wrote of the meeting in Freemasons Hall, she also mentioned a 'very serious conversation with Rachel about Captain Cresswell'. Frank Cresswell, Rachel's suitor, was *not* a member of the Society of Friends, which meant that Rachel would have to flout Quaker testimonies by marrying in church before a 'hireling priest' and so incur disownment. Attending such a marriage was equally unacceptable so that, if Rachel married 'out', her mother could not be present at the ceremony. There were already plenty of gossips who maintained that her family was too worldly and she was to blame. Both she and Joseph liked the young man, however, and felt he might be a steadying influence on Rachel. Since so many of her own sisters and brothers had married 'out', she could not regard the sin with such horror as those who remained strictly within the Society. Fowell Buxton, after all, was not a Friend nor was Samuel Hoare, but they were very much a part of her family and of her network of reform. She also secretly believed that Quakers were too strict about the question of marriage.

After discussion with Joseph Gurney and his wife, it was agreed that her sister Richenda's clergyman husband, Francis Cunningham, should marry the pair in church in Norfolk. Mrs Fry felt she was losing her daughter in every sense and was desolate when she left her in Runcton. In the days before the marriage her mother divided her time between shopping for the bride and visits to Newgate. Rachel's wedding day, 23 August 1821, has a large cross beside it in Betsy's journal; she was the first of her children to be married and she could not be present. She spent one of her improving days, calling on the widows and orphans in her district, and feeling forlorn. Rachel herself boasted, in a tactless letter to her mother, about a splendid public ball she had attended, knowing full well how much she disapproved. The meeting with the in-laws was not an unmitigated success either. The young couple invited the Frys to dinner with the Cresswells. 'Not high,' Mrs Fry wrote icily, 'though very kind.' Sometimes Betsy felt so humiliated and beset by difficult relatives that it seemed, she said, as though 'I could never again labour out of my own house and in my own Society, but that I cannot, dare not, give way to.'

During the winter months, the family stayed on at Plashet and Mrs Fry took the carriage to town once or twice a week on prison business. By now she was familiar with all the London prisons. With the help of local magistrates, she was trying to get matrons appointed in the women's section of the Cold Bath Fields House of Correction and at Clerkenwell prison.

At Christmas she visited the convict ships. 'A wonderful improvement' pleased her. The Ladies Committee now provided the convicts with work and work materials. Each woman convict on board received 'one Bible … one pair of spectacles, one comb, knife and fork and a ball of string'. The transport from prisons all over the country to the ships was still brutal in some cases. One poor wretch arrived on board with a fetter clamped around her ankle which had become embedded in the swollen flesh. When the sub-matron removed it, she fainted with the pain. Others came in irons. The ladies protested, wrote letters to Whitehall and spoke to their friends; Fowell Buxton raised the question of the convict ships in the House of Commons. Eventually, through lobbying friends in Parliament and badgering two kindly Admirals, Mrs Fry and her ladies forced a change in the system. The ironing of women prisoners on their journey to the convict ships was made illegal; another humane law was passed permitting the convicts to take children under seven with them and allowing nursing mothers to stay with their babies until they were weaned.

The reforms took years of hard, persistent work. Through
Elizabeth Fry's strenuous efforts, the conditions that the convicts met when they arrived in New South Wales were gradually
changing too. In the early days of transportation in the eighteenth century, officers and convicts used to board the women's
ships as soon as they docked at Botany Bay to take their pick of
the women. The custom was no longer openly practised, but since
the women had no shelter when they arrived, they were usually driven to begging or to prostitution. The Reverend Samuel
Marsden, a worthy Anglican clergyman who was chaplain at
Paramatta, had endeavoured for twelve years to have a barracks
built for the female convicts. As early as 1807 he had sent urgent
memorials to the Archbishop of Canterbury, to the Colonial
Office and to several Members of Parliament urging action. He
had received promises – but nothing else.

When he read about Elizabeth Fry in the newspapers he wrote,
in desperation, to beg her to use her influence. She received
his letter in February 1819 and began to bombard the Secretary
of State for the Colonies, Lord Bathurst, and Comptroller of
the navy, Sir Thomas Byam Martin, with correspondence on
the matter. By March 1820, building on the barracks had begun.
Mrs Fry was smoothly assured that by the time she had raised
the matter it was well in hand. It seems a singular coincidence
that action, delayed for twelve years, should follow within twelve
months of her intervention.

After Christmas Betsy spent a few days at Earlham with her
five-year-old son Gurney. There she felt at peace and at home.
For by now she was out of place in most domestic gatherings,
too sophisticated for many of the Plain Friends, too powerful for
genteel housewives and an oddity in high society.

She enjoyed the winter at Plashet managing the house, the farm
and the animals and pottering about in the flowerbeds. But the
Newgate 'season' was almost upon her. Such an aura of expecta-
tion surrounded her performance, such an air of near hysteria, that
it is hardly surprising that she found the readings 'exercising'.

John Randolph, the American Envoy to England, told a friend that he had seen the greatest curiosity in London.

> I have seen, sir, Elizabeth Fry in Newgate and I have witnessed there miraculous effects of true Christianity upon the most depraved of human beings ... I have seen them weep repentant tears while she addressed them. I have heard their groans of despair![5]

Maria Edgeworth, the novelist, a cooler witness, wrote to Elizabeth Fry in March 1822, assuring her that her main desire in coming to London was to 'become personally acquainted with the woman who has done the most good of any woman of this age.'[6] Nor was she disappointed. She thought Mrs Fry a delicate, Madonna-like woman, and was captivated, like everyone else, by her voice and manner and her effect on the prisoners.

In April Maria Edgeworth visited the Frys at Plashet and described them in a letter to her mother: 'happy, unpolished family, eldest daughter [Kate] too pert and talkative, her husband lisps and has an instinct for finding birds' nests.' Mrs Fry she found as delightful at Plashet as in Newgate.[7]

Yearly Meeting came round again with all the usual enter-taining and bustle in Mildred's Court and this time she feared that the bad feeling generated by Rachel's marriage would turn the tide against her. Each Yearly Meeting the men and women met in separate rooms to conduct the business of the Society and consider the members' fidelity to the Society's testimonies. On this occasion, Mrs Fry felt called to visit the Men's Meeting, which she was permitted to do if the women concurred with her 'concern'. Three other women, including her sister-in-law Elizabeth Fry, 'single Elizabeth, a faithful Friend', went with her. They were trembling. 'What an awful service it is for a poor weak woman to go amongst so many hundred men.' She delivered her message of prayer to the men to great effect. Many of them appeared deeply moved. 'Therefore what can we say, but that our merciful God was on our side ...' Elizabeth Fry felt very close to her God; He had become her awesome ally in a very personal sense.

Again that year she was pregnant, expecting her eleventh child at the age of forty-two. Her brother Joseph, always fearful for her health, sent her a present of wild duck and wrote to beg her to give up Newgate and her public life. In June Joseph's wife Jane died unexpectedly of pleurisy. Betsy of course travelled to Norfolk, although she felt 'really poorly', to comfort this cherished younger brother for whom she felt an almost maternal affection.

Back in London she found life hectic but entirely to her taste. She had just set off to town one morning when word came that she must return at once to receive the Princess of Denmark, who had invited herself to breakfast. Both the Prince and Princess, whom she had met through the Duchess of Gloucester, became friends and admirers of Mrs Fry. Then there were Italian noblemen to entertain to dinner, and the Hoares, and a host of company.

The baby was due in November and, to gather strength for the dreaded ordeal, she went to stay at Hunstanton in Norfolk with a gathering of the Gurneys – her widowed brother Joseph, his children, and her sister Rachel. Her own husband, her 'greatest comfort', watched over her health with great tenderness. For once she felt content to enjoy the sea air and the quiet. But her brother apparently could not resist calling a public meeting so that his famous sister could address the local residents. He was full of admiration for Elizabeth's modesty and eloquence.

At the end of October and with the Frys reinstalled at Plashet labour pains came unexpectedly. She feared she would die and called the family and the maids to pray for her. Again, she was rewarded in her prayers. Her infant son named Daniel – but always known as Harry or Henry – and her grandson were both born on the same day. Her journal was full of accounts of the 'darling little infants'.

For a month Betsy rested upstairs, carefully tended by the maternity nurse and almost as anxious about her baby's little ailments as she had been twenty-one years earlier, when her first child was born. There was, however, a significant difference.

When this baby was six weeks old she felt stirred to visit Newgate. She travelled the seven miles from Plashet to the City with the baby in her arms and took him into the damp and dirty prison. The prisoners and the Ladies Committee gave her a delighted welcome and she herself felt recharged. 'My dearest babe', she noted sorrowfully, 'suffered much by the rides to and from town, so that its little cries almost overcame me.'

Her sister Hannah Buxton had a baby in December, and in January Betsy went to stay with her sister Louisa who was expecting a child. Since childhood there had been friction between the two though now, of course, it was veiled. Louisa wrote pamphlets on the education of children which were highly regarded in their day. To Betsy, her sister's household seemed a model of order compared to her own. For her part Louisa admired her elder sister but could never quite comprehend the reason for her reputation. She applauded her achievements and fled her preaching.

Sandwiched between Mrs Fry's domestic duties was her public life, more demanding than ever. The previous year Sir Robert Peel had replaced Lord Sidmouth at the Home Office, much to her relief, for Sidmouth had never forgiven her for the Skelton affair. She was discussing criminal reform with Sir Robert and Fowell Buxton, dining at the Mansion House, and sitting for Charles Robert Leslie the portrait painter. With naivete, she rationalised the vanity of the portrait. She had agreed, she said, to her husband's request only because so many portraits of her had appeared already that 'it would be a trial to my family only to have these disagreeable ones to remain'. Besides, the useful employment would prevent the artist from drinking in low public houses.

As she sat impatiently, she dictated letters about Newgate to Kate and gave orders to her servants. In April she organised her first sale of the prisoners' work in their aid, sending round cards to friends in high society. Sir Robert Peel and his family were especially pressed to come, since their presence would be a valuable demonstration of support. Sir Robert pleaded his wife's 'delicate health' as an excuse. Nevertheless, the crowds swarmed into Squibb's Room in Savile Row to see Mrs Fry and the ladies of the Newgate Association selling quilts and stockings and baby clothes on the stalls. Over £319 was raised for the poor prisoners. Mrs Fry herself was, of course, the principal attraction and well aware of it, and though she told herself that she feared 'the pollution of the world' she enjoyed the fair enormously.

Despite all her efforts to raise money for them, when she went to visit the prisoners at Newgate they were troublesome. 'I met with such ingratitude I never remember,' she remarked, aggrieved. It seems remarkable that she did not meet with more open hostility. After all, if she had introduced reform into their lives, she had also taken away their pleasures; drinking, gaming, reading novels, even swearing to relieve the monotony. Many of the women she was dealing with were desperate characters. In December 1823 six women aboard a convict ship knocked down, beat and kicked the surgeon superintendent in an attempted mutiny.[8] Sometimes her own 'poor prisoners' must have been tempted to cheek or even hit the patronising Mrs Fry.

All the evidence given by her daughters, and in other biographies written in a similarly 'edifying' tone, present the Newgate prisoners as patient, ennobled, sinners, blessing their patron. It does not seem totally convincing. In a letter to *The Times* written in October 1833, two seamen, John Owen and John Richard Rice, rescued from the wrecked convict ship *Amphitrite*, testified that the Newgate prisoners on board had mocked and blackguarded Mrs Fry, who had been on board at Woolwich to read prayers to the women. 'It was Owen's place as boatswain to sling the chair for Mrs Fry and the other ladies when they came on board. He heard the Newgate girls wish she might fall overboard and be drowned.' Whether or not the story is accurate, (and nineteenth-century biographies claim that the *Amphitrite* was the only ship that Mrs Fry did *not* visit), the spirit of it seems unquestionably true. It is, incidentally, remarkable that she never once hints at fear of the convicts. She intimidated them, it would seem, by her absolute assurance.

A few days after the convicts had evoked her displeasure, she returned to Newgate. After the visit she wrote, 'the poor prisoners were quite cast down and very sorry for what they had done.' The source of their offence, probably gambling or swearing, remains undisclosed.

At home the Frys were entertaining lavishly and too frequently for Betsy's peace of mind. Yet when Joseph told her that he had taken a small place where he could go fishing with the children, she was upset at first at this further evidence of worldliness. However, she came to enjoy their pleasant summer retreat, two isolated cottages in the marshes at Dagenham, overlooking the river and surrounded by willow trees.

She was still breast-feeding her eleven-month-old baby, but she weaned him so that she could attend Bristol Meeting. Her journey to Bristol and Bath with her brother Joseph and her sister-in-law Elizabeth Fry, was, as always, a busy one: she held two public meetings and tried to persuade local magistrates to allow ladies into their prisons. It acted like a tonic to her spirits. She also met Hannah More, a great admirer of hers, her cousin Priscilla Gurney and her new sister-in-law, Lady Harriet Hay, brother Dan's wife. In six days the party had travelled about 280 miles, always on the move and fully occupied. She felt refreshed by the journey.

By the end of 1823, her public concerns were beginning to disturb her. The reasons were partly political. Peel's Prison Act of 1823 had been passed during the year. The Act set out to abolish the worst evils of prison life. In future local justices were required to inspect the prisons under their control and to make a quarterly report to the Home Secretary. Turnkeys were to become the salaried servants of the local authorities and fees or 'garnish money' paid by the prisoners were banned. Rules were laid down governing the health, clothing, diet, labour, education and religious observance of the prisoners. The indiscriminate use of irons was forbidden, and whenever a prisoner was subjected to a 'tyrannical punishment' the matter was to be reported to the visiting Justices of the Peace. Women were to be confined in a separate part of the prison, under the supervision of women officers. The Surrey Justices had decided to introduce covered vans to convey prisoners through the streets. Much of the Act seemed to draw on her experience of prisons and prisoners and her Newgate rules.

The main limitation of the new Act, however, was that unlike Mrs Fry's carefully supervised experiment in Newgate it failed to provide the machinery for law enforcement. Also many gaols in the country were not included. The Act only covered the prisons in the Cities of London and Westminster and in seventeen other provincial towns, and the one hundred and thirty county gaols.

In practice, the Act made the task of voluntary visiting Committees in the more negligent gaols almost impossible. Local authorities were resentful of interference and loath to increase the expenditure from the rates to pay for the reforms. Since inspection of their gaols was left to the local magistrates, they obviously did not welcome visits from pious ladies who would then report back to Mrs Fry in the capital. Her Committees from all over the country reported opposition to their efforts to go into the prisons.

'The burden and perplexity of the opposition in the prison cause is almost too much,' she complained at the end of the year, 'it is so much against my nature to take my own defence, or even that of the cause in which I am interested into my hands.'

VII

The Crash

On 21 April 1824, Joseph's forty-seventh birthday, his wife woke in floods of tears. She was distraught about his state of mind. Despite his many good qualities and twenty-four years of marriage, her husband was still so lacking in religion that she feared for him. That spring she was in an unusually nervous and depressed frame of mind. Exhausted after a journey into the Midlands on religious and prison service at the beginning of the year, she was suffering from a suspected miscarriage. She noted her symptoms meticulously: faintness, weakness and a glandular swelling under the arms. Since she was forced to remain at home, inactive, she became more fearful and introspective. Even an unexpected windfall of 'many hundreds, perhaps £2,000' failed to lift her spirits. Although the money was needed, with her large family and lavish expenditure, 'painful experience' had taught her to fear 'lest she should grow too attached to its value'. By now there seemed to be a pattern in these depressions. When she had been over-exerting herself, particularly when she heard criticism of her work, she would become genuinely ill and retreat from the world for a time.

In mid-April, after a 'very weak and faint morning', she did rally to attend a meeting of the Ladies British Society. Despite the setbacks, she felt encouraged to hear how many prisons were now visited throughout the country and of the improvements that the Lady Visitors had made.

The Society was seeking to rehabilitate the discharged prisoners as well as caring for those in prison. Thanks to Mrs Fry's prompting, a small home for nine ex-prisoners had been opened in 1822. They were also planning to open a home for what Mrs Fry called 'naughty little girls', children aged between seven and thirteen convicted of stealing or any other offence. These girls were to live under 'strict discipline and wholesome restraint', to learn reading, spelling, housework and needlework and, of course, receive instruction in the Scriptures.

In February 1824, Mrs Fry had applied to Sir Robert Peel, the Home Secretary, for permission to open the home. He gave his consent, on condition that the institution would be under her supervision. It ought, he said, to be supported by individual subscription and unconnected with public establishments. 'As a private individual,' Peel added, 'I beg leave to subscribe the amount of the accompanying draft, £20, in aid of the funds of the Establishment.'[1] Quick to seize an advantage, Mrs Fry thanked the Home Secretary for his liberal donation and asked his permission to make his generosity known to the public, adding 'I doubt not it will induce others to follow thy good example, more particularly as it proves thy approbation'.

But that spring of 1824, slumped in her depression, she was once again beset with doubts about her failure as a wife and mother. Yet she felt she had done all she could – '... as deep as my interest has been in the destitute and the forlorn, yet how much more have I been occupied with my own family.' Had she not, she added, been singled out by Providence to care for the downtrodden, then she would have been in danger of being 'pressed down out of measure by home cares and nearly to have sunk under them'.

Her prayers, her anxieties were on the same theme as usual, but more intense and distressing. By now her family were agreed that Mama was poorly and needed a rest. Kate, her eldest daughter, had already taken over the supervision of the household. Without too much protest, Betsy was persuaded to visit Brighton for the benefit of the sea air; but to imagine that she would rest idle, even in convalescence, was unrealistic.

One of the reasons for Mrs Fry's remarkable reputation was that she was seen as the spearhead of social reform. At that time of laissez faire, there was a dawning awareness of the need for social organisation, yet no statistical information or parliamentary enquiries to reveal the evils of society, nor social services to remedy them. It remained to outstanding individuals to take the initiative. The responsibility was heavy, particularly for a woman, since in order to be accepted by masculine society she had to personify the ideal of womanhood. At that time of her life Mrs Fry was acclaimed almost like royalty. Yet, unlike royalty, she was accessible. Hundreds of people came up to her after meetings, hordes called at her home, both at Plashet and Mildred's Court, poor people and ex-prisoners as well as members of her religious Society, customers of the bank and business, and the nobility.

At Brighton she was all but besieged by beggars in the street clamouring for pennies. Both at Earlham, where her father had helped to sustain the poor of the village and at Plashet, where she joined with the local gentry to relieve distress, her work with the destitute had been based on personal knowledge of families in the district. In the towns, she knew from experience, it was almost impossible to discover the real need. She had recently heard of the new experiments to encourage the poor to save for themselves, by means of Provident Societies. For her, however, care of the poor was a religious duty, laid down in the Scriptures. While she was convalescing at the seaside, she began to devise a plan which would combine the principles of self-help for the poor with visits to their homes to help with their problems. Through her personal reputation she attracted local dignitaries to patronise her new society. The bishop of Chichester agreed to be the patron, the Earl of Salisbury the president, and the Dean of Salisbury and Viscount Molesworth were amongst the vice-presidents of the Brighton District Visiting Society.

The plan was for the town to be divided into five areas with a team of voluntary visitors who would go into the homes of the poor. The poor were to be encouraged to save, by the Society adding to their savings from a subscription fund, much as the prisoners of Newgate were rewarded for thrift. Those in real distress were to be given financial help and imposters turned away. The first Annual Report of the Society was published in January 1825. Five years later, a member of the Committee reported: 'The families visited are improved in habits of cleanliness … the higher are not degraded but the lower are raised.' One of Mrs Fry's objects was to create a climate of concern between the classes. From that time onwards, she founded District Visiting Societies in other towns and played an active part in promoting their progress.

During her six week 'rest' at Brighton, according to family legend, she felt so faint during the night that she had to be carried to the window to gulp in the fresh air. As she looked out in the early dawn on to the shingly beach, she noticed a solitary figure pacing up and down the seashore. Intrigued, she enquired who he was, and was told that 'blockade men' – coastguards – patrolled the beaches at night to ward off smugglers. Her interest aroused, she made further enquiries. One day when she was driving down a narrow lane in her carriage, she hailed a blockade man walking by. When she asked him about his work and his family, the man replied politely but firmly that he was not allowed to speak to strangers – the local population were extremely hostile to the men who stopped the smuggling trade. Imperiously Mrs Fry gave the block-ade man her card and asked him to hand it on to his commanding officer, as she wished to make enquiries about the men's welfare. A few days later, the naval lieutenant in command of the coastguard station called on Mrs Fry. He was glad to be able to disclose to a sympathetic listener an account of the isolated life of both officers and men. They were on the watch all night, he told her, exposed to the worst of the weather and frequently set upon by smugglers. Since they were resented and regarded with suspicion in the district and had no friends, they often felt 'blockaded' themselves.

Here was another opening for her, another need to be fulfilled. She applied immediately to the Bible Society for Bibles and Testaments. She enjoyed travelling round in her carriage, distributing the books and talking to the men. They, in turn, were charmed by the strict Quaker lady, so dignified and gracious. In time she was to establish a system of libraries, which included some tales of travel and adventure as well as religious books, in coastguard stations throughout the country.

By July she felt well enough to move to the Frys' charming little cottages at Dagenham. The family was always more relaxed there; even Mrs Fry was content to leave the world behind in this willowy retreat, inaccessible except by boat. The youngsters enjoyed shooting snipe, fishing, boating (their dinghy was named *The Betsy*) and making up atrocious rhymes. Privately she felt frail and fearful but tried to conceal it. At the age of forty-four, she had borne eleven children, lost one and apparently suffered two miscarriages. She did not recover her health fully until the autumn. Even then, when they were able to move back to the large country house at Plashet, which had been undergoing repairs, she entertained less and cut down on the number of her engagements.

The following year, 1825, was to be one of her bustling years. She became embroiled in family matters in January when she discovered that William Fry, her brother-in-law, believed that he had been badly treated both by Betsy's brothers and by herself and Joseph when the bank had been in danger. She disliked seeming in the wrong and tried to placate him. 'If I had not to look to a very expensive husband and children, but only myself … I believe I could make almost any sacrifice to please him and his family.'

The epithet for her husband was fitting. He had recently visited Brussels and bought several Old Masters including a portrait by Rembrandt and the interior of a church by Canaletto, for he had excellent, if extravagant, taste. Betsy had little enjoyment of such luxuries and would have preferred 'a fine Christian simplicity'. In her case, this meant austere luxury.

Again in February she was advertising a sale of the prisoners' work, inviting influential friends and feeling thoroughly fatigued by it all. April was a busy month with the Annual General Meeting of the Ladies British Society and her Newgate readings. She launched yet another project, a Servants' Society, whose aim presumably was to find suitable employment for the servant class, care for their spiritual welfare and help them to save for old age – no details remain. 'No one knows what I go through in forming these institutions – it is always in fear.' Hardworking days were followed by sinking nights. She suffered from toothache again and frequently had to take opium to ease the pain.

Yet she seemed possessed, driven to 'expose herself' even more. Yearly Meeting of Friends came round in May with its duties of hospitality and crush of people. The lack of faith of her children was well known; Rachel, after all, had married out. Yet she particularly asked for a Meeting to be called for all the young people. Between 1,800 and 2,000 young men and women assembled on 23 May to hear her, including all her own children, except the baby. She poured out her heart and her mystic power can be sensed through the words in her journal:

> I was enabled to cast my burden for the youth, and my own beloved offspring amongst the rest, upon Him who is mighty to save and deliver … I had to ask for a blessing upon our labours of love towards them and that our deficiencies might be made up … I felt helped in every way, the very spirit and power appeared near, and when I rose from my knees, I could, in faith, leave it all to Him, who can alone prosper His work.

In June she hurried off to Norfolk for an aunt's funeral and returned 'to a great press of company, every day large dinners, noblemen and ladies and many others so that I am at times almost afraid for my mind and understanding.' In August there was more bustle. Her eldest son John was to be married to Rachel Reynolds, the daughter of one of her most intimate friends as a girl. This time the family could celebrate unashamedly. They dressed in their wedding clothes, 'the children looking sweet and very neat and I trust moderate ... we proceeded to London, my husband and I alone in the chariot, feeling the weight of the occasion.' At Meeting, Betsy noticed that her tears and prayers seemed to embarrass her son but attributed his coolness to the excitement of the occasion. The wedding party, a 'grand and hospitable entertainment', went off well, but when the couple came to live at Mildred's Court after their honeymoon John installed a piano in the house, much to his mother's disapproval.

In the middle of September she was travelling again in the Ministry, visiting Devon and Cornwall, where as a girl of eighteen she had struggled with family prejudice against her religion. She visited Liskeard, St Austell, Falmouth, and saw some of the wonderful scenery of the Cornish coast. This, she remarked, 'delighted me when my mind was at liberty'.

To the end of her life she was touchingly pleased if her family welcomed her home with warmth, secretly fearing that her piety and absorption in religion would alienate them. That November her homecoming was joyous, but the happy mood did not last long. Ten days later business worries and bankruptcy threatened once more. Money had been loaned again – on a very unsound basis in Mrs Fry's view. She felt, and perhaps rightly, that her presence was indispensable: '... my influence and aid appeared so important, that if absent I think I must have been sent for.'

There was another national crisis of confidence in 1825. All over the country a craze for speculation and investment, especially in the newly recognised states of South America, had produced 'bubble' companies. When these companies crashed, the run on money caused sixty country banks and six London houses to fail. One Sunday at the height of the crisis, a number of London bankers were called out of church by demands for gold from their country customers.

For months Elizabeth Fry's journals reflect her anxiety. From day to day she did not know whether the Bank could carry on, whether bailiffs would take away her property. When she looked into the state of accounts she was dismayed, but if she mentioned the matter to Joseph, he sulked and grew silent. She hints darkly at being kept in ignorance about something 'truly sorrowful' in the state of their private finances. Their situation was complicated by the fact that not only was Joseph well known in the City, but she was a public figure, and economies in their style of living – carriages, servants, expenses – had to be discreet. At Meeting she found it hard to concentrate on her prayers for worrying about the bills. In April they sold some valuable pieces of furniture.

> … my little monies are sunk to, I suppose, about a third of their value, and pay, I fear, no dividend at a time when I so much want it … I desire 'to do justly, love mercy and walk humbly with my God' but none can know until they are tried, the extreme difficulty of doing right.

Her brothers and sisters rallied generously to help her, with money to keep the Bank going and presents of clothes for her children. Her sister Louisa sent her a gift of £100. What was almost as important to her as anything was that her 'poor money' was safe. 'I am able to give freely to the poor through the abundant kindness of my dear Uncle Barclay and Cousin Hudson Gurney', she wrote.

Her brother Joseph wrote from Earlham advising her to withdraw gradually from the public eye, appear at Newgate less often and live a quieter life in the country. He should have known her better. At the Annual Meeting of the British Society, she gave a 'little general advice' to the large gathering of ladies. She was, of course, prominent at Yearly Meeting and visited five convict ships. She also travelled to Leighton Buzzard and St Albans to inspect the prisons. Later in the year she visited the family at Earlham and King's Lynn and she and Joseph agreed on a plan for a visit to Ireland that would include attending Meetings of Friends, and inspecting the prisons and lunatic asylums. In view of her brother's advice to her earlier in the year to retire from public life, the plan seems curious. In her journal she reveals that she had had a visit to Ireland in mind for twelve years, so it was presumably her influence that prevailed.

At six o'clock on a Monday morning, 3 February 1827, Betsy crept upstairs to say goodbye to her children – the youngest, little Daniel, was now four-and-a-half – and set off with her sister-in-law, Elizabeth Fry, and Joseph Gurney. On the journey Betsy drew a picture of the new Menai Straits Bridge for her children.

She was feeling unwell and wrote very tenderly to her husband: 'I felt my separation from thee and my tenderly beloved children during the voyage ... How I have missed thee, my dear love and did long for thee at Holyhead.' Betsy had never entirely lost her fear of water.

They stayed at a comfortable inn in Dublin and she had a good bedroom with a fire and a maid who enjoyed serving her. As usual she had a crowded programme, attending Meetings, visiting prisons, lunatic asylums – the state of the lunatics in Dublin gave her 'real pleasure' – a deaf and dumb institution and a nunnery. At least a hundred people called in to see her every day. Over 1,500 people thronged the Meeting House to hear her and hundreds were turned away. Brother and sister had to elbow their way through the crowds.

'Our dear sister was wonderfully enabled to surmount her bodily weakness and mental fears. I hardly ever heard such preaching as was hers that day,'[2] wrote her generous brother. She overcame masculine prejudice completely by her power. In Belfast, a clergyman who had been totally opposed to a woman addressing a congregation confessed after hearing her, that 'no one who loves the truth would dare to prevent them [women] preaching'.[3]

At another Meeting in the upper floor of a school, the crush was so great that Mrs Fry was terrified that the floor would give way and her brother was afraid that she would faint.

In a small inn in Galway, the friendly local mayor told them that the priests were so hostile that he would mount a guard of soldiers over the congregation to protect them. They assured him that no military presence was necessary. The Meeting was a resounding success and the poor Irish stamped their feet in approval at the close. In Limerick the multitudes that flocked after Elizabeth Fry when she visited the prison made it almost impossible to move about.

Back in Dublin they sat on the Judge's Bench and conversed with Judges Johnstone and Jebb, who were reformers, on the subject of capital punishment, while a 'crowded and inquisitive' assembly looked on.[4] Often, Betsy wrote home, she had a general on one side and a bishop on the other and sixty people pressing for a word from her.

On 12 April 1827, after three months of intensive activity, she fell ill with fever 'in one of my distresing, faint states' and the party had to wait for a week while she gained strength.

News of her fame and the crowds that mobbed her had reached her relatives in London. Louisa Hoare wrote to her son Samuel:

> Do you see the reports in the papers of Aunt Fry and her doings in Ireland? I wish you could see their letters. They are as entertaining and interesting as they are curious … Catholics, Protestants, high and low, learned and ignorant are drawn to your aunt by a sort of witchery; this witchery is, however, explained by the mighty power of the Gospel, manifested in a peculiar grace, combined with natural gifts. You may be sure Uncle Joseph bears his part too, though fame tells more of Aunt Fry …

One senses that Louisa still could not quite understand why her bossy, nervous elder sister aroused such admiration, whereas Joseph was extraordinarily sweet-natured about it. He knew that the crowds gathered to see Betsy and admired her unstintingly. By the end of their visit, they had intervened on behalf of a man condemned to death at Ennis in County Clare, a prisoner to whom Mrs Fry had spoken and who had since shown 'marked evidence of contrition and reform'. They had also visited Lord Wellesley, the Lord Lieutenant, twice and agreed to submit a report to him on their findings.

Their report, written by Joseph, using his sister's evidence, and published in both their names, pointed out the lack of employment and education in the country and the defective administration of justice. Almost twenty years before the famine in Ireland, the report called for more intensive cultivation of the land, so that if the potato crop failed, wheat would be a suitable substitute. It also called for higher wages, security of tenure and equal civil rights for all citizens, irrespective of their religion. As late as 1852 it was quoted in Parliament by Joseph Napier, then Attorney General for Ireland, in introducing measures to adjust the relationship between landlord and tenant. 'A better State paper on Ireland was never produced', he claimed.

It was the middle of May before she was home. Joseph Fry, who had missed her badly, went to meet her at Maidenhead to escort the party on the last stage of the journey. Almost immediately she arrived home she was claimed by official business. There was Yearly Meeting to absorb her, a visit to Lord Lansdowne, a fervent admirer of her work, who was now Secretary of State, and there were family sorrows. Fowell Buxton, her beloved brother-in-law, was very ill but soon recovered. With Rachel, however, the sister closest to her in age and intimacy, the illness was more serious.

On 20 July Betsy travelled to Brighton to be with her. She felt thankful, she wrote, to be able to return the 'unbounded kindness' of a sister so loyal and affectionate. It was Rachel who came to stay with her when she was in labour, Rachel who advised on the children's education and looked after the eldest girls when business was bad. At the time of her daughter Rachel's marriage, it was Rachel Gurney who helped Betsy to bear the shock of her daughter's alliance to a man who was not a Friend.

At the time of that difficult visit to Norfolk, when her daughter gave up her faith to be married into the Church of England, her sister gave her a present of a journal. Inside it is written 'Elizabeth Fry's Private Journal Book, given to her by her sister Rachel Gurney, who is to her and has been as much as one mortal can be to another'. She added, 'may our inexpressibly near union be a lesson to sisters to bear one another's burdens and to fulfil the law of love'.[5]

Nevertheless, when she was in Brighton with her ailing sister, Betsy could not resist enquiring about the charities she had founded during her own convalescence three years earlier. She held a meeting with the members of the District Society and discovered that the work was going well. The previous year the poor of Brighton had saved, between them, about £1,000 and many of the needy had been helped. She also called at one of the coastguard stations and found that the libraries she had had sent were useful to the men and their families. She then brought her sister home to Plashet to nurse until the end of the month. Even if Betsy's time was often taken up, Rachel greatly valued her company. In the carriage en route to Earlham she wrote to her sister: 'The quiet travelling has only been a luxury; both morning and evening have been delightful to me as to weather and scenery I have felt soothed and comforted, more than any-thing else.' It was Betsy, she said, who had enabled her to bear her illness. Later, when she was back at Earlham, Rachel wrote: 'Catherine is my constant comfort, Betsy is my greatest treat'.

That Betsy was deeply distressed and touched by Rachel's ill-ness seems plain. And yet, almost since the time that she had become a strict Quaker and developed her own inner life, her feelings were engaged principally in serving humanity, and only secondarily by individuals. Her passions were absorbed by her philanthropy and evangelist ambitions.

On 20 August her son John arrived by express coach from town to tell her that the news of Rachel from Earlham was so much worse that it was thought necessary for her to go at once to her brother Sam's house at Upton to decide whether or not to travel to Norfolk that day. 'On reading the different letters and seeking for a quiet mind, I believed that there was no such hurry and decided to wait until after Meeting on First day and early dinner with my family before setting off.' Her cooler judgement was entirely vindicated – Rachel lingered on for more than three weeks – but the incident reveals why her sisters believed that 'Betsy does not feel things as much as the rest of us'.

At the age of forty-seven and as one of the most famous women in the country, she was still conscious of her old feelings of inferiority and self-doubt when she was with them all at Earlham. The pious and affectionate brothers and sisters gathered beside the dying Rachel, languishing on the couch. Very often Betsy fell to her knees in prayers and thanksgiving. On 17 September the end came:

> About three o'clock this morning our most dearly beloved sister departed this life … They came to let me know about twelve o'clock, how she was going on; but at first I felt unequal to going to her and felt she did not want me; but gradually I found my tribulated, tossed spirit calmed, animated and strengthened, so that I joined the company round her bed, where I remained until the solemn close.

She had a taste for somewhat macabre detail and wrote in heir journal 'from the blue room – with my beloved sister's remains'.

> We were partners as children in almost all that we possessed … she was very strongly united in early life to Catherine [her eldest sister]. She was when young, beautiful, lively and warm-hearted and very attractive, so as even to excite in some of us, who were much less so, feelings of jealousy.

One cannot help admiring her honesty.

Betsy, of course, preached at Rachel's funeral and the very next day hurried, to King's Lynn to be with her daughter at her confinement. Two days after her sister's funeral her grandson was born. The following day, brother Dan sent for her to be with his infant son 'whose life hung by a thread'. Thanks to her nursing, the family believed, the baby was saved.

Grandmother, mother of young children, wife, aunt, sister and public figure, striving to play each part to perfection, surely Elizabeth Fry, if anybody, had a right to speak for the women of England. In 1827 her little book, *Observations on the Visiting, Superintendance and Government of Female Prisoners* was published. It contained a thinly-veiled plea for a more useful life for women.

In her introduction she wrote:

I wish to make a few remarks … respecting my own sex, and the place which I believe it to be their duty and privilege to fill in the scale of society … Far be it for me to attempt to forsake their right province. My only desire is that they should fill that province well; and although their calling in many respects, materially differs from that of the other sex and is not so exalted a one yet … if adequately fulfilled, it has nearly, if not quite, an equal influence on society …

No person will deny the importance attached to the character and conduct of a woman in all her domestic and social relations, when she is filling the station of a daughter, a sister, a wife, a mother or a mistress of a family. But it is a dangerous error to suppose that the duties of females end here … no persons appear to me to possess so strong a claim on their compassion … as the helpless, the ignorant, the afflicted or the depraved of their own sex … During the last ten years much attention has been successfully bestowed by women on the female inmates of our prisons … But a similar care is evidently needed for our hospitals, our lunatic asylums and our workhouses … Were ladies to make a practice of regularly visiting them, a most important check would be obtained on a variety of abuses, which are far too apt to creep into the management of these establishments …

In her diffident and apologetic manner Mrs Fry was advocating a radical change in women's status, urging opportunities for women outside the home that would inevitably bring further change. She did not champion professional paid work – the opportunities did not yet exist – but later was to form the initial plans for a nurses' training home in London.

The book, or pamphlet, contained practical advice on the formation of Ladies Committees, hints on behaviour towards prisoners and prison officials, notes on the need for employment of female officers in gaols, chapters on prison inspection, the classification, instruction and employment of prisoners and on their physical care, food, clothing, bedding and medication, and on rehabilitation. The book concluded with a passionate condemnation of capital punishment.

The great object of the Ladies Committees, she wrote, was 'the reformation of the prisoners'. It was unwise to talk to criminals about their crimes and the ladies must show 'as much confidence in the prisoners as circumstances will possibly admit … and entrust them with the care of various articles belonging to the Committee'. They should receive small rewards for good behaviour. She warns, from personal experience, of the dangers of ladies seeking to 'procure mitigation of the sentence of the criminal' and advises the ladies to obey precisely the rules of the prison and instructions of the magistrates.

She urged that prisoners be classified into four categories according to their moral character. She preferred iron bedsteads to wooden ones because they did not harbour vermin. Malt liquor (which she herself could not do without) was best excluded from prison except for prisoners on hard labour or in solitary confinement. As for wine and spirits they were entirely forbidden, except when used medicinally.

She believed employment and instruction were a means of preparing prisoners for discharge, a very enlightened view for the time, but was by no means soft on punishment:

No prison is complete which does not afford the means of hard labour. The tread wheel and hand-wheel or crank mill ... may be useful for the refractory and the depraved even among female prisoners, but then, its discipline ought to be applied ... only under strict limitations, for the female character is seldom improved by such rough and laborious occupations.

Ear-rings, curled hair and 'all sorts of finery and super-fluity of dress' were to be absolutely forbidden in tried prisoners. They were to wear close, plain caps not made of a transparent material.

If the long hair of female felons were cut off after their conviction, and afterwards kept short during their term of imprisonment, it would be found to act as a certain yet harmless punishment, and would promote that humiliation of spirit, which in persons so cir-cumstanced, is indispensable to improvement and reformation.

Thirty-five years later a prison matron described how effective and how cruel that punishment was:

The first inexorable rule to which the new prisoner has to submit and which is a trial that is always one of the hardest to bear is that of having her hair cut ... [they] clasp their hands in horror at this sacrifice of their external adornment, weep, beg, pray ... I can remember one prisoner delirious for a day and a night.[6]

In her *Observations* she recommended that although the women prisoners should be expected to attend the chaplain's service on Sunday, the Ladies Committee should take charge of their religious instruction during the week – a recommendation that subsequently was to lead to trouble.

Her pamphlet was enthusiastically received in reforming cir-cles, but despite her efforts the magistrates in country districts continued to refuse to admit the ladies into their prisons.

In the spring of 1828 Betsy was looking forward to a 'satisfactory wedding of one of my daughters'. Richenda, her third daughter, was engaged to Foster Reynolds, a silk merchant, a Friend and a good match. The young lovers travelled with her on a journey to the Midlands and Betsy felt quite jealous: 'They were so much engrossed by each other that I had not quite so much of their minds and hearts … as I should have liked.' She visited thirteen prisons, founded three new committees, reorganised others and attended a number of Meetings during the journey.

Richenda's wedding took place in June, the sun shone all day and the huge family party of about 130 relatives gathered at Plashet. A row of fine carriages waited in the road outside the Meeting House and the Meeting was crowded to overflowing, with numbers of smartly dressed neighbours drawn there out of curiosity. Although the wedding meal was cooked by Mrs Fry's own cook, the style and elegance of the occasion caused some of the Plain Friends to gossip and grumble.

Despite Betsy's pleasure at the match, she was upset later that summer by Richenda arriving at Plashet in a showy new dress. Others of her family were, she complained, 'a little gruff with me' and all in all Betsy really despaired of ever bringing up her children satisfactorily. For the first time in her journals, she openly confesses to a longing 'for a liberation from these responsibilities which at times lie heavily upon me'.

Travel, as always, was a way out. In the autumn she had another of her busy and successful journeys to the North with her husband. Away from home she suffered one deprivation. She could not be certain of the daily intake of drink which she needed more and more. In a private note to her daughter Katharine written from Listow near Bolton on 26 September 1828, she confided that she had been 'set off as I am apt to be for want of having really good porter for a day or two … I am becoming so delicate in these aspects that I am nearly ill if I cannot have these indulgencies.' In the same note she added, 'I am perfectly knocked up and ill. This morning I was obliged to go out of Meeting.'

Her craving for drink made her wretched and tearful and brought on 'miserable, hysterical tendencies'. Whether her addiction to drink was physiological or psychological, it was now an indispensable stimulus to her, both in her public role and in her private life.

But by now her public image was even more exalted. In mid-October in Liverpool she spoke three times at Friends' Meeting House, evidently captivating the reporter from *The Liverpool Advertiser:*

> A more musical voice and more distinct, correct and elegant enunciation we never heard … Her manner, however, though everything that is graceful and impressive is the least recommendation: the piety, benevolence and humility which pervade her sentiments and so signally influence her conduct are the chief merits of her public addresses.[7]

The local clergymen and other dignitaries at the Liverpool Town Hall met Mrs Fry with the aim of promoting a Provident and District Society modelled on the one at Brighton which was now doing well.

She had to break her journey at York to visit Benjamin Horner, her dentist. 'It makes my teeth sadly expensive, travelling so far for them,' she commented. The family party, which included their daughter Hannah, visited the Lakes and Mrs Fry 'had to scramble uphill and down dale after waterfalls in my old age'. Still, she enjoyed the journey and was pleased with Joseph who, she noted approvingly, had worked as hard as she had.

When she returned home at the beginning of November, she was feeling well and at peace in herself. Within a few days she was distraught. 'Without help,' she wrote on 15 November, 'it appears we cannot get through this Winter.'

For six days there was terrible uncertainty. Samuel Gurney this time was cautious about pouring more money into the bank. On 21 November 1828 the crash came. Frys Bank stopped payment.

While waiting for the bailiffs to come in to take an inventory of the property, she wrote, '… how striking to look round on everything and not think I can call one thing my own (except my children).' Her houses, land, furniture, would all have to be confiscated. Her journal that day ends with the prayer 'Thanks be unto the Lord who has remarkably blessed me in providing so for me individually that I have … always been able to pay everyone to whom I owed anything … in business dealings I have always promoted bright honour.'

Her wealthy brothers and sisters were once again marvellously generous to her. Louisa gave £236, Fowell Buxton and other relatives sent in gifts. Joseph's children sent her a portion of their pocket money and in her letter of thanks she wrote, '… if you like it, I propose buying with your money some of my own desks and things for my own room … when I use them I shall think of you and your kindness … *Pray keep this carefully.*'

For Mrs Fry, the bankruptcy was more than a personal disaster. Her own standing in the Society, as a Minister and reformer was called into question. The good name of the Society itself was affected, for then, as now, Quaker businessmen had a reputation for integrity and caution which was a steadying influ-ence on the volatile world of finance. A slur on a prominent member was a slur on the whole. The general public, too, were well aware that Elizabeth Fry's public philanthropy, her many journeys and donations, cost vast sums of money. Subscriptions to the Newgate Association were made out to the banking firm of Fry and Overend and wild rumours circulated. She was accused of drawing money from her husband's bank to fund her charities and run an extravagant household.

The Sunday after the bank stopped payment, the Fry family discussed the question of going to Meeting. Joseph, of course, was reluctant, but Elizabeth made up her mind that it was right for them to go. For him, though no record exists of how he felt, the humili-ation must have been acute. She sat up in the gallery with tears rolling down her cheeks. After a solemn pause, she rose and said, in a trembling voice: 'Though He slay me yet will I trust in Him …' She testified in simple words that her faith and love were as strong in adversity as they had been in times of prosperity. Her courage and dignity were as impressive as her words and members of the Society present wept with her.

The Gurney brothers, Joseph, Samuel and Dan, took the business in hand during that dismal December. They managed to salvage the tea trade and place it on a sound basis. Joseph Gurney was to run it with his nephews, including Betsy's son William, as partners. Joseph Fry was to become a salaried employee, with a monthly salary to be paid on the first of every month, so that he could not draw it in advance. He was to have an income of £600. Betsy's income was to be between £1500 and £1600.

They were now forced to move from the country house at Plashet. She dreaded parting with servants who had worked in the family for years, with the lovely house and grounds and her poor, yet they had no choice but to give up 'the dear Place'.

The Frys could not now pretend to be more than poor relations. Joseph Fry was, of course, extremely downcast, but the Gurney relations were principally worried about the effect of his depression upon Betsy.

She was poorly with a cough, bringing up a little blood. In the midst of all her troubles, however, she went with her brother Joseph to Newgate to take leave of a prisoner, due to be hanged for forgery the next day. 'If any may read this journal,' she wrote on that day, 5 December 1828, 'may it lead them to a most tender compassion for those in perplexed circumstances.'

As a bankrupt, her husband was in danger of being expelled from the Society and before Christmas she noted that his case was due to be brought before the Monthly Meeting. She prayed that they would act impartially. Already there were people both inside and outside the Society who were slandering the family and the bank – and even the Gurneys.

Many friends and colleagues did remain loyal. Letters of sympathy poured in, from aristocratic friends like the Countess of Derby, from the members of the Newgate Committee and the British Society, and from sympathisers with her work. 'Though my eyes are just now weaker than usual,' wrote the elderly William Wilberforce shortly after he heard the news, 'I must claim a short exercise of their power for the purpose of expressing to you the warm sympathy which Mrs Wilberforce and indeed all of my family are feeling on your account …'[8] Evidently in her reply to Wilberforce, she expressed misgivings about carrying on with her work in the prisons. Stoutly he reassured her of the propriety and 'absolute duty' of her renewing her prison work.

For months she remained at home, physically weakened by her troublesome cough and, despite her gallant efforts to submit to God's will, deeply depressed. All her life she had believed that prosperity was hers by divine right. She had implied as much in her first speech to the prisoners of Newgate. The good and righteous were rewarded. For once in her journals she sounded bitter. At Monthly Meeting members were avoiding them and others were only too ready to judge them. Joseph was being 'investigated' by a committee of the Ratcliff & Barking Monthly Meeting. Betsy, of course, felt the indignity: 'A Friend and his wife, much raised in life … visiting my husband as a delinquent.' Members of her own family 'queued' to disown him, she wrote. Certainly her brother Joseph believed that this 'painful justice' was necessary.[9]

She loved Plashet with its lawns and park and little farm even more passionately now that she had to give it up. But perhaps the most distressing effect of the bankruptcy was that her husband and children now felt fully justified in openly opposing the religious restrictions required of Plain Friends. Since many Friends – who were also creditors of the bank – had treated the family shabbily after the bankruptcy, she no longer felt able to oppose them. The children had invitations to parties where there were music and dancing late into the night – and she could not object to them going. Six months after his bankruptcy, the Monthly Meeting formally disowned Joseph. Their report stated that the failure of the banking house was due to 'dangerous advances made … on an extensive scale to persons not worthy of such credit, by which the property of others, confided to their care, was unjustifiably risked.' They added that their imprudent manner of conducting their business had brought 'great and lamentable loss' to a large body of creditors and 'reproach on our Christian profession'.

It emerged, in the course of the enquiry into Joseph Fry's business affairs, that the family had only become bankers since 1808, and before that date had run the tea and coffee importing business effectively. It seems reasonable to assume that the Gurneys, with their long and successful history of banking, had persuaded the Fry family to expand into a field in which they had no experience. The results were disastrous.

From the beginning, the Gurney family had dominated their marriage. Every year Betsy had visited Earlham at least once, and usually twice. Since the first crisis in her husband's business, she had confided in her brother Joseph not only her anxieties about their finances but also her disappointment at her husband's lack of religion. Now it was a Gurney, her brother Samuel, who offered them a home – a comfortable suburban house called The Cedars in Upton Lane, West Ham. It was not the country mansion she was used to but it was a dignified, red brick house, built in the style of Queen Anne, with a terrace in front and stone steps down to the formal gardens shaded by magnificent old cedar trees. Their grounds adjoined the larger pleasure grounds of brother Sam's mansion, Ham House – now West Ham Park. This was a mixed blessing, for it meant that she could never withdraw from the family.

'I suppose this is my last journal written in my little room at Plashet', she wrote on 1 June 1829. Leaving her home, she felt, was like a funeral.

By mid-June, she was settled in Upton Lane, her domestic staff reduced to her maid Chrissy, the housekeeper, cook and housemaid. She enjoyed the view. On a clear day she could see Greenwich Hospital and Park, the ships on the river and cows feeding in the meadow.

At the Yearly Meeting she had felt her new position acutely. For years she had been a leading personage, prominent at Meeting and able to offer hospitality to hundreds of members. Now, although she found Meetings a real consolation, she was at a loss to understand 'why such a change was permitted me'.

Incredibly, at the age of forty-nine, despite public disgrace and straitened circumstances, the strain of optimism in her fearful nature carried her through. Defying opposition from all her brothers and sisters, who thought it improper for her to venture on a religious journey at all, she set off to Stamford alone in the stage coach. From Ackworth in Yorkshire she wrote in her journal: 'enabled to minister, I trust with some authority and power ... visited one prison.'

VIII

More Cruelty than Before

Despite her brave gestures, it seemed unlikely that Elizabeth Fry would ever regain her standing and her confidence. She was nearly fifty, and on her twenty-ninth wedding anniversary looked back on a disastrous year: her husband's bankruptcy, her own illness, and her children's increased hostility to her religion.

'I have now had so many disappointments in my life, that my hopes, which have for so long lived strong, begin a little to subside', she wrote in a mood of despondency. Formerly, in dark moments, she had believed that Providence was supporting her, even in her trials. Now everything seemed overcast. The tea business was slack and there was talk of reducing their income even further. Repercussions from the bankruptcy were also limiting her religious calling.

In November 1829, a year after the crash, she had planned to join her brother Joseph on a religious tour of Suffolk. Since some of the largest creditors of her husband's bank lived in Ipswich she wrote, with unusual caution, to friends there to enquire whether her presence would be welcome. The answer was unexpected. Elizabeth Fry was not wanted.

'What a change,' she remarked bitterly, 'a family that used to be so glad to see me, so warm in pressing me to their house; and not even the least wish for my company.' A year after the crash she was still the victim of gossip and criticism. The style and show of Richenda's wedding in the summer before the bankruptcy still rankled.

Mrs Fry was accused of extravagance, of allowing music at the celebration. According to her daughter it was only an organ-grinder who had strayed into the grounds.

This kind of pettiness baffled her. She reflected endlessly on wealth and rank herself, yearning for the company of the 'high' and then reproving herself for such worldly preoccupations; and, despite herself, she thoroughly enjoyed a scandal, but petty gossip …

She would not, could not, allow that kind of trivial nonsense to deflect her from her duty. In the spring of 1830 she did attend Meetings in Suffolk and Norfolk with her brother but was disappointed to find that even he, this younger brother, who had been an ardent admirer, had now become critical of her tone when she preached. 'It might be but a fancy', she wrote, 'that I am not to most dear brother Joseph what I used to be, having become too dependent in outward things,' but added hastily that he and his 'dear wife' were 'most kind'.

Since Joseph himself and Gurneys Bank had been accused of being a party to Frys' failure, it seems likely that she had accurately detected a certain coolness in his manner. His famous sister had now become an embarrassment, an impediment to the bank and to his own position as a recorded minister.

Everywhere she met discouragement. When she visited Great Yarmouth, an Elder of the Society sent her a message, asking her particularly not to call at his house, since he so much disapproved of her conduct. This did not seem to trouble her unduly since, as she said, the criticism came only from hearsay. She sent him a message of love.

Yearly Meeting in 1830 proved another testing time. Her husband, obviously, did not attend but he also disapproved of the children being present, since he felt that they would have to face gossip and unpleasantness. Both he and his son William now refused to wear the Quaker coat and were openly hostile to the Society. Betsy, of course, felt the humiliation. She was also unable to keep open house as in the past and even if she invited one or two Friends home, she knew that they would receive 'a reluctant welcome'.

In spite of all her difficulties, she drew consolation from the Meetings and found the state of her Society 'very comforting'. She prayed affectingly for real improvement among Friends in those very matters which had touched her personally since the bankruptcy. She asked for 'less love of money, less judging others, less tattling' and 'more devotion of heart ... more real cultivation of mind ... more tenderness towards delinquents and above all more of the rest, peace and liberty of the Children of God'.

Disapproval from Friends prevented her travelling to Liverpool with her brother Sam and it rankled. In the autumn, however, she did make a journey with him to Sussex to the Quarterly Meeting of Friends. At Brighton Betsy was seized by an over-whelming desire to see the newly-crowned King William IV and his Queen. As a Quaker, she could not be presented at Court and she had set her heart on a meeting, perhaps as a salve for the humiliations of the past year. Page after page of her journal is devoted to her longing to see the Queen. In the end, she had to convey her blessings and her hopes through the Queen's lady-in-waiting, Countess Brownlow, 'an unexciting channel'. Poor Lady Brownlow had a wordy message: Mrs Fry begged that Queen Adelaide might promote the education of the poor, the general distribution of the Scriptures, the keeping of the Sabbath; that she would discourage parties and late nights and press for the abolition of capital punishment and of slavery. She also sent the Queen copies of two of her brother Joseph's books and her own *Observations on Prison Visiting*.

The Queen, apparently, could pass up the opportunity of meeting Mrs Fry. It was a disappointment. 'Time was,' she reflected in her diary, 'when even the sight of me was sought after and now I feel the day of curiosity is passed.' She wondered, 'Was it a wrong inclination that led me to see the Queen?'

When she returned to London she resumed her Newgate visits. In all the sorrow of rejection and disappointment, at least she could still feel 'much comfort in my Newgate visits ... having had but little company, I have been able, more than common to attend to the prisoners'.

Yet even the comfort of the prison cause was slipping away and her own position in it was changing. The new Whig government was committed to reform in every walk of life. In terms of penal reform, this meant a new and methodical approach to the problems in prisons. The laissez-faire society that had permitted prisons to remain pits of horror, and an unknown amateur like Elizabeth Fry to reform them, was giving way to a more ordered and organised system. The intellectuals in society, the lawyers, academics and journalists, were pressing for legislation to improve social conditions. Since she had come to live in London thirty-five years before, the city had swelled in size and population and life in it had become more complex and impersonal. There were newer roads, faster coaches, gas lighting in the streets. Shops were replacing the casual street-sellers. In the past year, Peel's constables in blue uniform had begun to plod the beat, replacing the old parish watchmen with their lanterns and the scarlet-waistcoated Bow Street runners. Still the crime rate soared. Political economists and utilitarian philosophers regarded crime and poverty as social and economic problems rather than moral and individual failures.

In 1829 Edwin Chadwick, a radical young criminal lawyer, published an essay on 'Preventive Police' in the *London Review*. In it, he rejected the prison system outright as too comfortable and too costly and advocated instead short, sharp terms of imprisonment followed by long periods of police surveillance for ex-convicts. He blamed the 'Howards and Frys', with their 'narrow sentiment and blind zeal', for transforming the prisons into comfortable refuges which attracted vagrants and beggars from the streets. His harsh, radical view reflected the mood of the times and was widely acclaimed. Informed opinion, inside and outside Parliament, was hardening against emotional methods of the pious and calling for a more scientific approach to crime and the criminal.

Despite Mrs Fry's 'miracles' at Newgate, the number of convicted prisoners had risen from 35,259 in 1817 to 121,518 in 1831.
The growth in population and better methods of crime detection
could not explain that away. The propertied classes in particular
– and it was in crime against property that the biggest increases
had occurred – were anxious for more effective solutions.

In 1832 Mr William Crawford, later to become one of the first
appointed Prison Inspectors, was sent by the British Government
to investigate the American prison system, then attracting a great
deal of attention. The system concentrated on separating prisoners in solitary confinement for their entire sentence, so that they
worked and slept in their cells with only their Bibles for company.
They even took exercise alone. A different form of the system was
used at Auburn prison in New York, where men and women were
allowed to work side by side in a central hall but were flogged
if they broke the rule of silence. Introduced by Evangelists and
Quakers, the system of isolation was said to have a 'purifying
influence on the criminal'.

Since the system was religious in intention, Elizabeth Fry
might have been expected to approve of it, but she had seen
for herself how damaging solitary confinement could be to the
criminal. The British Government, however, favoured the system
of separation and modified silence and the first penitentiary at
Millbank, completed in 1821, was looked upon as a model. There
each prisoner spent the first five days shut up alone and afterwards
worked in his or her cell for the first half of the sentence, leaving
it only for exercise or chapel attendance. Mrs Fry had seen young
girls who had been to Millbank on the convict ships. Illiterate and
terrified, they often became vacant-minded and remote when
deprived of any stimulus. She could not approve of separation.
To her credit she stood out against the growing body of opinion,
which included her own brother Joseph and Sam Hoare. She
argued consistently that being alone for months or years could
not possibly prepare prisoners to take up ordinary life on discharge. But prevention of crime was the preoccupation of the day,

not rehabilitation. It did not help that her beliefs were later entirely vindicated. In the United States of America, 'the separate system of imprisonment … resulted in deaths, suicides and insanity on a considerable scale'.[1] Nor did it help that the gradual erosion of her personal authority in the prison cause coincided with the years of public disgrace.

In January 1831 came another reminder that the old order was passing. Uncle Joseph of The Grove, who had been the first to encourage her in her calling, 'dropped down dead' in his house at Norwich. He was a Minister and to Betsy 'more like a father than anyone living'. Surrounded by her wealthy brothers and sisters at the funeral, she could not help reflecting bitterly on the injustice of her situation and was appalled by 'the evil of my own heart'.

In June that year the fever to see Queen Adelaide seized her again. She heard that she was to attend a sale held to raise funds for a hospital ship anchored in the Thames. Through the Duchess of Gloucester and other aristocratic friends, she contrived to be presented to the Queen. She spoke to Queen Adelaide 'almost entirely on benevolent objects' and congratulated herself on the fact that she 'did not enter on religious subjects with any of the royal party'. Of the Queen's replies, she does not record one word.

In the autumn she was travelling with her husband, troubled by her false teeth, a bad headache and stomach-ache. Now that fame seemed to have slipped away from her, she felt even more acutely her family's lack of sympathy with her religious ideals. The news that her daughter Hannah was to join the Church of England reduced her to tears.

New Year's Eve, 1832, found Elizabeth Fry on her knees by her bedside. The year ahead looked fraught with tension. Two of her children, twenty-six-year-old William and twenty-year-old Hannah, were planning to marry out of the Society, which was bound to bring her into conflict with Friends yet again. In the past year her son Joseph had been baptised and received into the Church of England.

She was anxious, too, about the mood of unrest amongst the people. After the defeat of the Reform Bill in September 1831, riots had broken out in the Midlands and a mob had attacked the Mansion House at Bristol. From Sunderland came alarming news of an outbreak of cholera.

Since it always appeared in the slums, cholera had been regarded as a disease of the poor, but even the experts did not know how the sickness spread. By February 1832, news from the City that cholera was as near as Limehouse caused panic. A Central Board of Health, set up the previous year, advised every town and village to take basic precautions: to designate certain buildings as reception centres and to arrange for the cleaning of infected premises. At first the existence of the disease was denied in London, as it had been in Sunderland, since it was bad for trade. With her usual shrewd courage, Mrs Fry gathered together some women from her Society and 'other kind and influential people' to do what she could. Although 'perhaps thought by some a busybody in it, yet more has been already accomplished than I could have looked for.'

She had a genuine interest in disease, born perhaps of her own hypochondria, and had acquired a certain amount of medical knowledge. When she had lived at Plashet, she had learnt how to inoculate children against the smallpox and periodically made a survey of the child population, with the result that she had kept the village free of the disease.[2] She could not, of course, halt the cholera. Nor did she altogether approve of the 'fast-day' proclaimed on account of the cholera on 21 March 1832. It was beyond the powers and scope of government to make people pray and fast and become holy.

On the day of the fast she was feeling anxious about having to appear before a Committee of the House of Commons on the subject of secondary punishment. By this time it was clear that the scheme of developing New South Wales partly by convict labour had proved an expensive failure. The shipment of the prisoners alone was costing about £300,000 a year. So the Government was anxious to find an alternative means of punishing criminals effectively.

From the tone of their report, it is clear that the Committee was the most hostile official body Mrs Fry had ever had to face. When she had given her evidence in 1818, she had been asked by the admiring officials to cite her list of achievements. This time she was challenged to state 'whether her views did not tend to the encouragement of crime rather than its prevention', an assumption that was implicit in many of the Committee's questions. Was not employment for women relaxation rather than punishment, they asked. She argued that prisoners disliked work of any kind and preferred prisons where, even if they were miserably housed, gaming, drinking and swearing were permitted. To keep criminals employed was important, she stressed, even if it meant that they had to make up an article one day and pull it to pieces the next. She held to the view that the object of imprisonment was to rehabilitate the prisoner, by means of employment and regular habits.

'Have the goodness to state the good effects that arise from needlework,' ordered one of the gentlemen. 'Nothing is so useful as needlework,' replied Mrs Fry, undaunted. 'The more women are employed in work suited to their sex, the better they go on … needlework, washing and ironing for example … tend to raise their moral standards, it raises them in their own estimation … I should wish to teach them any useful occupation, for working greatly tends to improve their moral character.'

The Committee was not interested in the psychology of the criminals or their private morals. They wanted to find a means of making imprisonment sufficiently unattractive to prevent crime. She admitted that it was difficult to know how to punish women. By now she disapproved of the treadmill because it could prove injurious to health. Those women sentenced to hard labour could be put to the crank-mill; cutting the women's hair short was undoubtedly a way of punishing them. But they were talking at cross-purposes. She was committed to elevating the prisoners; they wanted to punish them. The Committee tried again. Were there, they asked, any incorrigible characters who did not respond to the treatment?

Her answer was cautious and sensible. 'The very worst of women are improved in manners and habits ... they are no longer in the dirty and deplorable state they used to be, there is none of that daring, bold manner, but they are respectful, even the very worst of them ... to say they are really changed characters is going a long way.'

They pressed her further, seeking guarantees. Did she think that by a 'right system of prison discipline accompanied by religious instruction, we may hope for a change of character in the prisoners in general?' If the question was naive, the answer was considered and careful:

I am of the opinion that the efforts made in the education of the poor, the circulation of the Scriptures, affording asylums for the profligate, with other establishments distinct from prisons, as well as the regulations made in them, enforced by the Act of 1823, have produced an improvement in raising the moral standard of the worst class of women.

When she had first entered Newgate, she had preached to the women in gaol that it was their wickedness that had brought them into their miserable state. With fifteen years of experience of crime and criminals behind her and her own misfortune fresh in her mind, her view had broadened. She came near to acknowledging in her answer that the conditions of the poor were, in themselves, contributory causes of crime. Again, it was an answer that the committee was not ready to hear.

In recent years, she explained, her Committee had not had so much opportunity to influence the women sentenced to transportation, since the convict ships sailed so frequently that the women stayed at Newgate for a comparatively short time. As to the prisoners sent to Millbank Penitentiary, where prisoners worked for the first half of their sentences alone in their cells, she was disappointed, she told them, with those she had seen and implied that they would behave better under the ladies' care in Newgate.

Since the penitentiary was the first prison under the control of central government, built at a cost of half a million pounds, her reply was scarcely tactful.

Caroline Neave, the member of the Newgate Committee who ran the two refuges for 'naughty little girls' and for young women miscreants, gave evidence next. Since her home for the children had been opened, 103 girls had passed through it. The children were shoplifters or thieves' apprentices – one little girl had given a man the key to enter her parents' house, where he stole all their money. Only two children had been re-committed and four had returned to their 'evil course'. She assured the Committee that no corporal punishment was administered. If they were naughty, the little girls, aged between seven and thirteen, were placed in solitary confinement. 'Is that a dark cell?' asked an alderman with apparent eagerness. 'Nearly', came the reply. The children, she explained, were kept busy from morning to night with housework and needlework.

Her Westminster Asylum for young women had a similar record of hard work by the ex-prisoners which induced good conduct. The Committee was not unduly impressed. Again, Mrs Fry and her ladies were interested in reforming sinners, whereas Lord Melbourne who had succeeded Peel as Home Secretary, was rather more sceptical about the reformation of criminals.

Mrs Fry was, of course, aware of the hostile climate and anxious to impress the Committee with the necessity of having a Ladies Committee to visit every prison. She seems rather to have overdone it. 'I can tell', she said, 'almost as soon as I go into a prison ... from the general appearance of both women and their officers ... whether they are superintended by ladies or not.' She explained that the officers often came from a class of women 'not very high' and were liable to be corrupted and to grow familiar with the prisoners. When the Ladies visited, they ensured that a decent distance was maintained and the proprieties observed.

Could she, they asked, find female staff to superintend county penitentiaries? She admitted the difficulties of finding the right sort of person and added that in her view the Ladies Committees should select the prison officers.

In the course of her evidence she pointed out the plight of those in debtors' prisons where there was no separation between men and women. Some of them lived in luxury with huge hampers of food sent in, while others were in a state of near-starvation. She also drew attention to the neglected condition of untried prisoners.

She pleaded earnestly for some kind of subvention for the British Society. By the end of 1828, the Ladies had spent between £1,000 and £2,000 on prisoners sailing to the Colonies, providing them with haberdashery, scissors and schoolbooks; they had also laid out a great deal of money on the refuges. They were almost bankrupt. Although the Government gave them an allowance per head, they could barely meet their expenses.

When the Report on Secondary Punishments was published in August 1832, it disregarded Mrs Fry's evidence and advice almost offensively. In future, all women prisoners sentenced to transportation would first have to serve a term in Millbank Penitentiary. Hardest of all, only those prisoners convicted of trifling offences, and sentenced to one to two years' imprisonment, who 'have friends willing and able to receive them when discharged should … be allowed to remain'. This meant that the wretched women were penalised and banished because they were destitute and friendless. It was a cruel ruling, not assuaged for Mrs Fry by the reference to the good influence that 'assiduous attention and proper management appears to have affected on the most abandoned characters'.

The report recommended that 'every facility should be afforded to those benevolent persons' who visit the prisoners but they were to be granted no additional money. She knew that without legal enforcement provincial magistrates would continue to obstruct her Committees.

But in August 1832, when she journeyed through southern Ireland and in Wales with her brother Samuel, Lord Melbourne sent her a letter of recommendation stating that he was 'anxious that … the visiting magistrates should favourably entertain and second her benevolent intentions'. Her brother Joseph wrote to her from Earlham with cautious encouragement, too. He hoped, he said, that her influence, 'as far as it goes', would be beneficial.

The travellers – her sister-in-law Elizabeth was with them – were away for five weeks. Elizabeth Fry evidently preached with great power. In her journal she sounds a note of sincerity, on her work as a preacher and a woman, that is very different from the occasions when she speaks disparagingly of herself as a 'poor weak woman'. On 18 September 1832, she wrote:

> Though I believe we have scripture authority for it … yet I am obliged to walk by faith rather than sight, in going about as a woman in the work of the ministry; it is to my nature a great humiliation and I often feel it to be 'foolishness', particularly in large Public Meetings before entering upon the service; but generally, when engaged after a Meeting I mostly say in my heart 'It is the Lord's doing and marvellous in our eyes'. Such was often the case in this journey. I felt among Friends in Ireland as if my service was to lead them from all external dependence, either on their membership in the Society, their high profession or their peculiar testimonies … Above all, I endeavoured to lead all to the grand foundation of Christian faith and practice.

In Ireland, five years earlier, she had been almost mobbed and it seems that her following had not waned. Later, thanks to her influence, a prison for women was opened in Dublin.

She came home in September to her family and to yet another mixed blessing. Her son, William Storrs Fry was to marry Juliana Pelly, eldest daughter of Sir John Henry Pelly. She was delighted that he was to marry 'high' but there was the recurrent problem of marrying out. She had become almost resigned to being solitary on the day that her sons and daughters married. 'Here am I, sitting in solitude, keeping silence before the Lord on the wedding-day of my beloved son William,' she wrote in her journal. While she was alone she prayed earnestly for William and his bride and for all her family.

Three weeks after her son's wedding, her twenty-year-old daughter Hannah wrote to the Ratcliff and Barking Monthly Meeting, to explain that she too would have to leave the Society.

> I feel much that several of our family having pursued a different course to that of our beloved mother (who has done all that lay in her power to bring us up in the principles she loves and which have been so greatly blest to herself) may excite much surprise. The influence is known, but the counteracting influences that we have had in a remarkable degree from our earliest childhood are not known, but they have been powerful and various ...

Non-Quaker influences on the Fry children had undoubtedly been strong. They had, after all, partly through financial difficulties, partly because of their mother's frequent absences, been brought up by aunts and uncles, many of whom were members of the Church of England. It seems likely that mother and daughter collaborated on this letter, which justified and explained the family complications.

In November Hannah married William Champion Streatfield. Her mother could not be present at the ceremony, but thirty guests came home to Upton Lane to enjoy the wedding breakfast. 'The tears often flowed from my eyes in parting from this beloved child.'

Her large family of eleven children had now dwindled to the two girls at home, Kate, who was by now thirty-one and looked settled as her mother's secretary and helper and eighteen-year-old Louisa, and the two youngest boys.

She took what seemed almost like a royal tour of the family before Christmas. 'We have had the treat and great advantage of a visit from our dearest sister,' wrote Richenda, the vicar's wife. She helped her sister to set up a District Visiting Society for the poor in Lowestoft. 'It is like having an angel visitor, so full of grace and loveliness is she.' Despite the convention of exaggerated expression of the time, it is remarkable that several of her sisters refer to Betsy's presence as a 'treat'. With her pious exterior and her high-minded attitudes, it is an unexpected description, yet her visits seemed to inspire those she loved.

From the age of seventeen until her death, Elizabeth Fry's life is remarkably well documented, by her own detailed journals and by family references. However, from January 1833 until January 1837 the original journals are missing, with the exception of a handful of entries in the summer of 1833, and of the first six months of that year even the printed sources tell us nothing – there is no mention of Newgate, the British Society or Yearly Meeting. In the summer she went to stay in the Channel Islands. Her daughter explains in her memoir that with more of her children leaving the Society through marriage the 'press of interests and engagements had become too heavy on the reduced party at home'.[3] This seems unconvincing, since her engagements were reduced, not increased. A more likely explanation is that after the adverse Report of the House of Commons Committee, and all the journeys, she had suffered another of her bouts of nervous depression. In the public eye, as a prison reformer, and in the Society of Friends, her reputation had never sunk so low.

There are other family circumstances worth considering. The first half of 1833 was a vital time for them. Fowell Buxton was actively engaged in the last phase of the anti-slavery campaign – abolition was finally carried in August 1833. At the beginning of the year Joseph Gurney was considering standing as Whig Member of Parliament for Norwich, with an excellent chance of getting in. He had even visited London to consult with prominent members of the Society over the propriety of a Quaker Minister entering Parliament. By now Mrs Fry, with her notoriety, her husband who was a bankrupt and had been disowned by the Society, and her children who had resigned from it, was an embarrassment.

It seems curious, to say the least, that the Frys should be taking an extended holiday abroad at a time when the tea business was bad and their income drastically reduced. At the same time Joseph had undergone a mysterious transformation. He became religious, devoted to helping his wife in her worthy objects, and began to keep a journal. Rather sadly he lost his 'great love' for music which, he said, in an unusually expressive entry, 'seems to have passed away like a summer cloud, or died off like the leaves in autumn'.[4] Joseph Fry's 'powerful visitation of Judgement mingled with mercy' took place in May 1833. It is tempting to see in it the hand of his brother-in-law Joseph. For so long in his letters Joseph Gurney had commiserated with Betsy over her husband's lack of religion; he had propped up the family fortunes and was even now the stabilising force in their tea business. It seems possible that he exercised influence over his brother-in-law on this question too.

In her journal Betsy makes it clear that her 'dearest brothers' had made their journey possible, and it may have been pure philanthropy that inspired their help. By July 1833, she was happily settled into 'Caledonia Cottage' on Jersey with her husband, the two girls, her youngest son, and her maid, finding the island and the lush scenery delightful.

'I never saw so little poverty, no beggars whatever which is to me a real relief' – particularly as she had not 'even a shilling's poor money'. The party had letters of introduction to prominent island families and they spent a happy time visiting, exploring and picnicking. While her husband and the children were wandering and sketching, Mrs Fry would knock on the cottagers' doors with her tract-bag piled high with improving pamphlets, translated into French, and make conversation in her halting French to the astonished inmates.

By the middle of August she was sounding quite like her old self. To her satisfaction she had found her influence was needed:

there were prisons to visit, 'evils' to eradicate in the hospitals, religious meetings to hold for Friends and others. 'Religion', she confided to her diary, 'has been anything but bondage to me but has brought me a delightful freedom.'

Happy and engrossed, she drew up a set of rules for Jersey prisons, which were not, of course, subject to British laws. They echoed the reforms carried out on the mainland and included employment for prisoners, a proper system of payment for gaolers and religious instruction. She also established a charitable District Society. 'My dearest husband has very kindly united with me in my important objects', she noted on 12 August, and a week later, on their wedding anniversary, Joseph Fry prayed humbly in his journal 'to be a true spiritual helpmate … to aid and support her bodily powers and to cheer her under her frequent cares and anxieties.'

From Jersey Mrs Fry crossed to the islands of Guernsey, Sark and Herm, surveying the social services, ministering, making plans. In Sark she found its population of five hundred divided between members of the Methodist and the established Church and tried, as she did wherever she could, to create Christian unity between them. She was again over-exerting herself, but she was able to take short rests during the day. Very often when she felt tired out, after visiting or preaching, she would come home, take off her muslin cap, put a shawl around her head and a rug on her feet and fall fast asleep until her next appointment. After taking on the welfare of the poor, the sick, the imprisoned and the insane of the Channel Islands, she confessed in her journal to feeling 'too much driven'.

From Norfolk she heard that her married daughter, Rachel Cresswell, was seriously ill, though in her letters Rachel begged her mother not to return. 'I felt the pain of her not wishing to have me, though it saved me much trouble.' Worse accounts of Rachel's illness sent her mother hurrying back to England in the steampacket in November. The wind was high and the sea rough, and Mrs Fry's maid, her son Henry and even her little dog became ill. Her husband and daughters crossed to France as planned, while Betsy spent six weeks nursing Rachel back to health.

By now she seemed to be foraging for good causes. In April 1834, she set off again to Dorset and Hampshire for religious services. At Portsmouth she visited two hospitals and several prisons. With her two nieces, Priscilla Buxton and Priscilla Gurney, she travelled to the Isle of Wight. 'She was as zealous as we in the enjoyment of the scenery and the wild flowers', wrote Priscilla Buxton, who found her aunt's 'loving, hoping spirit' irresistible.

The following day the two girls left her at Freshwater, since she was feeling tired and wanted to rest. On their return, they received a message, asking them to join her at the coastguard station. 'We found her in her element; pleased and giving pleasure to a large group who were assembled around her.' Mrs Fry had spent the afternoon getting to know the local coastguards, asking them about the education of their children, their own opportunities for religious improvement. As a result of their conversation, and following on her earlier experiences she resolved to provide libraries for all the coastguard stations in Great Britain. Her husband worked extremely hard on the project, helping with the correspondence and despatches. In less than two years, over 52,000 volumes had reached five hundred stations on shore and forty-eight cruisers. The collections included schoolbooks for the children, and some tales of foreign travel, although the major part of them was of a religious nature.

'The celebrated Mrs Fry', thundered *The Times* on 1 February 1836 '... has extended her philanthropy to the men employed in the coastguards. Each station of the three Kingdoms has been furnished *at her own expense* with a library for the use of the crew ...'

Mrs Fry had learnt by then how damaging that sort of inaccurate publicity could be. Two days later she contradicted the statement. The expense, she pointed out, had been defrayed by the Government, her friends and the public. Since there were still libraries wanted for ships, she hoped that the Editor would encourage his readers to subscribe to the fund.

On her journey back to London from the Isle of Wight in 1834, she paused 'long enough to establish a library for the use of shepherds on Salisbury Plain'.

Again despite straitened circumstances all the family took a long journey in the summer up to the Highlands of Scotland. On her journeys she must have been something of a menace to the lower classes who were not as pious as she; everywhere she went she carried her tracts and her Bible. The postillions at the carriage window, the chambermaids and waiters in small Highland inns, all were invited, summoned, to attend Mrs Fry's readings.

After a month she tired of sightseeing. At the end of August she left Joseph and her two daughters in the Highlands to escort her son back to school, 'above all to attend the Meetings, see the Friends and visit the prisons here'. Admirers who had known her on her previous visit gave her a warm welcome and she occupied herself busily with the poor and her prison committees. In Edinburgh, Perth, Dingwall and Inverness, she formed new Ladies Committees. 'I came under the belief that duty called me to do so,' she wrote, '... I desire and earnestly pray to be preserved from an overactive spirit in these things.'

By 1835, it became clear that an official policy of harsher, more deterrent sentences had replaced Mrs Fry's vision of prisons that would regenerate the prisoners. In the eyes of the public, she had become a great national figure, a legend, a symbol of good, that was almost divorced from her real achievement. In the new harsh climate, her vision of reform was no longer taken seriously in political circles.

On 22 May 1835, the day after her fifty-fifth birthday, she was invited to give evidence to a Committee of the House of Lords, a Committee determined to introduce a regime of hardship and privation into the prisons.[5]

In her evidence she said that she had been 'much affected in visiting some prisons lately ... In some respects I think there is more cruelty in the gaols than I have ever seen before.' In some, prisoners trod the wheel for ten hours a day; in others, local magistrates punished men who broke silence by reducing an already meagre diet. 'If they are to be wholly silent and to be worked very hard,' Mrs Fry urged, 'their diet must be improved.'

She disliked the system of separation, she said, but wavered on the point when pressed; 'very nervous women in very difficult circumstances' would suffer greatly from it. 'I believe separation is excellent and highly valuable if it is properly managed.' Asked whether prisoners did not become contaminated by associating with each other at Newgate she became defensive. 'We are doing the best we can with a very bad system. Everything is as badly arranged as possible.' Improvements had been made since she had begun to visit, she told them, floundering. Indiscriminate visiting had been checked and the 'too great admission of porter and roast chicken'. Trying to appease a committee looking for improved discipline, she did herself less than justice. She had introduced, order, cleanliness and a semblance of self-respect to women who were degraded and despised.

She stressed the influence of religious instruction:

I have seen in reading the Scriptures to those women, such a power attending them and such an effect on the minds of the most reprobate, as I could not have conceived ... It has strongly confirmed my faith, and I feel it to be the bounden duty of the Government and the country that those truths should be administered in the manner most likely to conduce to the real reformation of the prisoner ... for though severe punishment may, in a measure, deter them and others from crime, it does not amend and change the heart.

Never, in her evidence before an official committee had she spoken her mind so eloquently on religion and never was a committee so little disposed to listen to her.

The Prison Inspectors made their first report to the House of Lords in March 1836. Their view of Newgate as a whole – and the men's side of the prison was indeed a disgrace – was highly censorious.

By a series of niggling criticisms and some more serious ones, they contrived to give the impression that the work of the Ladies Association was well-meaning but inept. They criticised the ladies' initiative in setting up a shop to sell tea, coffee, sugar, butter and snuff, which in their view were luxuries which should not be allowed in prison at all. More reasonably, they objected to the ladies classifying the women prisoners into grades. They referred to the want of clothing, soap, towels and space in the prison and remarked that the Gaol Act, which required female officers to take charge of female prisoners, was constantly infringed. What they did not acknowledge was that without an amateur like Mrs Fry, there would never have been a regulation of that kind in the first place.

They managed to make the ladies appear ridiculous in the matter of their visiting the male prisoners, a recent addition to their activities. They felt that these visits were 'inexpedient' and that the ladies might expose themselves to 'unpleasant sights'. One prisoner, for example, wore only a rug, no trousers. The ladies did not realise, they added, that the prisoners laughed at them and joked about them when they had gone. This was prejudice on the part of the Prison Inspectors, since the prisoners made fun of everyone in authority. Moreover, the evidence was somewhat suspect, in that it was provided by Dr Cotton, the chaplain, who had himself been criticised and partly usurped by the ladies.

It was recognised that more care was taken on the women's side at Newgate to limit the amount of beer to within the prison allowance and it had to be admitted that the men's side provided no instruction at all, except for the young boys.

Their objection to women prisoners being excused chapel on Fridays, when Mrs Fry gave her readings, on the grounds that the Gaol Act required prisoners to attend the Church of England service every day, was unquestionably a legitimate one. But it was concerning the instruction for women and the Bible readings that they were most cutting.

They paid lip-service to Elizabeth Fry, who 'had devoted much of her valuable time to the moral and religious instruction of depraved female inmates of this prison, who at that time were in such a lamentable state of degradation and disorder that it was scarcely deemed an act of prudence for any visitor to enter the wards'. Briefly they remarked on the improvement that she had achieved, adding significantly, 'whatever may be our opinion as to the propriety and advantage ... and expediency of encouraging generally the visits of ladies to well-regulated gaols, no one can for a moment doubt that in a miserable prison like Newgate, visits of the Ladies Committee have greatly contributed to lessen the depravity of the place, and cannot fail to be highly beneficial ...'

After more praise of the ladies for introducing order, cleanliness, employment and 'virtuous example', they came to the crunch:

> ... it is our duty to point out those parts of their proceedings which appear to us inexpedient and injudicious ... We think the introduction of the visitors who now attend on Fridays the readings to the women highly improper. On one occasion ...there were 23 visitors ... whilst ... only 28 prisoners could attend the lectures ... the sight of so many strangers distracted the attention of even those who were there ... These visitors furnish the prisoners with subjects for comment and conversation subsequently, to the exclusion of the better thoughts which might otherwise have been suggested by the lecture. They tend to dissipate reflection, diminish the necessary gloom of a prison, and mitigate the punishment which the law has sentenced a prisoner to undergo. Amongst the names recorded in the visitors' book ... we found those of several gentlemen. We submit that this is highly improper ...

Their objection to Mrs Fry exploiting her Friday readings for propoganda purposes does seem fully justified. The two Prison Inspectors were determined to dislodge her from the position of unorthodox authority that she held and they partially succeeded, although her Newgate readings were too well established and popular to be halted. Unfortunately no reaction of Mrs Fry's to the report on Newgate remains.

In June 1835, the month after she gave her evidence to the House of Lords Committee, Louisa left the Society of Friends by marrying out. Mrs Fry had long since become resigned to these weddings and compromised with her strict sentiments by allowing her children at least to wear decorative clothes. The wedding, according to an account written by two of her daughters, Hannah and Kate, was a lavish affair:

> Louisa you must imagine in a rich, white-flowered brocade, a crape bonnet and very splendid blonde fall [veil] ... The four bridesmaids were very pretty in satin and muslin over ... Last but not least our beloved mother in a stiff silk and suitable etceteras ... Then we all went to Church.

Mrs Fry, of course, stayed behind and prayed in her room during the ceremony but presided over the wedding breakfast:

> ... nothing could be more elegant ... cold fowls, pâtés, pies, potted things, crabs, lobsters, prawns, jellies, collared fish ... and ended up by strawberries and frozen cream ... the children had a table for sixteen in papa's dressing room with equally good fare. A bottle of hock, another of champagne and lemonade, with a bride's cake to themselves for their centre ... the bride went off without a tear in a light green silk bonnet and coloured muslin dress ...[6]

In her journal, Mrs Fry considered that she had seldom seen 'a more lovely party ... or a sweeter spirit'. However, after ten o'clock, when she and her brother Joseph retired, the youngsters began to dance quadrilles until almost midnight, when they finally withdrew after enjoying yet another elegant supper.

Mrs Fry, now in her mid-fifties, seemed to be constantly travelling. She journeyed to the South of England, to the Isle of Wight, and went on without her husband to Jersey and Guernsey to supervise reforms in the prisons. In 1836 she journeyed to Meetings in Sussex and Kent in March, to Dublin in April, and later in the summer to the Channel Islands for six weeks, holding meetings, forming committees, finding 'comfort and satisfaction' in her good works. Her sheer energy and stamina were extraordinary.

Two deaths in the family affected her. Joseph Gurney's second wife, Mary, died of typhus fever in 1835 at the early age of thirty-two, and in August 1836, Betsy received a letter from Richenda begging her to come home immediately because their sister Louisa was seriously ill. Characteristically, Mrs Fry decided that it was her 'duty' to remain in Jersey until she had completed her 'important business' with the hospital, the District Society and the prisons. When she reached England in mid-September Louisa was still clinging to life. Since she never had relished her sister's preaching, Louisa told her maid to inform Mrs Fry, when she called, that she was changing her nightdress, in order to avoid a sermon. But Betsy was there at the end, 'enabled to show her some marks of my deep and true love ...' She was genuinely shaken by the loss of her lively and generous younger sister. 'I do not like to enter life and its cares, or to see many or be seen. I like to withdraw from the world and be very quiet,' she wrote after Louisa's funeral.

Her retirement was not to last long. On 2 October, her son William brought her word to say that her husband and daughter Kate, travelling in Normandy, had been thrown down a precipice, their carriage broken to pieces. She set off immediately on the first packet ship to France. Fortunately she found Kate and her husband bruised and badly shaken but not seriously injured.

'So I have, at last, touched French ground,' Betsy Fry wrote triumphantly, 'William and I have not been idle; we have already visited the prison and the hospital.'

IX

Royal Commands

The first half of 1837 was devoted to family matters, a funeral, births and visits. She began the year with a nostalgic visit to Earlham. Her ministry, particularly among her relatives in Norfolk, sometimes gave rise to amusement. There her exploits were the source of endless family stories. On one visit she was summoned to the bed of a country squire, a close relative who was said to be dying. His bluff greeting took her by surprise: 'I am very glad to see thee, dear Elizabeth, and shall be very glad to talk with thee; but thee must just wait till these have done.' On the other side of the old man's bed two cocks were fighting ferociously.[1]

In February, she was called back to Runcton in Norfolk when her brother Dan's wife, Lady Harriet, died, leaving him with eight children. Here, too, she was welcomed and valued as a sister but Dan, who was now a successful banker and a member of the gentry, made it quite clear to her that he disapproved of women preachers and did not want any sermons in his house. She was not even allowed to read the Scriptures to the family circle. It was a relief, she reminded herself, to be able to stay quietly in her room in a household 'where I am not looked up to and depended upon for religious help'.

At nearby King's Lynn Rachel Cresswell was expecting another child and her mother was anxious to be with her. The young couple did not dare to interfere with her when she preached or read the Bible to them. But Betsy suspected privately that they found her religious services more of a trial than a comfort. She was determined, however, to be a model mother and do her duty 'even in the capacity of a lying-in nurse'. The only drawback was that the nurse was far more nervous than the patient. The night before the baby was born, Betsy was agitated and tearful, while Rachel lay patient and calm in between her pains. 'She is an example to me', wrote her chastened mother.

Rachel was not ready to be so generous towards her mother. In April, while she was still staying at King's Lynn, Elizabeth Fry preached from the pulpit in a public meeting held in a large Methodist hall nearby. The celebrated Mrs Fry naturally attracted attention and a huge crowd gathered. The family, both Dan and Rachel and Rachel's husband, Frank, were highly critical. But she was not prepared for the intensity of Rachel's reaction. When she came home, drained from her preaching, she found her daughter distraught. All her pent-up resentment of her mother 'deserting' the family during her childhood and making a public spectacle of herself exploded. 'I would rather have gone through another lying-in than it should have happened', she burst out bitterly. Her mother comforted and calmed her and recorded the incident in her journal. She did not reproach herself (although for years she had felt uneasy about the effect of her public duties on her children) but simply remarked on how little support she had ever had from her family in her religious calling.

Back in London public affairs again claimed her: the state of the female convicts in New South Wales, conditions in the national schools and prisons in Ireland, and the prisons in Jersey. After the 1835 Prison Act, which had stipulated that prisons in England and Wales should be visited by government inspectors, she had sensibly concentrated more and more on conditions overseas, although she was still active in Newgate. It did not occur to her that Joseph would resent her public work, since for years he had supported her patiently. When he did protest, Betsy's surprise was comical and contradictory. In her journal on 10 June 1837 she wrote:

This morning my dearest husband expressed his deep feeling at my constant engagements – I deeply felt it … for I make a point of always dining at home and spending evening and morning with him and my family, yet my mornings are much occupied by public and relative duties – ministerial, children, brothers and sisters and their children and others in illness and sorrow. I feel greatly cast down … desiring to be a constant, faithful, loving wife.

The problem was exacerbated by Joseph's life having contracted while Betsy's continued to epand. His business interests had dwindled and his 'reformation' – he had been reinstated as a member of the Society of Friends in May 1837 – meant that he no longer had a taste for concerts, or could enjoy a day out hunting. His wife, on the other hand, was constantly discovering new causes and new interests.

She took a very personal concern in the progress of the Royal Family. In June 1837 William IV died and the Princess Victoria was proclaimed Queen. Mrs Fry prayed for guidance and wisdom for the young Queen and added: 'I was with Lord Morpeth, who said the Queen behaved remarkably well when meeting the Privy Council, with feeling and much propriety.'

Her son Gurney, now twenty-one, was a constant source of anxiety to the family; he was unhappy, depressed and, according to his mother, 'without religious principle'. One gains the impression that he was suffering from a surfeit of religiosity. Their doctor was consulted about his morbid state of mind and he suggested, as a remedy, a journey on the Continent – with his father.

While they were away Betsy took the opportunity of escorting her brother Joseph, who was to pay a religious visit to America, to his ship in Liverpool. She made the journey with Sam Gurney and his wife, anxious in case she might be needed at home and yet determined to go. Hopeful as ever, she prayed at the age of fifty-seven 'that my very susceptible nature may be strengthened'.

In the cabin of the luxurious ship, she arranged flowers for her brother, put out his books and in the space of a few hours

Elizabeth Fry

organised a library of religious books for the crew, the passengers
and the steerage-class travellers. As the hour approached for sailing, she grew fearful that she would never see her brother again.
When his ship steamed out of port, she was seized by a violent
attack of toothache and almost fainted.

Back at home in Upton, she lived in a frenzy of activity. There
were the local poor to care for – they needed visiting, they
wanted a library, an infant school and a Provident Society. All
the needs were pressing, all her solutions practical and she drove
on relentlessly. Joseph, with more free time, was recruited to
write letters and keep accounts. He worked hard, but remained
in the background. 'I don't think my nature would lead me into
any sort of public service,' he remarked in his private journal.
One cannot help wondering what sort of comment upon his
wife that was.

She noted, in passing, that that summer she had ordered her
poor old pony 'Duchess', who had served her for many years, to
be killed humanely. 'He had been of no use to us for months,
his feet were all so sore that we feared he was mostly in pain,
besides as the pasture was failing, we could not afford to keep
him.' Nevertheless, she could not keep back her tears.

Plans for the women's prison in Ireland occupied much of her
time. She also launched herself gallantly upon a scheme to exert
more religious influence over her own children. They were all
married now, except for Kate, young Gurney and her youngest son,
Henry. She suggested that they should meet once a month in each
other's houses 'to consider how far we are really engaged for the
good of our fellow men'. After the discussion on matters of charity,
they could then, she hoped, read the Scriptures 'in an easy, familiar
manner', with everyone being free to ask questions or comment.
Her children, particularly the boys, were happy to help her with
any welfare work. But it was perhaps naive of Betsy to imagine
that they would enter into discussions of the Scriptures with her
with any enthusiasm. The meetings took place every month, but
for Mrs Fry there was never enough religion in them.

In the New Year of 1838, she fulfilled a long-held ambition: she travelled on religious service to France. Ever since the first accounts of Elizabeth Fry's work had appeared in the French press in 1818, her reputation there was remarkable. Their party consisted of Mr and Mrs Fry, Josiah Forster, an Elder of the Society, and Lydia Irving, a young Friend. They left England on 25 January 1838, armed with introductions to influential people. The crossing was cold and Elizabeth Fry wrote apologetically to her daughter Kate: 'I regret that so many indulgencies are wanted by me, for I find I cannot run rough as I should like to do. The warm clothing has been most valuable, the shoes and wristlets … but we had not enough wraps and I long for knee caps.'[2] In spite of the cold she was cheered to learn from the captain of the ship that in his opinion the sailors were much improved by the Testaments that Mrs Fry had provided.

Once she was settled in at an inn in Boulogne, she set about seeing that everybody was as comfortable as possible – and preaching to them.

> Picture us, our feet on some fleeces that we have found, wrapped up in cloaks, surrounded by screens … the wood fire at our feet. We have just finished an interesting reading in French, in the New Testament, with the landlady, her daughters and some of the servants.[3]

What made this journey particularly pleasing to her was that Joseph was with her, encouraging her in her pious works. 'When I look at my dearest husband and see the wonderful change wrought in him, it gives me encouragement,' she wrote to Kate. 'Mama is partial and, I fear, rather blind,' her husband interjected. They were like lovers again.

They occupied lavish apartments at the Hotel de Castille in Paris and the English Ambassador, Lord Granville, and many ladies of the French aristocracy combined to make their stay useful and pleasant. The French Minister of the Interior, Comte Montalivet, arranged admission to the different prisons. The visit became her usual round of visiting prisons, schools and hospitals but she seems to have regained her zest and confidence. She was constantly complaining that she was pressed and driven, but it was only at such times that she soared. She felt, she wrote to Kate, 'a wonderful access granted to the hearts of the French people,' and she added that she was 'not much troubled by flattery'.

For by now Mrs Fry was a sensation in Paris. On her second visit to the large women's prison at St Lazare, she asked if all the women prisoners – there were almost a thousand of them – could be assembled so that she might read to them. Even the gaolers and turnkeys, whom she did not want, crowded into the large hall to hear her. She chose the parable of the Prodigal Son, the passage she had read when she first opened her school at Newgate. With a French lady, chosen for her melodious voice, reading first, Mrs Fry followed in English with her comments. The same lady translated for her, sentence by sentence. She made her now familiar speech to the prisoners. Would they not like ladies to visit them, read to them, sympathise with them? Nods and murmurs of agreement came from all sides. Her sincerity and her tenderness melted them all. Before her arrival in their country, the French had rationalised Elizabeth Fry's dramatic success by suggesting that it was the result of her voice and manner. That she could produce a similarly striking effect on the prisoners in a foreign language in a foreign country appeared to the French people miraculous.

She was in her element, disturbed only by bad news from home about the behaviour of her son Gurney. She was distressed but prayed in her journal that before she left France she might see King Louis Philippe and his Queen. Of course, she fulfilled her ambition. She spent some time with the King and Queen and the duchesse d'Orléans, bombarding them with her pious hopes. Through her mission she had succeeded in arousing interest in the plight of women in prison, encouraged a more widespread distribution of the Scriptures and given away many copies of her own books on prisons and her sister Louisa's books on education. All in all, she was delighted with the trip – 'the most deeply interesting field of service I think I was ever engaged in'.

She came home triumphant. In April the largest gathering of ladies she could remember turned out to hear her give an account of her French journey and the state of the French prisons.

On her fifty-eighth birthday, a considerable age at that time for a woman who had borne so many children, she was torn between joining her brother Joseph in America and visiting Scotland. The Bill to reform the Scottish prisons was still pending and she was anxious to do what she could to oppose the introduction of solitary confinement. She decided to go north. Another Minister, William Ball, accompanied her, as well as her sister-in-law Elizabeth Fry, and an old friend of her husband's, John Sanderson. William Ball kept the journal of their visit. He described one meeting with 'an appalling audience', members of the Prison Discipline Society, magistrates and lawyers, where she reasoned that to place a human being 'intended by his great Creator for social life' in solitary confinement could lead to neglect, abuse and cruelty. Her vision in penal reform was nearly always enlightened. If, at that time, it had been couched in less religious language, if she had not been a Minister at all, she would perhaps have been better able to exercise her humane influence. At the same time had she not been a Minister, she would not, as a female, have had any influence at all.

At Paisley and Bridewell gaols a matron, Janet Stewart, was appointed in August 'at the suggestion of Mrs Fry'. By September Betsy was home again, to find that the family were content and pleased to see her. Gurney, her troublesome son, had left the Society and married out, and the responsibility apparently settled him.

By December she was again planning her travels. She told the members of her Monthly Meeting of her intention to visit France and other parts of Europe and received their consent in the usual form of a certificate. Privately, she had one grave doubt.

She expected trials 'particularly doubting my health bearing being without malt liquor … as I think I suffered much when last in France for want of it, but if the Lord calls me there I must be willing to suffer for his name's sake.' Before she left, she organised a large and successful sale to boost the funds of the British Society who were now working with ex-prisoners as well as continuing their work of visiting prisons, convict ships and supporting the refuges. Largely because of her energetic participation and influential friends, over a thousand pounds was raised.

The party travelling to France consisted of Elizabeth and Joseph Fry, their children Katharine and Henry, and Josiah Forster, the Quaker Elder. Money for her journey came in from her generous family. Sam Gurney gave her £200. They sailed for France in March 1839. At Boulogne, where she had organised a District Society, the party met an enthusiastic welcome. Flowers and wine brightened their apartments. So many people came in to visit Mrs Fry – charitable ladies, poor people, resident English living on straitened means – that she hardly had time to eat breakfast or change her dress. The carriage was surrounded by people begging for books.

In Paris their reception was equally enthusiastic. They were invited out to dine by Lord William Bentinck and entertained by the English Ambassador. She feared and loved the adulation. She made an extensive tour of the Paris hospitals, including the Lepers' hospital, where an English maid was one of the patients – Mrs Fry comforted her and left her with a gift of money. She also formed a Ladies Society to visit Protestants in prisons and hospitals. At St Lazare Prison, which she had visited twice the year before, she was pleased to find that female officers had been introduced.

In April, Mrs Fry met the duchesse d'Orléans again, who told her to her gratification that her visit was a blessing to the city. 'It is a friendship to cultivate,' she noted, 'as she will most probably be the Queen of the French!'

The day before they left Paris she brought her report on the state of the prisons to the Prefect of Police and obtained permission for her newly formed Committee of Protestant Ladies to visit the Protestant prisoners. She was personally granted leave to visit all the prisons in France. 'We have the great satisfaction', she wrote from Fontainebleau, 'of hearing that a law is likely to be passed for women prisoners, throughout France, to be under the care of women.'

A large party came to take leave of her and stayed until half-past-twelve at night. The French had taken Mme Fry to their hearts, this grandmother with twenty-five grandchildren and such a zest for reform and for work. But her own family was beginning to grow restive. At first the visit together had been a great success. She found Joseph's presence at the Meetings a support, he 'filled an important place', she found. But by the end of her stay in Paris, both Kate and Joseph were beginning to feel aggrieved at her going out so much without them and resentful at the public clamour. She herself was obviously finding their presence cumbersome.

The journey from Lyon to Avignon was a delightful experience for them all. She always warmed to the spring and in early May, with the snow-capped Alps in the distance and the grass ready to be cut, the countryside was alive with lilacs and laburnum, philadelphus and roses, pinks and carnations, acacias in full bloom and yellow jasmine growing wild in the hedges. 'It is a sudden burst of the finest summer combined with the freshness of spring.' The party enjoyed a visit to the Roman aqueduct and Avignon.

By mid-May, when they had settled at Avignon, Joseph and Kate were again feeling very neglected and depressed. Betsy was taken up with her usual round of engagements, visits to prisons and refuges; she had time to visit only one school, a school for women. She also visited the homes of some of the poorer Protestants and read with them, and held a 'very important Meeting of influential people'. In her sermons she stressed the importance of reading the Scriptures, observing Sundays and 'having proper books in the house particularly in the kitchen'. Most important of all she emphasised family worship.

In her own family, however, there was no peace. Even when she was with them, she seemed elusive. It was a comfort and a blessing, she persuaded herself, to have them there but 'difficult to perform all my duties satisfactorily and particularly to the satisfaction of all my dear companions'.

From Avignon they journeyed to Nîmes, a centre of Protestantism, where she visited 'a scattered body of people professing the principles of the Society of Friends', who had suffered persecution for their faith in the past. In the great Maison Centrale, with its 1,200 prisoners, she saw men working in complete silence in a vast workshop. She asked permission to enter a dark cell for violent prisoners where one man was chained by the hands and feet. Mrs Fry spoke to him quietly and told him that sometimes when she had seen prisoners in his plight, she had pleaded on their behalf for their chains to be freed. However, she had to have a sincere promise of good conduct in the future. Such was her influence that, as soon as the chained man gave her his word that he would behave well in future, he was set free.

The carriage, with an attendant van carrying hampers stocked with sugar, coffee and candles, journeyed on to Marseille, where she visited a convent, a home for delinquent boys, the town prison and the hospital. At Hyères, the party rested and spent two quiet days on the shores of the Mediterranean, enjoying the hot climate and the lazy scene, taking their meals on the hotel verandah overlooking the blue sea, shaded by vines and orange groves. Two days were enough for her and then she insisted they must be off to Toulon, to form charitable societies and hold Meetings. The Protestant pastor took her to visit the Bagnes, or prison of galley-slaves, where the prisoners slept upon boards, were chained in pairs to a large iron rod and fed on a diet of bread and dried beans. Although the pastor had proved accommodating in taking her aboard the prison ship, he was not prepared to have a woman preaching in his temple; instead 'Josiah Forster and myself had a large public meeting partly in the open air.'

At Toulouse discontent in her family threatened to erupt. Joseph was suffering from the heat and the rest of the family were exhausted. Mrs Fry was still eager to crowd in as many duties and experiences as she possibly could. 'My husband was rather discouraged,' she noted when setting off before five in the morning with Josiah Forster to visit the theological training college for ministers of the Protestant Church at Montauban. There was a fitting welcome for her. The Dean escorted her into the chapel where the professors and students were waiting to hear her. Josiah Forster spoke first but, she noted, was 'flustered and did not speak clearly'. Then it was her turn and she dwelt on the conditions in the prisons in France, her opinion of the general state of their nation and the extreme importance of their future calling. Clearly she made her usual outstanding impression and the pastor, who had interpreted, prayed for her. 'I have seldom felt sweeter peace in leaving a place than Montauban.'

Reluctantly, at Joseph's insistence, she agreed to rest for a few days in the cooler climate of the Pyrenees. They had a 'sweet, quiet lodging' at Bagnères-de-Luchon and made excursions into the mountains. One day they rode up a steep mountain pass and down into Spanish territory. Mrs Fry had come prepared with little books of extracts from the Scriptures. She presented them to two startled Catalan peasants, dressed in brown costume with scarlet sashes, and as they rode along, she stopped the party to scatter the Scripture books in the manger of a cow-shed or lodge them on a door-nail.[4] At the Catholic church at nearby Barèges, the priest warned his flock from the pulpit against the little books that Protestant visitors were distributing. He remarked particularly on one lady 'who went up into the mountains to give them away'.

While she was 'resting', she prepared a lengthy paper for the French Minister of the Interior with observations on the state of the prisons she had inspected and her recommendations for their reform. A shorter version of the paper was made for the Prefect of Police.

Both Joseph and Kate resented her obsessive need to work, and when it was of a written nature they usually found themselves obliged to help her. They had suffered from the constant travelling, her endless engagements and the stream of visitors who crowded into their apartments every day. For them the journey had become a penance.

They were to travel home through Switzerland where there would be more public engagements. 'I very seriously laid before my husband and Katharine my doubts how far I could go on with this journey unless there was more peace and brightness to be felt,' she said, adding, rather hopefully, 'they kindly entered into my feelings.' At Bagnères-de-Bigorre, before their departure, she founded a fund for poor people who came to bathe in the waters and in the local prison, through her intervention, two prisoners were freed from their chains. In terms of her public 'performance', of the influence she had had in creating a more humane attitude towards prisoners, her visit had been a triumph.

But her family had suffered through her excessive zeal. She even had a serious disagreement with Josiah Forster who disapproved of her ecumenical form of Christianity. She warned her audience on the Continent against allowing their particular doctrines to militate against true Christianity and tried to find some point of reconciliation between Protestants and Catholics in a divided France. In this, she was very like her mother. Forster was shocked by her insistence on the broad principles. Mrs Fry bemoaned 'how little he appeared to have fully understood my ministry since in this land'.

At Grenoble matters came to a head. It was August, they had been travelling for five months and the family party was uncomfortable, exhausted and disillusioned by what they had seen. In the evening 'Katharine poured out her heart upon her very great disappointment in the journey, first expecting to receive real spiritual benefit and she thought she had suffered real loss ...'

Joseph too was bitterly disappointed and told his wife that he thought the journey had created a rift between them. Betsy was crestfallen. She had hoped that the journey 'would be blessed to us and laboured so to take my beloved family with me for their good'. No doubt she sincerely believed what she said, although the family had seen so little of her. She took it for granted that they had to travel at her pace and at her direction. As usual she was cramped by her position as a woman and by what men and, not unnaturally, her own family expected of her.

> I think it would have been better for me to have had a clear and better understanding with my husband and Josiah Forster before we set off. My fear of women coming too forward has led me to have a man who I really esteem … who takes part in the service of meetings.

Their journey through Savoie proved pleasant. She dared not give away her tracts there for fear of imprisonment. The party travelled through Switzerland and found that even in remote villages the name of Elizabeth Fry was known and the peasants came to stare and one or two to ask her counsel. In Geneva, Lausanne and Berne she visited prisons but in her journal she remarks triumphantly that from Thun she had 'almost entirely devoted myself to my dearest husband and children … we had some sweet times together'.

At Heidelberg, Mrs Fry congratulated herself on giving in to Joseph. She had wanted to visit a well-known German pastor, but for once Joseph asserted himself and told her that he wished to see the minister on his own. Betsy agreed, thinking it right to give in to Joseph when not 'called' to do otherwise. 'But where the will of my God is concerned,' she wrote, 'then I must have my way and my dearest husband is quite disposed to yield.' By then, however, it was rare that Mrs Fry did not assume that the will of her God was directly concerned in all her personal activities. They arrived back in England after six months' extensive travel.

For four weeks in the autumn the house in Upton Lane was full of family, children and grandchildren, brothers and sisters. She was genuinely pleased to have them, but as soon as she had stayed at home for a few weeks she grew restless. In November her daughter Rachel was again in labour and Mrs Fry was glad enough to travel to King's Lynn to be with her. While she was staying with the Cresswells, she was horrified to discover that her seventeen-year-old grandson Frank was destined for the army. Naturally, as a Quaker, she disapproved and prayed 'for a way of escape ... from this un-Christian way of life'. By Christmas her prayers, and her machinations, had turned young Frank from a prospective officer into an apprentice in the bank. Her brother Samuel Gurney, at Mrs Fry's prompting, offered to take his great-nephew into the bank in Lombard Street and teach him the business.

She was already planning another sortie to the Continent by the New Year. At home she was disturbed about the state of England, about the 'infidel principles in the form of Socialism gaining ground', and the 'Popish doctrines' practised in many churches, but 'our young Queen' was a source of satisfaction and comfort to her. The Queen sent Elizabeth Fry a present of fifty pounds for the refuge for female prisoners. Through Lord Normanby, the Home Secretary, Queen Victoria was familiar with her work and her recent tour of the Continent had made a heroine of her again in England.

On 1 February 1840 nine days before Queen Victoria's marriage to Prince Albert, Elizabeth Fry was granted an interview with her. She was asked to be brief and only to reply to the Queen's questions. 'This was very cramping', Betsy complained. The Queen asked her about her work at home and abroad and received a short sermon in reply. Mrs Fry expressed her satisfaction 'that she [Queen Victoria] encouraged various works of charity and I said it reminded me of the words of Scripture "with the merciful will I show myself merciful" ... after a little more she made a sort of sign for us to withdraw, when I stopped and said that I hoped the Queen would allow me to say that it was our prayer that the blessing of God might rest upon the Queen and her Consort … Lord Normanby said the Queen was pleased, much pleased with our visit.' But Mrs Fry was not content to leave the matter there. She wrote to the Duchess of Kent 'expressing more fully my desire for the Queen, really speaking my mind as to the example she should set'.

After recording at length her visit to the Queen she turned to what she called 'a much more deeply interesting subject … our much beloved daughter Louisa was delivered of a lovely girl', but the baby died twenty-four hours after she was born. 'The events of this week have been very serious,' she wrote, 'got through Louisa's labour and my visit to the Queen.'

Although she was conscious of time passing, conscious of her age – she was in her sixtieth year – it was not allowed to inter-fere with her travels. In February she embarked on a journey to Belgium, Holland and Germany. She did make one concession and, before she left, made a will leaving her money to her husband and children, trying to be fair to them all. But almost twenty-three years after her first taste of public life, she was again fully launched and triumphant.

Power had always intoxicated her, the power of the monarchy, the sense of her own power. Had she not been driven by a desire to serve God, her ambition would have made a monster of her. As it was, she wrought havoc with her own children. Yet she believed tenaciously that power had been given to her to save prisoners, to succour the poor, to right injustices. She swept through Europe as if possessed, dignified, modest and utterly ruthless.

It was easier this time without her own family. She travelled in regal style with her brother Samuel Gurney, by now a very wealthy man, and the party stayed in large apartments in the best hotels. Samuel's daugh-ter Elizabeth and her friend Lucy Bradshaw accompanied them, the two girls acting as helpers to the older members of the party. William Allen, a recorded Minister and Josiah Forster also joined them. They arrived in Ostend on 27 February 1840, where they received an order from the Belgian Government granting permission for them to visit the prisons.

Elizabeth Fry was delightfully cheerful. Her brother Samuel was an ideal travelling companion, 'so able, so willing, so generous'. She found her niece Elizabeth 'sweet, pleasant and cheering'. She must have felt the contrast between her contented niece and her daughter Kate, always so fearful of travel. They visited Bruges and travelled on to Ghent, where Mrs Fry spent an afternoon in an atrocious prison. One of the cells was formed of angular pieces of wood, so that standing, leaning or lying down was painful for the prisoner. In Brussels she wrote in her journal, 'the most important duties were a long visit to the King in which we represented fully our view of the Prisons'. There were, of course, the usual meetings, dinner parties and grand visits. By the time she reached Rotterdam she was feeling unwell, her chest hurt her and she found the service given in the grand hotels was not what she was accustomed to.

'Chambermaids don't grow in Holland except when you want your bed warmed,' wrote her niece, '… Aunt doesn't care for it, but I think she generally values the opportunity of talking to some "dear waiter".'[5] Of course Aunt Fry was well-equipped with tracts and holy books in German and French and busily giving them away. Travelling with her on the Continent was truly like travelling with royalty. 'Inasmuch as I am the hem of Aunt's garment,' wrote her niece, 'they are all kindness itself.'

At Minden the party slept at a 'true German inn – neither carpet nor curtain', visiting Friends, holding Meetings. Since she did not speak a word of German, Mrs Fry had to rely entirely on interpreters, but her reputation flew ahead of her and everywhere her reception was rapturous. In Hanover, she wrote to the King and Queen about the state of their prisons. In one deplorable prison, untried prisoners were chained to the ground until they confessed to their crimes, whether they were innocent or guilty.

Evidently her letter impressed the Queen. On the day of her departure, the Queen's Chamberlain arrived with a message that the Queen wished to see the whole party.

'We were received with ceremonious respect, shewn through many rooms to a drawing-room where were the Queen's Chamberlain and three ladies-in-waiting to receive us ... We were sent for by the Queen – a very Queen like fine person.' The King was too ill to be present and Mrs Fry and the Queen had a long and serious conversation. She lectured the Queen of Hanover on 'the difficulties and temptations to which rank is subject – the importance of their influence – the objects incumbent upon them to attend to and help in Bible Societies, Prisons'. Then she read her formal address, in which she asked the Queen to patronise ladies visiting the prisons.

Her earnestness, her piety, her extraordinary reputation combined to make her irresistible. 'This year', she noted with satisfaction, 'I have had intimate communications with the Duchess of Gloucester, Princess Sophia, Our Queen, the Duchess of Kent and the King of the Belgians.'

In Berlin the astounding performance was repeated. A splendid room of the Hôtel de Russie was filled with a 'fine company of the higher classes'. 'It would be impossible', wrote her niece, 'to describe the intense interest and eagerness which prevailed when our aunt rose.' She described the story of her early days in Newgate, which always animated her, the changes that had been brought about through the ladies' visits and ended with an eloquent appeal to those present to join in the work of visiting and redeeming the prisoners.

The novelty of this English lady in full sail was again irresistible. Princess William, sister to the late King of Prussia, gave the scheme her wholehearted support and invited the Committee of exquisitely dressed ladies to hold their first meeting in the Palace. Elizabeth Fry arrived looking stately in a beautiful full silk coat, a pair of light gloves and a new cap. When the carriages reached the palace, the Princess herself came out to meet them and the Committee stood about the elegant suite of rooms, drinking chocolate while waiting for the rest of the royal family. When the meeting began, Mrs Fry was seated in the middle of the sofa with the Crown Prince and Princess and the Princess Charles on her right and Princess William, Princess Marie and the Princess Czartoryski on her left. A table was placed before her with pens, ink and paper and the rules for the new Association translated into German. After describing the work of the Society in England, she asked the Prince and Princess if they would permit a short time for prayer. They all bowed assent and Elizabeth Fry knelt down and asked blessing on the whole state, from the King in his palace to the prisoners in the dungeon. The Royal family then invited Elizabeth Fry's party to visit them again before they left Berlin.

Meanwhile, at home, she had been sadly missed, for no matter how trying Joseph might find her presence, he felt her absence still more. 'I long for the time when we shall see thee again my dearest, in occupation of thy own seat at table ...'[6] He wrote this letter in March and sent it to Hanover. His next letter sounds an exasperated note: 'It would be truly kind to tell us not only where you have been, but where you will be for about 10 days, thy last letter had not even a date or the place and time.' Poor patient Joe Fry. He ended his letter by saying that he was trying to find some news to tell her but could not remember anything except that their son John had let his house to a stranger, whose name he had forgotten.

It had in some ways, been an unsuitable marriage, Joseph was plodding and dull, except in the forbidden areas of art and music, where he had far more sensibility than his wife, while she – she was Elizabeth Fry, the wonder of many lands.

In Berlin Mrs Fry was very happily obsessed. She called at the Ministry of Justice to report on the state of the prisons in Prussia and in the drawing room of her hotel apartments received a Committee of twenty men who wished to discuss the question of prison discipline with her. On this occasion Mrs Fry asked her niece to chaperone her. 'She does not like to be alone with so many gentlemen.'[7] She managed to cram into her stay an inspection of a large hospital and a religious service held in a combined workhouse and prison for the benefit of the inmates.

By May the exhilaration and exertions of the past months had affected her health. She developed a cough and cold and 'an extraordinary infirmity of mind'. While her companions travelled to Dresden, Mrs Fry rested quietly at Leipzig, accompanied by her maid and a Mr Byerhaus, a young German gentleman who had placed himself at her disposal during her stay. The weather was mild and spring-like and friends visited her with gifts of oranges and books and a fine print of 'Prisoners at Worship'. Despite her reputation for delicacy, she had a remarkably robust constitution when work was demanded and in two days she was well enough to move on to Düsseldorf to inspect the Association for Prisoners in the Rhine and Westphalia. This charity was founded as a direct result of her work at Newgate by a Pastor Fliedner, a German clergyman who had been so impressed by her readings that he had returned to his own country resolved to improve the prisoners' welfare. The objects of the Prussian Association were similar to those of the English Association except that their first objective was to maintain order in the prisons. After that in importance came classification of the prisoners according to their crime, finding work for them and offering them spiritual solace through the services of a chaplain.

Six miles from Düsseldorf at Kaiserswerth, an ancient town on the Rhine, was Pastor Fliedner's other institution, also a tribute to Elizabeth Fry's inspiration.

In 1834 on a visit to London to raise funds, he had spent a day at Mrs Fry's home, talked over his plans for training women as nurses and accompanied her on one of her 'visits of mercy' to Newgate. Two years later Pastor Fliedner had established an institution for training Protestant deaconesses to tend and nurse the sick. 'Of all my contemporaries,' wrote that remarkably devout man of Mrs Fry, 'none has exercised a like influence on my heart and life.'

She was greeted at Kaiserswerth with rejoicing: 'The 8th of May, 1840 was a great holiday to us,' he wrote later, '... truly her friendship was one of the "all things" which God, in Sovereign mercy has worked for my good ... Thus may my happiness be estimated, when in 1840 Mrs Fry ... came in person to see and rejoice over the growing establishment at Kaiserswerth.'[8]

For Mrs Fry, too, the day was marvellous. She peered into every room, examined the rules, addressed the deaconesses on their calling. Here in Kaiserswerth, her long-cherished dream of women leading useful lives was realised. At the Institution, twelve young women were training to be teachers while twenty deaconesses worked in the wards, nursing the sick.

For years she had been aware of the appalling conditions in hospitals but her energies were wholly taken up with her prison work. In 1827, in her book on prison visiting, she had called upon ladies to better conditions in 'our hospitals, our lunatic asylums and our workhouses'.

Two years later, in 1829, the Poet Laureate Robert Southey had written to Amelia Opie, seeking to enlist her sympathy and, through her, to involve Elizabeth Fry in hospital reform – the two women had been friends since girlhood. The poet, in his letter, urged Amelia to establish societies for improving hospital management 'so as to do for the hospitals what Mrs Fry has done for the prisons'.

Amelia wrote to Betsy and sent on Southey's letter. Mrs Fry replied encouragingly, stressing the importance of the cause, but did not fulfil Southey's hopes by volunteering to organise the campaign herself. At that time Elizabeth Fry was still trying to live down the scandal of her husband's bankruptcy and was meeting opposition in her public life. Without Mrs Fry to command, Amelia Opie was simply not equipped to launch a national campaign and the idea was allowed to founder.

However, the visit to Kaiserswerth fired Elizabeth Fry with new enthusiasm to reform conditions in English hospitals. The hospital nurse of those days was almost invariably a heavy drinker and a slattern, despised by the physicians. Florence Nightingale believed that hospitals preferred 'that the nurses should be women who had lost their character',[9] so that they would fit into the system without causing trouble. Some of them slept in the wards with their male patients.

On her return to England in May 1840, Elizabeth Fry envisaged a new type of nurse to work in the hospitals. She drew up detailed plans for a training school for Protestant Sisters of Charity. The Sisters were to spend a probationary period working in the wards of a large public hospital. The first eight were trained at Guy's Hospital. If accepted, they were to live in a nurses' home in the City, tending the poor of the parish and going out to stay with patients when needed. The services were to be free for those who could not afford to pay; the better-off were asked to pay a small charge.

Mrs Fry persuaded her brother Sam's wife, Elizabeth Gurney, to put her plans into practice, but she herself invited the Dowager Queen to become Patroness of the establishment. Lady Inglis agreed to become their President.

The Fry nurses wore a neat, plain uniform and received a stipend of £20, rising to £23 after three years' service, as compensation for their hard work and piety. At the home, they were expected to attend prayers and they were encouraged to read the Scriptures to their patients as well as tend to their physical needs. By the time the Crimean war broke out in 1854, there were over forty of these pious, respectable women with nursing experience. A handful of the 'Fry Sisters' accompanied Florence Nightingale's party to Scutari.

Florence Nightingale, Elizabeth Fry's junior by forty years, wrote of the reformer with admiration. It was certainly due, in some degree, to Mrs Fry's influence that she escaped from the tyranny of the drawing-room to follow her calling. According to legend, in the 1840s, when Florence Nightingale was a girl in her twenties, she visited Mrs Fry and poured out to the older woman her hopes, her frustrations and her passionate desire to serve God through nursing. Mrs Fry is said to have recommended her to Kaiserswerth. Miss Nightingale did in fact receive her first nursing training there in 1851, although later she was to complain that 'the nursing was nil and the hygiene horrid' at that pious institution.[10]

In 1846 Florence Nightingale received – and treasured – the Year Book of the Kaiserswerth Institution from Chevalier Bunsen, the Prussian Ambassador. Bunsen had been a close friend and admirer of Mrs Fry and his son married Sam Gurney's daughter.

In this, as in her main work of prison reform, Elizabeth Fry's passionate desire to lead a useful life herself and to encourage other women to work for the improvement of their own sex had disturbed the placid, vapid lives of countless Victorian women. By working outside the home, she and her followers had broadened the horizons of their fellow women and changed for ever the confines of respectable femininity. She, however, could never quite bring herself to acknowledge the consequences of her feminism. As a 'poor, weak woman', she had won a place for *herself* in the world of men. But despite her achievements and the public's regard, she remained timid and unsure of herself beneath her stately appearance.

'If I live to the day after tomorrow,' she wrote on 19 May 1840, two days before her birthday, 'I shall be sixty years old – this is a considerable age to attain, beyond what I could have hoped for.'

X

Heroine of Europe

The object of life, Elizabeth Fry had once said, was to follow Christ. In her own way she had tried so hard to keep that vision bright. She never lost her sense of urgent compassion for suffering. Yet as she grew older, she was drawn more and more to indulge the worldly side of her nature: the love of pomp and flattery; the calls on friends in high life; and the court gossip she so enjoyed about the Queen and Prince Albert. She preached simplicity and humility in Meeting House, but could be seen, almost every week, visiting Duchesses and Dukes, Lords and Ladies, her Quaker bonnet bobbing up incongruously from their elegant carriages. Her recent journey through the Continent, travelling in high style in the interests of the downtrodden, had suited Betsy admirably. She used her influence, she persuaded herself, to ease the sufferings of the wretched. Even on her rare visits to Buckingham Palace or Windsor, the Queen or Prince Albert would not be spared a sermon, and through her influence with the monarchy abroad, many prisons had been reformed. Yet in her sixties, as in her teens, she was intensely introspective and spiritually ambitious. She felt the contradiction. She could neither give up the seductive thrill of mixing in high society, nor avoid the feeling that it was corrupting her. In later life, however, she was more inclined to justify herself.

To the world at large she appeared circumspect. On 17 June 1840, Lucretia Mott, an American Friend visiting England for the

World's Anti-Slavery Convention, heard Elizabeth Fry give an account of her extremely successful mission to the Continent to a meeting of the British Society held at Westminster. Mrs Mott noted in her diary:

> E. Fry unassuming, meek – modest – nothing very striking, has done immense good to the poor prisoners by moving in her own and God's sphere rather than in man's and the Devil's.[1]

Mrs Mott was remarkably generous to a woman who could command an admiring audience, considering that she herself and the other women delegates from America had been refused seats on the floor of the Convention on the grounds of their sex. Lucretia Mott represented a faction of the American Abolitionists who championed the rights of women as well as of slaves. Ironically, the World's Anti-Slavery Convention in London was to be remembered as the springboard for the movement for women's suffrage in America.

Elizabeth Fry did not spring to the defence of her rejected sisters, although among the English abolitionists, who were mainly Friends, she had immense influence, and her own brother-in-law, Fowell Buxton, led the anti-slavery lobby in Parliament. She seemed rather inclined to ignore the issue, and the day after the convention closed, sat beside the chairman at a meeting of the British and Foreign Anti-Slavery Society, the hosts who had insisted on the ban, although the women delegates from America were barred from the platform.

Over three thousand people packed into Exeter Hall for the meeting. Mrs Mott recorded the scene: 'E. Fry & Duchess of Sutherland introduced – much clapping – taken to front seats on the platform – after repudiating such exposure of ladies – rather inconsistent.' Lucretia Mott's criticism evidently came to the ears of Mrs Fry, who had also been indiscreet enough to allow her niece, Sam Gurney's daughter, to sit on the platform too. After the meeting Elizabeth Fry apologised to Mrs Mott for her conspicuous position. It was the inconsistency of her opponents, the British and Foreign Anti-Slavery Society, that she found objectionable, Mrs Mott replied. She told Mrs Fry that her prominent place was 'just the seat she ought to have occupied in a *Prison meeting*'.

Elizabeth Fry's own journal does not give the impression that she felt any embarrassment at her seat on the platform on feminist grounds. She was caught up in her usual agitation at living in the limelight. She was responsible for inviting the Duchess of Sutherland, 'one of the highest persons in the Kingdom, the duke is said to have £400,000 a year', and obviously delighted to be sitting between the Duchess and the Duke of Sussex, the chairman.

To be on the side of the afflicted slaves was, she considered, an honour. But there is no evidence to suggest that she approved of women's suffrage or desired any more freedom for her own sex than the freedom to work for ennobling causes. She had always been curiously conservative in her attitudes, except where they concerned penal reform. She idolised the monarchy and abhorred the idea of socialism. Despite her own turbulent and finally unsatisfactory family life, she was constantly praying to be a dutiful wife and mother and she idealised the family.

At this stage in her life, therefore, she was unlikely to take up the women's cause. Consequently in the history of the women's movement, in America, Elizabeth Fry has a poor showing. Elizabeth Cady Stanton, a pioneer in the crusade for women's rights in the United States, condemned her for publicly shunning Lucretia Mott: 'If Mrs Mott was conversing with a circle of friends on the lawn, Mrs Fry would glide into the house. If Mrs Mott entered at one door, Mrs Fry walked out the other.'[2] According to Elizabeth Stanton, Mrs Fry not only avoided Mrs Mott but made a veiled attack on her at a rather grand Quaker tea-party held in Tottenham. After tea Mrs Fry prayed 'against the apostasy and infidelity of the day in language so pointed and so personal that we all felt that Mrs Mott was the special subject of her petition'.

Lucretia Mott herself gives a more dispassionate account of the afternoon's gathering. 'There was much conversation – reading scripture – way opened by William Ball for anyone to speak who had a wish to – E. Fry asked if that included women.'[3] By asking the question it seems clear that Elizabeth Fry had allied herself with the women. One man present did want to impose a ban of silence upon the women but the host, William Ball, an admiring colleague of Mrs Fry's, would not hear of it. After William Lloyd Garrison, the leader of the American Abolitionists, had spoken, 'E. Fry followed in prayer – that our mission might be blessed in breaking the fetters of the poor captive – but above all blessed to ourselves in bringing us to the unsearchable riches of Christ'.[4] Mrs Mott does not seem to have found Elizabeth Fry offensive and readily gives an account in her diary of Mrs Fry's own expla-nation of her reluctance to take sides on the question.

After the prayers, refreshments were handed round in an adjoin-ing room and Elizabeth Fry spoke of her brother Joseph's visit to America, where he had been since 1837. He had differed fundamen-tally with William Lloyd Garrison on religious grounds and disliked Garrison's promotion of women's rights. 'I do not approve of ladies speaking in public even in the anti-slavery cause except under the immediate influence of the Holy Spirit. Then and only then all is safe,' he had written in a letter to his children in July 1838. Mrs Fry could not publicly oppose a brother who had for so long supported her. At the tea-party Lucretia Mott noted that she asked 'to be excused from visiting our land as anything like dissension was particularly unpleas-ant to her'. Betsy had always deferred to male Gurney prejudice except when religious inspiration had set her free.

She had never been especially generous towards her colleagues, towards the women in particular. All the generosity in her nature was expended in her philanthropic work. She had so little time; she could not take on more; nor would she cross her brother Joseph. She was devoted to him; he had been her confidant for years in spiritual and business matters, and she also depended on him for financial support.

Two months after the tea-party, Joseph returned home in Sam Gurney's coach-and-four to a grand family gathering at Earlham. The old house overflowed with generations of Gurneys. It was almost like the old days.

> Aunt Fry amuses herself among the trees and flowers. Our Aunt Cunningham [Richenda] flits to and fro. Our Aunt Buxton [Hannah] talks to everyone with childish pleasure and flow of spirits. Our Aunt Catherine is soon overdone ... At the head of the family group our uncle Joseph, full of calm dignity ... saying droll things as in old times and showing his nine books of sketches brought home from the West Indies with great pleasure ...[5]

This picture of the enchantment of Earlham drawn by one of Sam Gurney's daughters does not quite match Mrs Fry's first feelings on that visit. Before Joseph arrived she was anxious and apprehensive, wondering whether she would be able to establish her old intimacy with her brother. After she had had a private talk with him, she was much relieved, even 'surprised at my own foolish fears ... my foolishness was partly about money matters ... I abhor in myself a discontented feeling, even for a moment in money matters – my Lord do so marvellously provide for me. This morning Joseph gave me £200.'

Joseph's generosity and the spell at Earlham helped her to enter into the golden mood of the family. She described the visit eloquently in her diary.

> It was like days that are passed when a large party of us took a beautiful drive and walk on a fine bright day by the sea, over a fine heathy land upon the little hill. Surely the sun shone upon us in every way.

She drove back to London in fitting style, in Sam Gurney's coach-and-four – the use of Sam's coach was part of Joseph's gift, to be deducted from the £200. However, when she drove it to Meeting that autumn her stylish carriage provoked criticism in the newspapers. The public were eager for any titbit about Elizabeth Fry.

By her standards the winter and spring were quiet. She travelled to the Midlands to visit Quarterly Meeting of Warwickshire, Leicestershire and Rutland and to visit Friends in Birmingham. That spring of 1841, William, her second son, fell ill with inflammation of the lungs. Her youngest daughter Louisa gave birth to a boy in March and Betsy, who was with her, was thankful when it was over. Not only did Louisa withstand the actual birth well, but she herself was 'not overwhelmed either'.

But after the baby was born, Louisa was ill for some months. In May it was discovered that she had an abscess above her navel. On 30 May, Elizabeth Fry wrote anxiously:

> In the very depths of affliction O Lord, our dearest Louisa being again extremely ill, I, in my hurry, gave her a wrong medicine of a poisonous nature: my fright at first was inexpressible …

The doctor was summoned and Louisa was given an emetic. Betsy poured out her prayers in her journal.

> Permit me gracious Lord, in this deep emergency to entreat Thee to save my beloved child with an everlasting salvation, and, if it be Thy blessed will, grant her a little revival that I may never have the weight of believing that her end was accelerated by my carelessness. Be very near to her, granting her Thy peace and the joy of Thy salvation.

There was in her prayers an egoism unashamedly human. She stayed with Louisa and nursed her until she was almost better. 'The query now comes closely home,' she wrote, 'Am I called again to the Continent or not?'

In England she was by now a peripheral figure in penal reform as far as the professionals were concerned On 2 April 1843, to her astonishment, she even found she 'had difficulty in getting into Newgate', when she unwisely took along a party of her aristocratic friends. She still busied herself with her prison visits and a Society for the Patronage of Discharged Prisoners but she missed the urgent sense of involvement of the past.

Earlier that year she had visited the 'model' prison, designed on the separate system, being built at Pentonville. What she saw appalled her, and in July she wrote to Colonel Joshua Jebb, who was in charge, to protest:

> … the dark cells … should never exist in a Christian and civilised country. I think having prisoners placed in these cells a punishment peculiarly liable to abuse … in the cells generally the windows have that description of glass in them that even the sight of the sky is precluded … I am aware that the motive is to prevent the possibility of seeing a fellow prisoner; but I think a prison for separate confinement should be so constructed that the culprits may at least see the sky … My reason for this opinion is that I consider it a very important object to preserve the health of mind and body in these poor creatures; and I am certain that separate confinement produces an unhealthy state of mind and body …

Her appeal was ignored and the prison was completed the following year.

On the Continent, by contrast, her advice was eagerly sought. Ever since her return to England a year before she had corresponded regularly with the Prussian Royal Family who urged her to return. The Queen of Denmark also expressed a strong desire to meet her.

After his visit to the West Indies, during his American journey, Joseph was drawn to visit the Continent to persuade slave-owning governments of the advantages of emancipation that he had seen for himself. So it was natural to plan an expedition together. Mrs Fry, of course, intended to continue to crusade to improve prison conditions.

They were to travel to Holland, Germany, Prussia and Denmark. Joseph's daughter Anna and Sam's daughter Elizabeth Gurney made up the party, together with Elizabeth Fry's own maid, Mary.

They left England on 31 July 1841. The crossing was comfortable but a small upset put them all in a flurry. Just as they were about to disembark, Elizabeth Fry could not find her expensive new bonnet. All the ladies searched the cabin until at last Mrs Fry called out that her brother had sat on it. Dismayed they looked at the squashed and now completely unrecognisable hat. Fortunately the ladies were able to straighten it, though even if it had been destroyed, no doubt Joseph would have found a way of having a new one made quickly for her. The wealthy banker spent his money freely, determined that the party should travel in the utmost comfort.

'We live in rather too much luxury, I think and as to eating and drinking there seems no end to it,' commented Elizabeth Gurney, herself the daughter of a prominent banker. 'Uncle's unbounded generosity makes us travel "en prince".' This Betsy Gurney was a great favourite with Mrs Fry, 'almost a daughter'. She in her turn admired her aunt greatly and wrote of her visits to 'dungeons and palaces' with enthusiasm and affection.

Despite the holiday atmosphere, both Elizabeth Fry and her brother took their missions extremely seriously. She had been in Holland the previous year and found her second visit more satisfactory. She was known to the Secretary of the Interior and several prison authorities and could accomplish more in her brief visits. At the women's prison at Gouda, twelve miles outside Rotterdam, she was pleased to find that some of the improvements she had recommended, including the employment of more women gaolers for the female prisoners, had been put into practice. At other prisons, the Committees of Visitors she had initiated were helping to introduce a more humane regime.

Sister and brother had letters of introduction from the Duchess of Gloucester and Prince Albert to the Dutch Royal Family. 'Although they are only Mrs Fry and Mr Gurney,' wrote young

Betsy, 'they are of the first English family and expect to be treated like Dukes.' Three days after their arrival in The Hague, the pair were summoned to the Palais du Rois for a conference with King William II. The King wore regimental uniform, the Queen, a sister to the Tsar of Russia, a full and beautiful morning dress of white, while Mrs Fry appeared before them in a plain, brown silk dress, draped with a dull brown silk shawl, exquisite and expensive presents from her own family.

The King obviously found her fascinating – even at her age she could exert a magnetism – and began to talk to her in an informal way, asking her about her work in prisons. She wrote afterwards: '... he said he heard I had so many children, how could I do it? This I explained, and mentioned how one of my daughters now helped me in the Patronage Society.' She sensed his mood and spoke to him 'very boldly but respectfully' about the conditions in the prisons in his land. She then tactfully drew attention to her brother, mentioning his recent visit to the West Indies. Joseph spoke plainly to the King of the need to abolish slavery in the Dutch dominions and pointed out the damage done by enlisting negro soldiers on the Gold Coast.

Then Mrs Fry called the King's attention to the lack of religious education in Holland. It was forbidden, since there were Jewish as well as Christian children in the schools. The King explained this law to her, but she was unruffled, declaring that Bible education need not transgress the spirit of their law. 'Religious principle', she assured the King earnestly, 'is the only true foundation of virtue.' The King listened patiently and at the close of the conference, Elizabeth Fry blessed the Royal Family with fervour and at some length. 'The King took me by the hand and said he hoped God would bless me. I expressed my desire that the blessing of the Almighty might rest on the King, the Queen, their children and their children's children.'

From The Hague, the English party drove on to nearby Amsterdam, where Joseph called a meeting of wealthy businessmen to try to convince them of the practical and financial advantages of abolition.

Betsy Gurney wrote:

> Many stiff Dutch slave owners present. Uncle took wholly the Expediency side of the Question, remembering the love of Dutchmen for the Money part of the Story. Aunt then rose and hoped some of them … would take a higher ground and shew the Christian and the right side. But alas! I fear there were few there that would take that to heart … Nevertheless they were caught by what she said … in fact Mevrow Fry is a very great person in Holland as well as over the rest of the world …

From Holland they travelled in the carriage to Bremen in Germany, where Mrs Fry was almost mobbed by crowds wanting to shake her hand and receive one of her little tracts. At the museum, brother and sister held a religious meeting where their solemn ministry was greatly appreciated by a large crowd. One of the German pastors present blessed the Quakers. Turning to Elizabeth Fry, he said, 'Your name has long been to us a word of beauty.'

In many of the cities of Europe where work of a religious or philanthropic nature thrived – and the two were nearly always connected – the name of Elizabeth Fry was honoured. In Hamburg she met a Fraülein Sieveking, with whom she had corresponded for years. The latter had established a 'Society of the Ladies' Committee' for 'succouring and nursing the sick and helpless poor' and finding work for the unemployed. Through her journeys Elizabeth Fry spread knowledge of new welfare methods across the continent of Europe.

At the end of August, the party crossed the Baltic in a steam packet bound for Copenhagen. Peter Browne, Secretary to the British Legation, met them at the harbour with the news that the Queen had booked apartments for them at the Hotel Royal. Despite the grand hotel and 'rather too much luxury', Betsy Gurney noticed that her Uncle Joseph was worried by fleas and Aunt Fry slept badly because the sheets and blankets were too narrow to cover her.

The day after their arrival, the Queen of Denmark, who was herself sincerely religious and eager to help Mrs Fry and her brother, travelled to Copenhagen from her country residence especially to meet them. She sent first for Elizabeth Fry but the rest of the party were called for shortly afterwards. Their time in Denmark was divided between prisons and palaces. In the police prison, Elizabeth Fry was deeply distressed to find two Baptist ministers, Peter and Adolph Munster, in solitary confinement. The two brothers had been imprisoned for nine months for their religious work, since it was illegal, at the time, for dissenters to worship in public.

On the fifth day of their visit the English party was invited to dine with King Christian VIII at his country estate. When they arrived the Queen met them and took them for a stroll around the beautiful grounds. But Mrs Fry could scarcely take in her surroundings, she was so apprehensive. (The King had a reputation for religious bigotry.) After half an hour they were summoned to the drawing room where the King greeted them most cordially. Dinner was at four in the afternoon.

'Imagine me the King on one side and the Queen on the other and only my poor French to depend upon,' Betsy wrote home, describing in detail the gargantuan meal of soup; melon; yams, anchovies, caviar, bread and butter and radishes; meat; puddings; fish; chickens and game; and the table piled high with fruit. 'The fashion was to touch glasses; no drinking healths. The King and Queen touched my glass on both sides.'

After the meal Elizabeth Fry strolled with the King and Queen to the drawing-room window and steeled herself to talk to him seriously about the state of the prisons, mentioning the good features as well as the bad. She had, she said, a petition for him which she meant to make before leaving the palace. But first the King went to a private room with Joseph, who talked at length about the desirability of abolishing slavery in the Dutch West Indies. After an hour had passed, Mrs Fry joined them and begged the King for religious tolerance in his land. She spoke of the Munster brothers and pleaded for their release. 'I did my best, in a few words, to express my mind and very strongly I did it. I gave also Luther's sentiments upon the subject.' King Christian was visibly moved by her plea. At the close of the visit she prayed simply and with great feeling for the Royal Family and their own causes 'to Him who can alone touch the heart'. At a farewell meeting with the Queen and the Princess of Denmark, according to her impressionable niece 'there was not a dry eye in the room' during Elizabeth Fry's address. 'Many dined with us before we left, but several ladies, young and old, dropped off from the tables, drowned in tears ...'

'Wherever she travelled on the Continent, crowds gathered, bringing fruit, pineapples and cherries, and bunches of flowers to the carriage and begging for tracts. From Denmark they returned to Hamburg, travelling on to Hanover, Berlin, Silesia, Dresden and Halle. Everywhere they went they inspected the prisons and made recommendations. They were entertained handsomely by members of the Prussian Royal Family.

Her very personal interest in each prisoner conveyed to the authorities a vivid picture of life in gaol. Thanks to her visit, the Munster brothers, imprisoned in Denmark, had been freed. The overall effect of their tour was to alert people throughout northern Europe to the misery inside prisons and the need for more religious tolerance.

But by now these long journeys, the constant movement and the strain of public speaking had become a drain on her health. By the time the party reached Berlin she was feeling ill, 'hardly able to walk or use her arms'. As far as possible she concealed her ailments from her party as she feared it would diminish her in their view, and somehow, whenever she preached in public, she was able to transcend her physical illness.

Joseph was now anxious to be home quickly – he was to be married in three weeks for the third time – so six horses were harnessed to the carriage for maximum speed. Inside a board was arranged to make a sofa for Elizabeth Fry so that she could lie down when the others travelled on the outside seats. A 'providential' supply of port wine eased her pain, but she was uncomfortable, with little appetite and diarrhoea.

She felt ill and worried that she was becoming a drag on her party. 'I had a little debt to my companions which I endeavoured to pay by giving each a little advice and a blessing before we left Ostend,' she wrote in her journals.

The travellers arrived at Dover on 2 October where Joseph Fry was waiting anxiously. He was shocked at the sight of his wife weak and exhausted, with her limbs stiff and swollen. Her brother, too, when he realised how ill she really was, which, in his haste to get home, he had overlooked, was full of remorse. She travelled home slowly, staying a few days at Ramsgate, looked after carefully by Kate, then moving on to her son William and his wife and ending up in Norfolk with Frank and Rachel. All the children were kind and thoughtful and she was touchingly grateful. More and more now she seemed to need to drink wine and she prayed not to become 'unduly devoted to the good things of this life or partake of them beyond the limits of true Christian moderation'.

At Christmas she was relying on half a grain of opium a day to soothe the pain in her bowels. She wrote of a 'very serious conversation' on religious subjects with Queen Victoria. 'I think her a very superior pious woman. I am sorry she is under so much High Church influence. I was treated with the utmost kindness and respect by her. She gave me a book, the account of the King's death, that she kept on her table since about the time he died.'

No doubt Queen Victoria considered Mrs Fry herself, almost forty years her senior, a 'very, superior, pious woman'. It is even conceivable that she may have modelled herself on this rare woman who combined the roles of mother and public figure.

Meanwhile Elizabeth Fry's health was delicate and she could not go to afternoon Meetings. In the first week of January 1842, the amount of opium she was taking to ease her pain and diarrhoea had increased to a grain a day. (The common dosage was only a quarter of a grain.) She slept badly and woke with the old feelings of sinking and faintness swamping her. She kept a record of her diet in her journal:

> I take meat three times a day, no fruit whatever, very little veg-
> etables, a little rice, a tumbler of porter or ale twice a day at
> luncheon and dinner and port wine as required. Dr Elliot says
> I require a pint a day in the present low state of my blood and
> constitution. I believe I should be better without, but of course I
> try to do with a smaller quantity.

She was becoming more and more dependent on her 'medicine' at a time when religious circles in America and England were beginning to denounce drink as an evil. Her own brother Joseph had become a total abstainer by then which upset her. Her atti-tude to drink and strong medicines was rather like her attitude towards high society. There were inherent dangers in them, but for Elizabeth Fry they were indispensable. All her life she had encouraged the view that her case needed special treatment. Her constant prayers and supplications against the abuse of 'these valuable helps' reveals how uneasy she felt. '… continue to find opium needful to keep me in pretty good health,' she wrote on 11 January, 'but thankfully accept it as a gift from the Lord.'

Her social life was to become exceptionally demanding that month so that she needed all her strength. The previous autumn the husband of one of her most loyal helpers in Newgate, Sir John Pirie, had been elected Lord Mayor of London and he and his wife were eager to help Mrs Fry in her work. Lady Pirie came to visit her in Upton Lane to beg her to attend a grand banquet to com-memorate the laying of the foundation stone of the Royal Exchange in mid-January. She pleaded ill-health but Lady Pirie came back and reminded her that there would be a number of influential guests present including Prince Albert, the Duke of Wellington and government ministers, who could help her with her prison cause.

At the last minute she decided to attend. She arrived at the Mansion House late, muddy and flurried. Because of the crowds, the carriage could not drive up to the door and she had had to jostle through the mob, with the result that she was spattered right up to her knees. Bundled upstairs, she had 'the most hurried and confused dressing, the Lord Mayor waiting at the bedroom door, sending for me again and again'. She walked into the drawing-room on the Lord Mayor's arm, wearing a brown silk gown and a white silk shawl, composed and stately and looking extraordinarily distinguished among the ladies with feathers in their hair and gowns of brilliant colours.

She made a formidable guest. She launched unashamedly into propaganda for her causes and her prisoners. Sir James Graham, the Secretary of State, was cross-questioned about the new prison under construction for women prisoners; Lord Aberdeen, the Foreign Secretary, appealed to for his help with her campaigns in Europe; Lord Stanley, the Colonial Secretary, asked about the state of the colonies and the conditions of the women convicts there. From all the gentlemen she extracted a promise that they would ask their wives to patronise her sale, to be held in April in aid of the prisoners.

At dinner, sitting between Sir Robert Peel and Prince Albert, she began straight away to lecture the Prince about the management of the royal nursery and the need for religious education for the royal children. She also voiced her concern about the prisons. Punishments were becoming too harsh and the gaolers held too much power. Would he tell the Queen? In fact she over-estimated the power of the monarchy and her methods made her unpopular in some government circles.

Evidently Prince Albert steered the conversation onto a more general level, for she admitted that there was some entertaining talk about her journey and the food and manners in Europe. 'The Prince talked a great deal to me as well as my speaking to him,' she wrote, 'we both felt, I believe, as if we had long been friends.'

She tried to persuade Sir Robert Peel to visit the new prison at Pentonville and see for himself the dark cells that she disliked so much. She also raised the question of the severity of punishments and the degree of power held by the gaolers, realising, perhaps, how little hope she had of seeing reforms carried out.

When dinner was over, she informed both the Prince and Sir Robert that she could not, in conscience, rise for the toasts, since she disapproved of that means of displaying goodwill, although she expressed her prayers for the wellbeing of all. When 'God Save the Queen' was played, however, Elizabeth Fry felt it safe to rise to her feet. That, she felt, was a hymn. Although no formal toast was proposed to her health, in his toast to the Lady Mayoress, Sir Robert Peel included some highly flattering remarks about Mrs Fry. He said, she remembered, that 'there was not a table in Europe that would not have been honoured by my presence'.

Her attendance at the banquet was noticed and criticised by the newspapers and a member of her Society sent her a disapproving letter – her very presence among all the pomp and ceremony offended. And there was worse to come.

At the end of January 1842, the King of Prussia came to England for the christening of Queen Victoria's eldest son, Edward, Prince of Wales. Mrs Fry was invited most pressingly to the Mansion House, since the King wanted to meet her again. Although it was a Sunday, she agreed, provided that there would be no toasts. That morning Katharine and Joseph accompanied Elizabeth Fry to Meeting and afterwards to the Mansion House where the waited for the Prussian King, who had attended the service at St Paul's Cathedral.

'I have seldom seen any person more faithfully kind and friendly than he is,' wrote Elizabeth Fry. The two friends discussed the marriage of the Princess Mary of Prussia and the christening of the Prince of Wales. Betsy told the King that she thought the pomp of the christening ceremony 'undesirable'. Since the King was related to the British Royal Family and was their guest, the remark was hardly tactful. To King Frederick, however, she was a saint and could do no wrong. He arranged to visit Newgate the following Tuesday, to hear her read to the prisoners, and accepted an invitation to luncheon at her home afterwards.

His proposed visit aroused comment in court circles. She was, after all, only a commoner living in an ordinary suburban house. 'There were difficulties raised about his going to Upton', Elizabeth Fry wrote in her diary, 'but he chose to persevere.' Her family had misgivings about the visit too. Surely Ham House, with its pleasure gardens, her brother's impressive residence next door, was a more suitable place to receive a King. Katharine Fry thought their own home was 'ill calculated for the reception of such a guest'. 'To the feelings of some,' she wrote sourly, 'this Royal visit was a source of mortification rather than pride.'[6] Nothing spoilt the day. Mrs Fry met the King at Newgate, accompanied by the Lady Mayoress and the Sheriffs. As they walked up to the wards together, he gave her his arm. All sixty women prisoners were neat and clean, standing round the table. They sat down, the King, the Sheriffs, the ladies of the Committee and the prisoners, and Elizabeth Fry began to speak.

> I felt deeply but quiet in spirit – fear of man much removed … expressed my desire that the attention of none, particularly the poor prisoners, might be diverted from attending to our reading by the company … but that we should remember that the King of Kings and Lord of Lords was present, in whose fear we should abide and seek to profit by what we heard.

After reading from the Bible she knelt down to pray for the prisoners and for the King of Prussia and his kingdom.

From the gates of the prison she hurried to her carriage, arriving back at Upton to find the parish celebrating. Flags were flying, church bells ringing and crowds of charity schoolchildren lined the churchyard wall shouting and cheering as she went by, while police on horseback kept the road clear.

Her carriage arrived at her home shortly before the King. 'I had to hurry to take off my cloak and then went down to meet him at his carriage door.' In the drawing-room, decked with flowers, Elizabeth Fry presented her huge family party to the King – her daughters and daughters-in-law, sons and sons-in-law, her married sisters and brothers and twenty-five grandchildren present.

Before the meal there was a solemn silence. The luncheon, she wrote afterwards, was 'truly handsome, fit for a King but not extravagant'. The King asked for a second helping of oyster soup, a dish that he had never tasted before. From her account it is clear that the royal guest thoroughly enjoyed himself and felt at home with her. After her prayers for the King and Queen of Prussia, a deputation of Friends arrived to read an address. The King stayed far longer than his schedule allowed and seemed reluctant to leave. 'He wept aloud at parting and hardly let me leave hold of his arm the whole time I was there except at table.'

Naturally enough, the affair brought Mrs Fry further publicity and criticism. So, with brother Joseph's financial help, she went with her husband to stay in Brighton for a rest. She felt ill and weak again, yet when she returned to London she told her Women's Monthly Meeting that although her health was poor she proposed to retain for a few months longer the certificate which gave her permission to travel in the Ministry. She still nursed the hope that she would be able to travel to the Continent.

By April 1842 she was taking more opium and more wine, on her doctor's orders. When she tried to cut down she felt weaker. She was convinced that these were the only medicines which could help her. That summer Samuel Hoare lent Betsy his house at Cromer and her brother and sisters from Earlham came to stay in the village to try to rally her. At sixty-two, she was beginning to fear that her powers were failing; she dreaded becoming senile and a burden to her family. When she heard that Frank, her eldest grandson, was to join the army after all, she no longer had the energy to oppose the prospect. The one thing, however, that never failed to rouse her was the opportunity to work for the poor.

At Cromer, Joseph Gurney and his wife Eliza had noticed

the fishermen, who were out of work in the summer months, lounging on the cliffs. They held a service for them in their dining-room and Joseph, Eliza (herself an acknowledged Minister), and Elizabeth Fry spoke to the fishermen. From her sister-in-law's account,[7] it seems that Mrs Fry preached with great sweetness and solemnity to the men and they were touched and sobered by her care. Before long she was organising a library, and planning a reading-room where they could drink tea and coffee. Her scheme was completed that winter. News from the Prison Committee that the Government had finally agreed to appoint matrons to travel with the women on the convict ships delighted her. It was a measure that she had worked for for many years.

Perhaps most encouraging were letters from overseas. In Denmark, as a direct result of her visits to the prisons and her personal appeal to the King, new prison buildings had been added, the prisoners' cells were to be heated in the winter and the prisoners were now given employment. Members of the newly-formed Prison Committee in Denmark were empowered by royal decree to visit the prisons and distribute religious literature. In Prussia four new penitentiaries were being built under the special direction of the King. From Düsseldorf and Hamelin came encouraging reports of a new concern for the prisoners' welfare. Mrs Fry's great exertions had not been in vain.

By the New Year her health was improving and, as she grew stronger, she became restless. Her children still caused her much anxiety. Katharine, her mother's aid in all her work, was now in her forties and unlikely to marry, but her mother could not understand why she should feel discontented. Her youngest son Harry, about to enter the tea business with his brothers, also seemed unhappy, just when she thought she had settled him satisfactorily. 'I am very much devoted to them and to all my family and attend little, very little to public service,' she wrote in February 1843. 'May my God grant that I may not hide my talent as in a napkin.' She prayed with rather less fervour that she would not enter the public arena unless divinely inspired. The truth was she was bored with her family and longed to go abroad again. She brightened up considerably at the prospect of a religious mission to France with Joseph and his new wife Eliza. Meanwhile, she tried guiltily to play the good mother and, as usual, overdid it. Her daughter Hannah was seriously ill that spring and her mother hurried to nurse her. She was greatly distressed when the invalid's husband made it clear that he thought she was doing more harm than good. 'It is rather humbling after being so much to my children hardly to be permitted an entrance into the sickroom,' she wrote. For once Joseph reproved her for worrying so much. It showed, he said, a want of faith.

It was the paradox of her life that she could bring comfort, consolation, hope and religion to thousands and yet failed miserably with her own family. She did not admit it to herself but her children were a disappointment to her. Not one of them had turned out either distinguished or pious and only Richenda, who had married a Quaker, remained in the Society all her life. She preferred her sons to her daughters; they did not resent her duality. William, her second son, was the favourite, and that March he invited her to dine with an important guest.

'We had to meet Lord Ashley at my son William's to consider the subject of China and the opium trade,' she wrote solemnly. She was delighted with Ashley, an ardent churchman and an aristocrat, and thought him 'quite a Wilberforce'. 'He is a man devoted to promoting the good of mankind and suppressing evil.'

Her own use of opium, however, had always been 'medicinal' and when she crossed the channel on a blowy April evening in 1843, she was grateful for a quarter of a grain, taken with wine and biscuits, to soothe her. Katherine accompanied her on the journey to watch over her mother's health, but Betsy considered it 'best for my dearest husband to remain at home'.

All the party were concerned at her weakness when they landed at Boulogne, but despite their efforts to persuade her to turn back, she insisted on travelling on to Amiens, where she held a Meeting. Only the women in the party were allowed into the large prison, run by nuns, at Clermont-en-Oise. There, they saw over a hundred female prisoners making lace in one of the huge rooms, while the nuns sang hymns. Mrs Fry persuaded the Mother Superior to allow her to preach to the twenty-two nuns and the lay sisters. With Katharine translating, she spoke encouragingly to them, stressing the importance of bringing religious principle as well as good discipline into the lives of the 900 prisoners in their charge. Then Elizabeth Fry spoke of her own work at Newgate. 'How good she is,' exclaimed the Mother Superior as Mrs Fry concluded her strange religious meeting with a few words of prayer in French.

In Paris she was greeted with enthusiasm and affection, but on her visits to the King and Queen, the duchesse d'Orléans, and to the prisons, her sonorous voice lacked its power, she was noticeably weaker and tired quickly. She relied more and more on Katharine. When she was summoned to call on the duchesse d'Orléans at the Tuileries she found it difficult to make herself understood in her halting French and had to send for her daughter to act as interpreter. Her own account of her stay in France lacks the enthusiasm and zest of former years.

On their previous visit together, Joseph had counted it 'a high privilege' to accompany Elizabeth Fry and praised her preaching. This time he was newly married to a woman who was herself a Minister and understandably had less time for his sister. Although her sister-in-law, who was an American, professed to be in awe of Elizabeth Fry and was reluctant to visit the King and Queen with them, she soon found her tongue in the presence of Louis Philippe. Eliza Gurney's address to the royal couple made a striking impression and, for once, Mrs Fry was overshadowed during the royal visit. However, the next day a beautiful Bible with engravings arrived for Betsy from the Queen.

The Quaker party was invited to dine with M Guizot, the French Foreign Minister. After the topics that usually concerned them had been discussed – abolition, prison reform and equality for the Protestant minority – Elizabeth Fry made a special plea.

Would the French Premier assist the King of the Sandwich Islands in his campaign to introduce teetotalism? The King of those islands, Kamehameha III, had written to Mrs Fry explaining the evil effects that drink had had upon his people and pleading for her help. To people all over the world she was a symbol of righteousness and she tried valiantly to use her unique position on their behalf.

Mrs Fry inspired great affection wherever she went and before she left Paris at the end of May, friends – French and English, Catholic and Protestant – came to see her and loaded her with presents. Her carriage was packed with luxury provisions, air-cushions, handsomely bound Bibles, a fine picture and a writing-case. There were presents too for the others in the party. Katharine was given expensive sketching materials and paints. The evening before she left, Betsy spoke to a large assembly, rising above her frailty in her prayers. 'I was tired and poorly, my flesh and heart ready to fail, but the Lord strengthened me and I felt really helped by a power quite above myself.'

Since her first visit to France six years earlier, a bill to reform the prisons had been brought before the Chamber of Deputies and her Ladies Committees all over the country were visiting the prisoners. Once again Mrs Fry's compassion for women prisoners had rescued them from isolation and neglect.

She arrived home at the end of May 1843 in time to attend one or two sittings of the Yearly Meeting and to be present for the annual report of the British Society. She was feeling better and, for once, could record in her journal that no great anxieties oppressed her. By July she seemed to be quite her old self, travelling to Hertford for a Meeting and entertaining a large party of delegates from abroad in her garden. But later in the month she caught a chill and felt once again overtired and anxious. She was distressed and made ill by the continued criticism from Friends (probably of her worldly life among the aristocracy) and by her failing memory. Her sister-in-law, Elizabeth Fry, who had so often travelled with her in the Ministry, was ailing too, and Joseph decided to rent a house at Sandgate, hoping that the sea air would do them both good.

The stay at Sandgate was not a success. The house faced south, was built under the cliff and Mrs Fry disliked it intensely. She found the little resort dull, their house hot and the beds hard. 'My nights are sad', she wrote wistfully, 'yet my dearest husband likes it so much that I must stay.' It was a new experience for her to be idle and obedient. She became so irritable in her illness that she wondered whether she could be a truly religious person and prayed touchingly for more grace. A month later she was still discontented and yearned to go to Norfolk, where her family had prepared for them. Joseph, for once, would not give way. He was apprehensive about the effects of a journey.

In September, to Betsy's relief, she was moved to Tunbridge Wells where her daughters Louisa and Hannah nursed her carefully. She was grateful for a good bed where she could sleep soundly but her appetite remained poor and even the presents of pheasant and wild duck from Norfolk could not tempt her. She wrote of 'an almost constant need of stimulants that appear greatly to relieve, and I should almost say to keep me alive'.

By now the wine and opium she took daily to allay her anxiety and soothe her pains were almost certainly contributing to her physical and mental distress. She suffered from what she described as 'a great sense of exhaustion in the stomach and general restlessness'. She had great pain and stiffness in her joints, perhaps a form of rheumatism. It was a vicious circle. Because she was forced to be inactive, her need for drugs increased; yet while she was ill there was little hope of a return to the public service that could lift her out of her depression.

In the autumn she came home to Upton Lane. Louisa and her family came to stay so that her two daughters could take turns in nursing. She could not get downstairs, so from October onwards controlled the household from her room, insisting that meals be served on time, household prayers strictly observed and the servants kept busy. She liked the windows to be open and the rooms thoroughly aired, even in illness. Her own personal toilet was important to her and it took time and patience to get her dressed to her satisfaction.

Her daughters and Betsy's visitors were expected to read to her and they naturally chose books of a pious nature. But one afternoon her daughter was reading a religious biography to her mother when Mrs Fry interrupted, saying that she could not bear any more. It was too affecting. 'How I feel for the poor, when very ill, in a state like my own for instance, when "good" ladies go to see them.' Religion, she explained to her astounded listener, was often thrust too forcibly on a sufferer. It should be introduced tactfully and gently, she said, reminding her daughter of the tenderness of Jesus' 'tone and manner to sinners'. For Betsy, religion had always come through her inner being, not through man's ministrations.

The infrequent entries in her journal at this time were, as usual, full of quotations from the Scriptures but now she looked for passages suited to her condition. When she could, she wrote letters and sorted out her tracts but there were hours, tedious hours, to be got through. Joseph was wonderfully patient with her, holding her hand while she muttered to herself, again and again:

Come what, come may,
Time and the hour run through the roughest day.

By March 1844 she was recovering a little, able to be moved from one room to another in a wheelchair and quite determined, despite Joseph's misgivings, to travel to Bath to take the waters. Hannah and Fowell Buxton were there, she needed company and the change seemed to do her good. Her son William, with his little daughter Emma, came to join them and by the time she returned to Upton, she felt in better health. During July two deaths in the family set her back again. Her sister-in-law Elizabeth Fry died after a long illness, and it was a terrible shock to Betsy when her little grandson Gurney Reynolds, died suddenly. She began to dream again, as vividly as in her youth, but now it was of graves opening up all around her. With William's help she managed to attend Meeting at nearby Plaistow one Sunday morning. She was pushed in her wheelchair soon after the Friends had assembled and after a profound silence addressed the gathering in a strong, clear voice on the subject of the death of the righteous.

William had found his parents a suitable house at Walmer by the sea and soon afterwards she was moved there. It was an unhappy summer. She had barely been there a fortnight when news came that scarlet fever had swept through William's family. Within two days of contracting the illness Juliana, his second daughter, died, then three of the servants caught the fever and were looked after by Mrs Fry's own 'Nursing Sisters'. Finally William himself became ill and died within a fortnight of his daughter.

Joseph and Katharine were afraid that the shock would kill Betsy. Of all their children William had been the favourite, the most attentive, calling in to Upton every morning on his way to London. But in a curious way Betsy seemed to rally with the sorrow. When she returned home she began to minister again, to walk a little and drive in the small pony-chair that her son Joseph had given her, while others strolled by her side. She invited William's widow Julia and the remaining children to stay with her and tried to console them. It seemed to distract her from herself.

'Favoured with a tranquil easy night, thanks be to my God,' she wrote in one of the last few entries in her diary, 'I am attended to with the utmost kindness by my dearest husband, my sweet daughter Louisa and my maid Mary.'

There were four more deaths in her family that winter: her sister Louisa's child and her infant son, Hannah's husband, and, hardest of all, Fowell Buxton. Betsy herself clung to life and in the spring of 1845 fulfilled her desire to see Earlham again and spent a few happy days there. Although she was frail and a little forgetful, she was taken to Meeting in Norwich two Sundays in succession in her wheel-chair – the time of Meeting was delayed until eleven o'clock for her. She spoke to her old friends in her full, rich voice, never faltering; she could still quote whole passages from the Bible.

In May, she attended two of the women's sittings at Yearly Meeting in London and in June the Annual Meeting of the Ladies British Society was held at Plaistow, near her home, instead of at Westminster, in order to spare her the journey. She spoke to them almost with her old power and invited the committee to take refreshments at her home. Later that month she held a little party in the garden at Upton for Harry, her youngest son who had recently married. The union gave her pleasure since she liked Lucy and she belonged to a Quaker family of impeccable respectability.

In August she was moved to a pleasant house in Ramsgate, overlooking the sea, where her children and grandchildren came to visit her. However frail she appeared, her old dominance did not leave her. She liked her sons around her, and of her daughters there was now only Katharine. On September 13 1845 she wrote to her son Joseph:

> I deeply feel that from very long and continued illness I can be very little to your dearest father in his latter days and I feel it most important that his sons should be his helpers and comforters. I can no longer take pleasant little walks with him as I used to do, no longer make his table cheerful … I wish us not long to be left without some of you here … if we cannot afford to keep open house, we must live a little in common … were I rich, I would pay all your expenses, journey, etc., but this I cannot do. I feel certainly very poorly … I think that you cannot expect that you will very long have a mother to come to …

The letter ends with her usual prayers and exhortations. Three weeks later, on 13 October 1845, she died after a stroke which had rendered her unconscious. Almost before she was buried she had become a legend of piety and philanthropy.

Over a thousand people thronged to Elizabeth Fry's funeral which took place in the Friends' burial ground at Barking.

There is no appointed funeral service among Friends, who gather in quiet, expectant worship beside the grave. The vast crowd stood in silence; Joseph Gurney was the first to offer a prayer; and afterwards a Meeting was held in a spacious tent, especially erected for the occasion.

Seen as a whole, her life had been a triumph. From a sheltered background and without formal education or training, she had won herself a place of honour in the courts and governments of the world. Even before her religious conversion, she had been determined to use her talents to some purpose, to find a meaning in her life. Instead of succumbing to a life as a genteel invalid, she battled with her own frailty and with the injustices of her time. Two hundred years after her birth, despite the sanctimonious clothing of her thought, she seems a brave and modern woman. Through her personal courage and involvement, men and women all over the world have been enabled to recognise, in the prisoner behind bars, their own face. For her signal achievement was to acknowledge the humanity of the prisoners and to consider their individual human needs. That so little progress has been made in finding humane and satisfactory methods of treating and rehabilitating them is a comment on our indifference rather than her vision.

Elizabeth Fry has been regarded as a saint in the past, and it is not difficult to understand why. She had the gift of touching people's hearts by her own deep religious feeling and her passionate concern for good. But she had great faults as well as great gifts, of which she was acutely and painfully aware. She was proud, selfish and ruthless. Domestically she was inadequate, overanxious and neglectful, ready to sacrifice her family at any time for her cause. Yet she was remorseless with herself too, forced by her circumstances to create a new role in life for a woman, since her duties as a mother and Quaker minister were in direct conflict with the assertion of herself that her reforming crusade demanded. Relatives and friends, even Kings and Queens, remembered Elizabeth Fry all their lives and from her fanaticism flowed a wave of tolerance and compassion which swept through nineteenth-century Europe.

Sources

NOTE

I have drawn heavily on primary sources in writing this book, principally Elizabeth Fry's own journals. There are forty-six volumes in all, forty-four at the Library of the Society of Friends and two at Norfolk Record Office. It was often instructive to compare her original outpourings with the heavily edited two-volume transcript made by her daughter, Katharine Fry, which is now in the British Library Manuscript Department.

Her relatives were all prolific writers, even for their time. They kept journals, wrote scores of letters and some of them wrote books. Apart from the main sources mentioned in the Bibliography, I have seen journals and letters of Elizabeth Fry's circle, owned by descendants, friends and individuals throughout the country, who generously allowed me to look at them.

CHAPTER I: 'A FLY-AWAY STATE'

1. George Pickering, *Creative Malady*.

CHAPTER II: THE TRANSFORMATION

1. John Gurney's Household Account Book; 2. Rachel Cresswell, *A Memoir of Elizabeth Fry*; 3. John Gurney's Household Account Book.

CHAPTER III: 'A CAREWORN WIFE AND MOTHER'

1. Manuscript letter, Joseph Gurney to his sisters at Earlham, February 1805, Gurney Correspondence; 2. Augustus Hare, *The Gurneys of Earlham*, Vol I; 3. Joseph Gurney to his sisters at Earlham, February 1805.

CHAPTER IV: 'LAUDABLE PERSUITS'

1. ed J. Braithwaite, *Memoirs of Joseph John Gurney*, Letter to John Talwin Shewell; 2. Evidence given to a House of Commons Committee on Employment of Boys in Sweeping Chimneys by the Society for Superceding the Necessity of Climbing Boys, 1817; 3. *Memoirs of the Life and Gospel Labours of Stephen Grellet*, Vol I; 4. Local History Department, Newham Library; 5. Joseph Gurney to Elizabeth Fry, 2 March 1813, Gurney Correspondence; 6. Gurney Correspondence.

CHAPTER V: 'QUITE A SHOW'

1. *Edinburgh Review*, July 1821; 2. *ibid*; 3. Mrs Fry's Evidence to the House of Commons Committee on Prisons, 1818; 4. Gurney Correspondence; 5. Susanna Corder, *Life of Elizabeth Fry*; 6. Mrs Fry's Evidence; 7. Fowell Buxton, *Origins of the Prison Association*; 8. Corder, *Life of Elizabeth Fry*; 9. ibid; 10. Report of a Select Committee on the Prisons of the Metropolis, Mrs Fry's Evidence, 1818; 11. R & S Wilberforce, *Life of Wilberforce*; 12. Cresswell, *A Memoir of Elizabeth Fry*; 13. House of Lords Debate on Prisons, 3 June 1818; 14. Research and Historical Department, Bank of England; 15. Anthony Babington, *The English Bastille*; 16. Cresswell, *A Memoir of Elizabeth Fry*.

CHAPTER VI: THE NATIONAL CRUSADE

1. Corder, *Life of Elizabeth Fry*; 2. ed Braithwaite, *Memoirs of Joseph John Gurney*; 3. Backhouse Papers, University of Durham; 4. Manuscript letter, 20 July 1819, Gurney Correspondence; 5. Corder, *Life of*

Elizabeth Fry; 6. Gurney Correspondence; 7. ed Christine Colvin, *Maria Edgeworth's Letters from England*; 8. Charles Bateson, *The Convict Ships, 1787–1868.*

CHAPTER VII: THE CRASH

1. Peel Papers, CXVIII, General Correspondence, 1–26 February 1825; 2. ed Braithwaite, *Memoirs of Joseph John Gurney*; 3. *ibid*; 4. *ibid*; 5. Hare, *The Gurneys of Earlham*; 6. *Female Life in Prison by a Prison Matron*, 1862; 7. reprinted in *The Times*, 17 October 1839; 8. Gurney Correspondence; 9. Minutes of Ratcliff and Barking Monthly Meeting, 23 April 1829.

CHAPTER VIII: MORE CRUELTY THAN BEFORE

1. *Babington, The English Bastille*; 2. *Cresswell, A* Memoir of Elizabeth Fry; 3. *ibid*; 4. Joseph Fry's Private Journal, Gurney Papers; 5. Papers of the House of Commons, March 1836; 6. J. Menzies Wilson & H. Lloyd, *Amelia: The Tale of a Plain Friend.*

CHAPTER IX: ROYAL COMMANDS

1. Hare, *The Gurneys of Earlham*; 2. Egerton Manuscript 3672–5, British Library; 3. *ibid*; 4. Cresswell, *A Memoir of Elizabeth Fry*; 5. *Elizabeth Fry's Journeys 1840–1841*; 6. Egerton Manuscript 3672–5; 7. *Elizabeth Fry's Journeys 1840–1841*; 8. Corder, *Life of Elizabeth Fry*; 9. Cecil Woodham Smith, *Florence Nightingale*; 10. ibid.

CHAPTER X: HEROINE OF EUROPE

1. ed F.B. Tolles, *Slavery and the Woman Question—Lucretia Mott's Diary*; 2. E. Stanton, *History of Woman's Suffrage*, Vol I; 3. ed Tolles, *Slavery and the Woman Question*; 4. *ibid*; 5. Hare, *The Gurneys of Earlham*, Vol II; 6. Katharine Fry, *Manuscript History of the Parishes of East and West Ham*, Local Studies Department, Newham Library; 7. Hare, Vol II.

Bibliography

Anley, Charlotte, *The Prisoners of Australia*, London, 1841

Anon., *Female Life in Prison, Memoirs of a Prison Matron*, London, 1862

Babington, Anthony, *The English Bastille*, London, 1971

Bateson, Charles, *The Convict Ships*, Glasgow, 1959

Braithwaite, J. B., (ed.), *Memoirs of Joseph John Gurney*, 2 vols.,
    Norwich, 1854

Brayshow, A. Neave, *The Quakers: Their Story and Message*, London, 1927

Buxton, Charles, (ed.), *Memoirs of Sir Thomas Powell Buxton*, London, 1848

Buxton, Sir Thomas Fowell, *An Inquiry, whether crime and misery are pro-
    duced or prevented by our present system of prison discipline*, London, 1818

Carpenter, Mary, *Our Convicts*, 2 vols., London, 1864

Colvin, Christine, (ed.), *Maria Edgeworth, Letters from England*, Oxford, 1971

Corder, Susanna, *Life of Elizabeth Fry*, London, 1853

Finer, S. E., *The Life and Times of Sir Edwin Chadwick*, London, 1952

Fry, Elizabeth, *Observations on the Visiting, Superintendance and
    Government of Female Prisoners*, London, 1827

Fry, Katharine, & her sister, *Memoir of Elizabeth Fry with Extracts from
    her journal and letters*, 2 vols., Philadelphia, 1847

Geldart, Mrs T., *Memorials of Samuel Gurney*, London 1857

Greer, Mrs, *Quakerism or the Story of my Life*, Dublin, 1851

Grubb, Sarah Lynes, *A Selection from the letters of London*, 1848

Gurney, Joseph John, *Notes on a visit made to some of the Prisons in
    Scotland and the North of England in company with Elizabeth Fry*,
    London, 1819

– *Report addressed to the Marquess Wellesley, Lord Lieutenant of Ireland, by Elizabeth Fry and Joseph John Gurney*, London, 1827

Hare, Augustus, *The Gurneys of Earlham*, 2 vols., London, 1895

Hibbert, Christopher, *The Roots of Evil*, London, 1966

Inglis, Brian, *Poverty and the Industrial Revolution*, London, 1972

Johnson, R. B., (ed.), *Elizabeth Fry's Journeys on the Continent, 1840–1841, from a diary kept by her niece Elizabeth Gurney*, London, 1931

Kent, John, *Elizabeth Fry*, London, 1962

Lucas, E.V., *Charles Lamb and the Lloyds*, London, 1898

Menzies-Wilson, J., and Lloyd, H., *Amelia: The Tale of a Plain Friend*, Oxford, 1937

Mott, R. F., (ed.), *Memoir and Correspondence of Eliza P. Gurney*, Philadelphia, 1884

Perkin, Harold, *The Origins of Modern English Society 1780–1880*, London, 1969

Plumb, J. H., *England in the Eighteenth Century*, London, 1950

Pringle, Patrick, *The Prisoner's Friend: The Story of Elizabeth Fry*, London, 1953

Ruggles Brise, Sir Evelyn, *The English Prison System*, London, 1921

Seebohm, Benjamin, (ed.), *Memoirs of the Life of Stephen Grellet*, 2 vols., London, 1862

Shillitoe, Thomas, *Journal of the Life, Labours and Travels of Thomas Shillitoe*, 2 vols., London, 1839

Timpson, Rev Thomas, *Memoirs of Elizabeth Fry*, London, 1847

Tobias, J. J., *Crime and Police in England, 1700–1900*, Dublin, 1979

Tolles, F. B., (ed.), *Slavery and the Woman Question, Lucretia Mott's Diary*, London, 1952

Trevelyan, G. M., *British History in the Nineteenth Century and After—1782–1919*, London, 1937

Turberville, A. S., (ed.), *Johnson's England*, 2 vols., London, 1933

Vansittart, J. (ed.), *Katharine Fry's Book*, London, 1966

Whitney, Janet, *Elizabeth Fry, Quaker Heroine*, London, 1937

Wilberforce, R. and S., *Life of Wilberforce*, London, 1839

Woodward, Sir Llewellyn, *The Age of Reform*, Oxford, 1962

Woodham-Smith, Cecil, *Florence Nightingale*, London, 1950

REPORTS

Report of the Committee on Prisons within the City of London, 1818
Report of the Select Committee on Secondary Punishments, 1832
Prison Inspectors' Report on Newgate Prison, 1836

UNPUBLISHED SOURCES

Fry, Elizabeth, 46 volumes of her manuscript journal – 44 in Friends
    House Library, London, 2 in the Norfolk Record Office, Norwich
Fry, Joseph, private journal, Friends House Library
Fry, K., History of East and West Ham, Newham Reference Library,
    London, Local Studies Department
Gurney and Fry correspondence, British Library, Department of
    Manuscripts, Egerton Mss 3671–3675
Gurney, Joseph John, examined copy of private journal, Friends House
Gurney Mss, Friends House (and Eddington, A. J., *The Gurney
    Manuscripts: Synopsis of the Contents*)
History of Barking & Ratcliff Monthly Meeting of the Society of
    Friends with particular reference to the Frys and Gurneys (thesis,
    D. Bambridge), typescript, Newham Library
Notes on the West Ham associations of the Buxton, Fry, Gurney and
    Pelly families, (F. Sainsbury, 1961), typescript, Newham Library

Index

Aberdeen, 138, 140

Aberdeen, Lord, (Foreign Secretary), 253

Ackworth, 56, 191

Adelaide, Queen, 195, 198

Albert, Prince, 230, 239, 246–7, 255–6

Alderson, Dr, 26, 33

Allen, William, 231

Alnwick Castle, 56

Amiens, 261

Amphitrite (convict ship), 165

Amsterdam, 247

Angelzaark, Mr, 104; Mrs, 117

Anti-slavery, British & Foreign Society, 240–1; campaign for, 206–7; World's Convention, 239, 240; American abolitionists, 240–3

Ashley, Lord, 260

Association for the improvement of female prisoners in Newgate, (Newgate Committee), formation of, 117 *and see* Newgate

Association for prisoners in the Rhine & Westphalia, 235

Auburn prison, New York, 161

Avignon, 225

Backhouses, the, 144, 145

Bagnères-de-Bigorre, 228

Bagnères-de-Luchon, 227

Ball, William, 223, 242

Bank of England, 132

Barclay, Robert, 17; Uncle (E.Fry's), 176

Barèges, 227

Barking, burial ground, 267; Monthly Meeting, 92, 137

Barns, Nurse, 86

Bath, 166, 265

Bathurst, Lord, 161

Belfast, 177

Belgium, E.Fry's journey to, 301; King of, 232, 233

Bell, Catherine, 180 *and see* Gurney

Bentinck, Lord William, 224

Berlin, 233, 235, 250, 253

Berne, 229

Berwick prison, 240–1

Birkbeck, Jane, 126

Birmingham, 244

'blockade men', 172

Boulogne, 221, 224, 261

Bow, 102

Bramerton, 18

Bradshaw, Lucy, 231

Bremen, 248

Brick Lane, 41

Bridewell prison, 141, 223

Bridges, Sheriff, 117, 120

Brighton, 146, 170, 171, 179, 195, 258; District Visiting Society, 171, 206

Bristol Meeting, 166

British & Foreign Bible Society, 92–3, 173

British Society, 157, 169, 174, 176, 188–9, 203, 224, 239–40, 263, 265

Broadstairs, 146

Browne, Peter, 248

Brownlow, Countess, 195

Bruges, 232

Brussels, 232

'bubble' companies; financial collapse of, 175

Bunsen, Chevalier, 238

Buxton, Anna, 99, 100; Mrs Hannah, *see* Hannah Gurney; Priscilla (E.Fry's niece), 209; Thomas Fowell, 81, 82, 84, 85, 112, 115, 254, 155, death of children, 154, 158–60, 160, 162, 179, 187, 206, 240, 265, death, 266

Byerhaus, Herr, 235

Cedars, the, Upton Lane, (the Frys' home from 1829), 190 *and see* Upton Lane

Chadwick, Edwin, 148

Channel Islands, 206–7, 208, 215

Charlotte, Queen, 133

Chichester, bishop of, 171

cholera outbreak, 199

Clare, Suffolk, 59

Clerkenwell prison, 160

Clermont-en-Oise prison, 261

Coalbrookdale Quaker colony, 51, 53, coastguards, 172; libraries provided for, 209–10

Cold Bath Fields House of Correction, 112, 160

Colegate, 26

Committee(s), House of Commons, 117, 126–8, 131, 135, 199–203, 206; House of Lords, 210–14; Newgate *see* Newgate; of Protestant Ladies (in Paris), 224–5

compters (committal prisons), 97

convicts, 135, 259, in New South Wales 218, 261

Copenhagen, 248–9

Corporation of London, 123, 128

Corresponding Society, 26

Cotton, Dr, (chaplain of
Newgate), 113, 117, 212

Court House, the, Norwich, 17

Covent Garden, 42

Coventry, 74

Crawford, William, 197

Cresswell, Cpt Frank, 159, 160,
218, 251; Frank (son), 230,
259; Mrs Rachel, *see* Rachel
Gurney

Crome, old, 23

Cromer, 20, 156, 259; Hall, 156,
259

Crouch, William, 33

Cunningham, Rev Francis,
107, 159; Mrs Richenda, *see*
Richenda Gurney

Dagenham, the Frys' cottages at,
166, 173

Darby, Deborah, 51, 89

Darlington, 144, 145;

Denmark, 245, 249–50, 259; royal
family of, 163, 245, 249–50

Deptford, 135

Derby, Earl of, 142; Lady, 142, 188

Devonshire House, 68, 158

Dilwyn, George, 68–9

Dingwall, 159

District Visiting Societies, 171; in
Boulogne, 224; in Jersey, 215;
in Lowestoft, 206

Doncaster prison, 140

Dover, 251

Dresden, 235, 250

Drury Lane, 42

Dublin, 177, 178, 204

Dunbar prison, 141

Durham prison, 140, 155

Düsseldorf, 235, 259

Earlham Hall, 21, 22, 25, 26, 27,
28–9, 30, 32–3, 42–3, 45, 46,
47, 51, 54, 55, 56, 57, 58, 59,
63, 65, 67, 70, 73, 76, 81, 85,
87–8, 92–3, 94, 101, 102, 103,
107, 114, 116, 156, 161, 176,
180, 181, 190, 204, 217, 243,
259, 266

East Ham, 65

economic depression, 95–6,
106–7, 111

Edgeworth, Maria, 162

Edinburgh, 210

Edward, Prince of Wales, christening of, 256

Edwards, Edward, 90

Elliot, Dr, 252

Ely, 76

Enfield, Dr, 28; Henry, 29, 33, 54

Ennis, County Clare, 178

Falmouth, 175

Fliedner, pastor, 235

Fontainebleau, 225

Forster, Josiah, 221, 225, 226, 227,
228, 231

Fowell Buxton, Thomas, *see*
Buxton France,
E.Fry's visits to, 215, 221–2,
223–8, 261–2, prison report,
224, 227
Freemasons Hall, 158, 159
Freshwater, 279
Friends, Society of, *see* Quaker
Fry, Mr and Mrs W.S., (Joseph
Fry's parents), 65, 66, 69, 76,
77, death of 'Mother Fry', 77,
death of William Storrs, 85
Eliza, (J.Fry's sister-in-law), 67, 76
Elizabeth, (J.Fry's sister), 162, 166,
177, 204, 223, 263, death 265
Elizabeth (Betsy), née Gurney,
of Earlham, (1780–1845), birth,
15; ancestors, 15–6; parents, 17;
early childhood and education, 19,–24; mother's death,
25; early notions of religion,
30, 32; reactions to William
Savery, 34–8, 42, 43, 46; early
'good works', 46–7, 52–3; her
'school', 47, 53, 58, 61; encouragement at Coalbrookdale
Quaker colony, 50–1; courtship
by Joseph Fry, 55–61; marriage,
62–3; dominance of Betsy in
partnership, 61, 63; at Mildred's
Court, 67–8; loss of religious
inspiration, 68, 72; birth of first
five children in London, 72–83;
periods of depression, 75–6;,
78, 83–4, 145, 169, 170, 189,

190; first public appointment
as visitor to the workhouse
in Islington and first intima-
tions of her 'power' over an
audience, 79; death of Mr Fry
senior, 85; move to Plashet
and life at Plashet, 86; birth of
sixth child, 86–7; death of Mr
Gurney, 87; and the psychological release it gave her to speak,
88; recorded as a minister, 92;
seventh child, 92; ill-suited to
domestic life, 81, 92, 103–4,
124–5; eighth child, 94; visits
Newgate in 1813, 99–100; at
Newgate in 1816, 112; 'school'
in Newgate, 113, 114, 115, 119,
regulations, 120–1, adopted
into prison system, 122–3; sets
up Newgate Association, 117;
importance of prison cause as
outlet for E.F.'s self-expression
and talents, 114, 124, 137; appetite for admiration, 46, 57, 100,
118, 125, 129, 133, 144, 154, 158,
162; love of grand company, 43,
47–8, 49, 56, 233, 254; strug-
gles against worldly temptations, 29, 47, 48, 56, 66, 193–4,
239; incurs family and public
censure and gossip, 94, 101–2,
124, 129, 136, 137, 185, 187,
193, 244, 254, 256; charismatic
powers, 101, 113, 116, 117, 122,
128, 142, 144, 222; clash with

Lord Sidmouth, 130–3; evidence to House of Commons Committee on prisons, 126–9; opposition to capital punishment, 128–30, 136, 158; concern for convicts, 135, 161; dependence on the Gurneys, 106, 107, 116, 154, 190; prison reforming tour in the North of England and Scotland, 139–44; description of E.F. in Glasgow, 141–2; miscarriage(s), 152, 169, 173; concern for lunatics, 143–4, 153, 177; meets with opposition to reform, 167, 196–8, 203, 210; concern for coastguards, 172, 209; *Observations* published, 182–4; collapse of Fry Bank and effect on E.F., 186–190; leaves Plashet and moves to Upton Lane, 190; evidence to hostile House of Commons Committee on secondary punishment, 199–203; visit to Channel Islands, 206–8; to Isle of Wight, 209; to Highlands, 210; evidence to hostile House of Lords Committee, 210–4; first continental tour, 221–3; second continental tour, 223–9, and family dissension during it, 227–9; third continental tour, 231–7; received as a celebrity, 128, 129, 133, 136, 137, 140, 141, 142, 154, 171, in Ireland, 177–8, 185–6, on the continent 222–3, 223, 224, 250; visits Kaiserswerth, 235–6, and promotes hospital reform and nursing sisters in England, 236–42; clashes with American feminists, 239; fourth continental tour, 246–51; dines at Mansion House, 253–4; visited by King of Prussia at Upton Lane, 259–60; ill-health, 260–3; dependence on opium and laudanum, 41, 57, 74, 103, 254, 256, 258, 261, and on drink, 41, 73, 74 ,85, 224–5, 251, 252, 256, 261; death at Ramsgate, 264; burial at Barking, 264

Joseph, of Plashet, (1777–1861), 55, 57, 59, 60, 61, 62, marriage to Betsy Gurney, 62–3;, 65, 66, 68, 71, 72, 73, 74, 75, 83, 85, 86, 91, 92, 94, 103, 105, 117, 136, 144, 151, 155, 156, 163, 164, 166, 169, 180, 186, appreciation of fine art and a spendthrift 173, 176, bankruptcy 187, disowned by the Society 188–9, 194, 198, 'transformation' 207, 208, 209, 215, 218, 219, 221, 224, 225, 226, 227, 228, 229, 230, 231, 233, 234, concern for Betsy's health, 250, 254, 258, 261, 262, 263, 264

their children: general, 136, 137, 207, 208, 231, 257

Daniel (Harry/Henry), 163,
    177, 207, 208, 220, 224, 257,
    264
Elizabeth, 92, death, 105
Hannah, 95, 107, 186, 198, 205,
    as Mrs Streatfield 214, 258,
    261
John, 78, 83, 100, 107, 151, 174,
    180, 234
Joseph, 87, 107, 198, 263, 265
Katharine (Kate), 72, 80, 107,
    108, 109, 124, 126, 139, 144,
    155, 162, 164, 170, 185, 205,
    214, 215, 220, 221, 224, 225,
    228, 232, 251, 254, 257, 260,
    263, 264
Louisa, 103, 107, 144, 155, 205,
    214, as Mrs Pelly 231, 244,
    261, 263
Rachel, 75, 82, 105, 107, 125,
    126, 137, 138, 154, 155, 159,
    as Mrs Cresswell 162, 174,
    176, 208, 217, 218, 230, 251
Richenda, 83, 100, 107, 151,
    185, as Mrs Reynolds 193,
    258, son's death 262
Samuel (Gurney), 106, 107,
    155, 219, 220, 222
William, 81, 100, 107, 151, 188,
    194, 198, 204, 215, 244, 251,
    258, 263, death 263
William (Joseph's brother), 68,
    71, 76, 95–6, 173
Frys Bank, in difficulties 96, 176;
    crash 187, 188

Galway, 30
Garrison, William Lloyd, 242
Geneva, 229
Gentleman's Magazine, 124, 133
George III, 29
Germany, 231–6, 245, 248
Ghent, 232
Glasgow, 139, 141
Gloucester, Duke of, (Prince
    William Frederick), 29, 33,
    132, 158, 159; Duchess of, 157,
    163, 198, 233, 246
'Goats' (Dutch Meeting House in
    Goats Lane), 23, 35, 62
Gouda prison, 246
Gracechurch Street Meeting
    House, 49, 68
Graham, Sir James, (Secretary of
    State), 253
Granville, Lord, 221
Greenwich hospital, 190
Grellet, Stephen, 97; first visit to
    Newgate, 87–99, 103
Grenoble, 228
Guernsey, 208, 215
Guizot, Monsieur, 259
Gurney: Catherine (E.Fry's
    mother), 18, 19, 20, 21, 22, 23,
    25; John (E. Fry's father), 15,
    18, 19, 20, 21, 25, 26, 27, 33, 34,
    37, 51, 53, 54, 55, 56, 58, 59, 62,
    78, death 87, 88;
    their children: **Betsy** (Elizabeth)
        see Elizabeth Fry
        Catherine (Kitty), 18, 19,

25, 26, 27, 48, 53, 55, 59,
60, 61, 62, 84, 180, 181,
243
Daniel, 86, 88, 94, 107, 136,
166, 182, 188, 217, 218
Hannah, 31, 72, as Mrs
Buxton 82, 84, 85, 164,
243, 262
John, 53, 55, 76, 80, 84, 87,
88, 94, 96, 101, 103, 104,
death 105
Joseph John, 24, 78, 92, 101,
102, 106, 112, 114, 126,
129, 137, 139, 140, 143,
144, 152, 157, 159, 163,
166, 176, 177, 179, 186,
187, 189, 190, 190, 193,
198, 204, 206, 207, 214,
215; visit to America
219, 223, 242, 245, 246,
247, 248, 249, 252, 256,
258, 259, 265; and third
wife Eliza 256–7, 258–9,
259
Louisa, 21, 28, 30, 32, 33, 45,
as Mrs Hoare 80, 84, 97,
164, 176, 178, 182, death
215, 222
Priscilla, 21, 31, 55, 82, 87,
94, 129, 155, 156, death
156
Rachel, 18, 19, 25, 26, 27,
37, 41, 45, 54, 59, 72, 95,
105, 107, 116, 163, 179,
death 181, 182

Richenda, 24, 31, 35, 37, 44,
87, as Mrs Cunningham
107, 136, 159, 205–6, 215,
243
Samuel, 26, 74, 83–4, 107,
112, 156, 181, 186, 188,
190, 195, 203–4, 219, 224,
230, 231, 237, 238, 243
Anna (E.Fry's niece), 246
Elizabeth (E.Fry's cousin and
sister-in-law), 80, death 84
Elizabeth (E.Fry's niece), 231,
232, 233, 234, 240, 246
Hudson (E.Fry's cousin), 23,
96, 176
John (E.Fry's grandfather), 16
Joseph of the Grove (E.Fry's
uncle), 27, 29, 34, 35, 48,
198
Priscilla Hannah (E.Fry's
cousin), 50, 51, 166
Priscilla (E.Fry's niece), 209
Richard (E.Fry's uncle), 58,
62, 80
Gurneys Bank, 15, 34, 87, 106,
194

Haddington prison, 144
Hague, the, 247
Halle, 191
Ham House (now West Ham
Park), 181, 190, 255
Hamburg, 248, 250
Hamelin, 257
Hanbury, aunt, (E.Fry's), 144

Hanover, 232; royal family, 232, 233, 234, 250

Harcourt, Lady, 133

Hay, Lady Harriet, 166, death 214

Heidelberg, 229

Hempstead, Norfolk, 62

Herm, 208

Hertford, 260

Hicks, Mr, 154

Hoare, Hampstead family, 43; Mrs Louisa, *see* Louisa Gurney; Samuel, 80, 82, 96, 112, 116, 154, 159, 197, 256

Holland, E.Fry's visits to, 231, 232, 245–8; Dutch royal family, 245–8

Holyhead, 177

Horner, Benjamin, 186

Hughes, Joseph, 65

Hunstanton, 163

Hyères, 226

Inglis, Lady, 237

Inverness, 210

Ipswich, 94, 193

Ireland, 177–8, 203–4, 218, 220

Irving, Lydia, 221

Isle of Wight, 209, 210, 215

James, Mary Ann, 130, 131

Jebb, Colonel Joshua, 254; Judge, 178

Jersey, 207, 208, 215, 218

Johnstone, Judge, 178

Judd, Hannah, 25

Kaiserswerth, 235, 236, 237–8

Kent, 215; Duchess of, 231

Kett, Elizabeth, 18

King, Jane, 68

King's Lynn, 84, 87, 88, 176, 182, 217, 218, 230

Knowles, Molly, 44

Knowsley, 143

Lakes, the, 74, 186

Lancaster, Joseph, 71; E. Fry adopts educational methods of, 104

Lancaster prison, 155

Lansdowne, Lord, 158, 179

Lausanne, 229

Lea, river, 76

Leeds prison, 155

Leighton Buzzard prison, 176

Leipzig, 235

Leslie, Charles Robert, 164

Limerick, 178

Limehouse, 199

Lincoln prison, 155

Liskeard, 175

Liverpool, 142, 155, 186, 195, 219

Liverpool Advertiser, 186

Lloyd, James, 28, 48

London Review, 196

Louis Philippe of France, 222, 259, and Queen, 222, 259

lunatics, E. Fry improves conditions of, 143, 153

Lyon, 225

Mackintosh, Sir James, 157, 158

Maidenhead, 179

Mansion House, 133, 164, 199, 253, 254

Maria (convict ship), 135

Marsden, Rev Samuel, 161

Marseille, 226

Martin, Sir Thomas Byam, 161

Mayor of London, Lord, 123, 252

Melbourne, Lord, (Home Secretary), 202, 203

Menai Straits bridge, 177

Midlands, E.Fry's visits to, 169, 185

Mildred's Court, 67, 68, 70, 71, 73, 74, 77, 78, 79, 82, 85, 87, 95, 96, 99, 105, 109, 112, 117, 126, 153, 162, 171, 175

Millbank penitentiary, 197, 201, 203

Minden, 232

Molesworth, Viscount, 171

Montalivet, Comte, (French Minister of the Interior), 221

Montauban, 227

More, Hannah, 166

Morpeth, Lord, 219

Mott, Lucretia, 240, 241, 242

Munster, Peter and Adolph, 249, 250

Napier, Joseph, (Attorney General for Ireland), 282

Napoleonic wars, 95

Neale, Molly, 18

Neave, Caroline, 202

her evidence to House of Commons Committee, 202

Newcastle-upon-Tyne prison, 141, 155

Newgate, prison and committee, 97–101, 111, 112, 'school' 113, 114, 115, Association (Committee) formed 117–118, 119, regulations 120–1, 122, 123, 124, 125, 126, House of Commons report 126–9, 130, 131, 132, 133, 134, 135, 136, 140, 141, 151, 152, 157, 159, 162, 163, 164, 165, 166, 167, 174, 176, 187, 188, 195, 196, 201, 206, House of Lords report 210–4, 218–9, 221, 233, 234, 235, 236, 254, 255, 259; governor of (*see also* Newman), 99, 114, 117, 118, 119, 134; matron of 120, 123

Newman, Charlotte, 130, 131

Governor, of Newgate, 99, 114, 117, 118, 119, 134

Nightingale, Florence, 236, 237, 288; E.Fry's influence on, 237

Nîmes, 226

Norman, Molly, 52; Nanny, 81

Normanby, Lord, (Home Secretary), 230, 231

Normandy, 215

Norwich, 15, 18, 21, 22, 26, 28, 32, 46, 47, 48, 65, 198, 206, 263; prison, 112

Notes of a visit made to some of the prisons in Scotland and the North of England in company with Elizabeth Fry, 143, reactions to, 152
Nottingham, 155

Observations on the visiting, superintendance and government of female prisoners, 182–4, 195
O'Connor, Mary, 115
Old Bailey, 97
Opie, Amelia, 26, 43, 236
Orléans, duchesse d', 222, 224, 259
Ostend, 231, 251
Owen, John, 165
Oxford, 74

Paine, Thomas, 26–7
Paisley prison, 223
Paramatta, NSW, 161
Paris, 152, 221, 224, 225, 259, 260
Peel, Sir Robert, (Home Secretary), 164, 166, 170, 196, 202, 253, 254
Pelly, Sir John Henry, 204; Juliana, 204
Pentonville prison, 245, 254
Perth, 210
Peterloo, 153
Phillips, Richard, 93
Pindar, Peter, 44
Pirie, Sir John, (Lord Mayor of London), 252, 253, 254; Lady, 252, 253, 254

Pitchford, John, 31
Plaistow, 363, 264
Plashet, (the Frys' home in Essex), 55, 59, 65, 69, 76, 86, 96, 102, 107, 108, 109, 112, 116, 117, 144, 151, 152, 160, 162, 163, 171, 173, 180, 185, move from 188, 189, 190. 199
Portsmouth, 209
Prison Act of 1823, 166–7, 212
prison conditions, general, 111, 112, 140–1 *and see* Newgate
Prison Discipline Society, 223
Protestant Ladies, Committee of, 224
Protestant Sisters of Charity ('Fry nurses'), 237
Provident societies, 171, 220
Prussia, 233, 234, 235, 238, 245. 250; King's visit to England 254, and to Upton Lane, 254–7
Pyrenees, 227

Quaker (Society of Friends), dress 17; consequences of marriage 'out' 17, 154; language 16; in the eighteenth century, 16–17; procedure at Yearly Meeting, 162; worship 16, 23
Quarterly Meeting, Dorset & Hants 106, Suffolk 94, Sussex 195, 215, Warwick, Leicestershire & Rutland 244
Ramsgate, 251, 264

Randolph, John, (American envoy), 162

Ratcliff & Barking Monthly Meeting, 189, disowns J. Fry 190, Hannah Fry's letter to, 205

Regan, Denis, 86

Reynolds, Foster, 185, death of son Gurney, 262; Mrs Richenda, *see* Richenda Gurney

Reynolds, Rachel, 174

Reynolds, Richard, 50, 51

Rice, John Richard, 165

Rotterdam, 232, 246

Rousseau, Jean-Jacques, 26

Runcton, 107, 159, 217

Russian asylums, E.Fry's influence on, 153

St Albans prison, 176

St Austell, 175

St Lazare prison, 222, 224

St Martin's Lane Meeting House, 97

St Petersburg, 153

Salisbury, dean of, 171; Earl of, 171; Plain, 210

Sanderson, John, 223; Mary, 215

Sandgate, 260, 261

Sandwich Islands, King of, 260

Sark, 208

Savery, William, 34, 35, 36, 37, 38, 42, 43, 44, 45, 46, 79, 51, 68, 89

Savoie, 229

Scotland, E.Fry's visits to, 137–43, 210, 223

Servants' Society, 174

Shaftesbury, 106

Sheepwash, Yorkshire, 56

Sheffield, 155

Sheriff(s), 114, 117, 120 *and see* Bridges

Siddons, Mrs, 24, 43

Sidmouth, Lord, (Home Secretary), 128, 131, 132, 133, 164

Sieveking, Fraülein, 148, and her Society of the Ladies' Committee, 148

Silesia, 250

Sims, Dr, 87, 102

Skelton, Harriett, 131, 132

Smith, Rev Sydney, 13

Smithfield, 98

Society of Friends, *see* Quaker

Society for the improvement of prison discipline and the reformation of juvenile delinquents, 158

Society for the patronage of discharged prisoners, 245

Sophia, Princess, 153, 233; adopts E.Fry's reforms in Russian asylums, 153

Southey, Robert, 236

Spitalfields weavers, 97

Stamford, 191

Stanley, Lord, (Colonial Secretary), 253

Stanton, Elizabeth, 241

Stewart, Janet, 223
Stratford, 74
Streatfield, William Champion,
    marriage to Hannah Fry 205,
    death 263
Suffolk, 94
Sunderland, 199
Surrey, 105
Sussex, 145, 215; Duke of, 241
Sutherland, Duchess of, 240, 241
Switzerland, 228, 229

Tasburgh Meeting House, 80
Thun, 229
Tottenham, Quaker tea-party in,
    241
Toulon, 226; prison, 226
Toulouse, 227
transportation, 132, 134, 136, 161
    and see convicts
Tunbridge Wells, 261

Upton, 181 *and see* Ham House
Upton Lane, (the Frys' home,
    The Cedars), 190, 204, 205,
    220, 230, 252, 255, 261, 262,
    263, 264

Venning, John, 153; Walter, 153
Victoria, Queen, 219, 230, 251,
    253, 254

Wakefield prison, 141, 155
Walmer, 263
Walpole, Sir Robert, 16
Warwick Castle, 74
weavers' friend, the, 16
Wellesley, Lord, 179; J. J. Gurney's
    and E.Fry's report to, 179
Wellington, Duke of, 252
Wensum, river, 21
West Ham, 190; Park *see* Ham
    House
West Indies, 243; J.J.Gurney's
    efforts to emancipate slaves,
    245, 247, 249
Westminster asylum, 202
Westmorland, 74
Wilberforce, William, 129, 189
William IV, 195, 219
William Frederick, Prince *see*
    Duke of Gloucester
William, Princess, 233, 234
Williman, Sarah, 25, 87
Wollstonecraft, Mary,
Woolwich, 165

Yarmouth, Great, 194
Yearly Meeting, 68, 70, 124,m
    137, 155, 162, 174, 176, 179,
    191, 194, 206, 260, 264
York, 56, 155, 187

Also by Tempus:

Agatha Christie: The Finished Portrait by Dr Andrew Norman
September 2006, ISBN 978 07524 4990 1

Vanessa Bell by Frances Spalding
November 2006, ISBN 07524 4033 0
'A sensitive and scholarly biography.' *The Times*
'Excellent.' *The Guardian*
'An excellent biography: it could hardly be bettered.' John Russell, *TLS*

Enid Blyton: The Biography by Barbara Stoney
November 2006, ISBN 07524 4030 6
'Admirably fair ... the issues are faced and discussed with honesty and tact'
Daily Telegraph
'This biography finds exactly the right tone.' *Sunday Times*

A.A. Milne: His Life by Ann Thwaite
November 2006 ISBN 07524 4085 3
'Compelling, meticulous and very sensitive. I absolutely loved it.' *Andrew Motion*
'[Thwaite] has a Coleridgean gift for getting into the feel of her subject – the man, the age, the style.' *London Review of Books*
'In you my father has found the perfect biographer.' *Christopher Robin Milne*

Arthur Conan Doyle: Beyond Sherlock Holmes by Dr Andrew Norman
February 2007, ISBN 978 07524 4187 0

That Singular Person called Lear: The Extraordinary Life of the Author of the Owl and the Pussycat by Susan Chitty
February 2007, ISBN 978 07524 4137 5
'Deliciously amusing' *The Literary Review*
'A thorough and fascinating biography' *The Sunday Telegraph*

Frances Hodgson Burnett: Beyond The Secret Garden by Ann Thwaite
February 2007, ISBN 978 07524 4138 2
'A glittering, lively story.' *The Observer*
'A model biography' *Daily Telegraph*

Elizabeth Robins by Angela V. John
March 2007, ISBN 978 07524 4028 6
'A sympathetic portrait based on meticulous scholarship' Judith P. Zinsser,
Miami University
'A detailed, authoritative study of a remarkable woman' *Norma Clarke*

Edmund Gosse: A Literary Landscape by Ann Thwaite
March 2007, ISBN 978 07524 4136 8
'Consistently absorbing and entertaining.' *The Observer*
'Magnificent ... It is one of the finest literary biographies of our time.' John Carey,
The Sunday Times
'Extremely enjoyable.' *Daily Telegraph*

Marie Stopes and the Sexual Revolution by June Rose
March 2007, ISBN 978 07524 4200 6
'Hugely entertaining' *The Literary Review*
'A fascinating account of a fascinating woman' *The Sunday Times*

If you are interested in purchasing other books published by Tempus,
or in case you have difficulty finding any Tempus books in your local bookshop,
you can also place orders directly through our website

www.tempus-publishing.com